Managing an Effective Operation

Paul Graves qualified as an electronics engineer while completing an apprenticeship with Rolls Royce Ltd, Aero-Engine Division, Derby. He joined the Specialist Division of Rolls Royce and Associates Ltd, working on the management of the design and supply of nuclear reactor systems, and was located in Derby, Barrow-in-Furness and Dounreay in Scotland. He then became Engineering Manager of Fisher Controls Ltd (a part of the Monsanto company) at their Lewisham plant, where they designed and manufactured major electronic instrumentation systems for defence and industrial applications. He progressed to become Director and General Manager of the Lewisham business, a post he held for five years before joining Sundridge Park Management Centre in Bromley, where he is Programme Director for several core management programmes and specializes in operations, technology and quality topics. In recent years he has worked in the USA, Europe, Russia (including Siberia) and SE Asia.

Eddie Fowler has over thirty years' experience in human resource management. After ten years in the steel industry, he worked in heavy-electrical engineering, plastics and high tech electronics. Latterly, he worked in the headquarters of a major international services company.

He has had responsibility in all the aspects of HR–employee relations, pay and benefits management, training and development, recruitment and employment law.

For the past ten years he has worked in management development as a corporate executive and consultant. He was responsible for initiating and developing a management development strategy for some 3000 managers in the services company and has advised on the design and implementation of competence-based management training programmes.

For the past five years he has been a standing committee member of MCI.

Managing an Effective Operation

Paul Graves and Eddie Fowler

**the Institute
of Management**

F O U N D A T I O N

BUTTERWORTH
HEINEMANN

Butterworth-Heinemann Ltd
Linacre House, Jordan Hill, Oxford OX2 8DP

R A member of the Reed Elsevier plc group

OXFORD LONDON BOSTON
MUNICH NEW DELHI SINGAPORE SYDNEY
TOKYO TORONTO WELLINGTON

First published 1995

British Library Cataloguing in Publication Data
A catalogue record for this book is available from the British Library

ISBN 0 7506 2031 5

Composition by Genesis Typesetting, Laser Quay, Rochester, Kent
Printed in Great Britain by Clays, St Ives plc

Contents

Series adviser's preface

This book is one of a series designed for people wanting to develop their capabilities as managers. You might think that there isn't anything very new in that. In one way you would be right. The fact that very many people want to learn to become better managers is not new, and for many years a wide range of approaches to such learning and development has been available. These have included courses leading to formal qualifications, organizationally based management development programmes and a whole variety of self-study materials. A copious literature, extending from academic textbooks to sometimes idiosyncratic prescriptions from successful managers and consultants, has existed to aid – or perhaps confuse – the potential seeker after managerial truth and enlightenment.

So what is new about this series? In fact, a great deal – marking in some ways a revolution in our thinking both about the art of managing and also the process of developing managers.

Where did it all begin? Like most revolutions, although there may be a single, identifiable act that precipitated the uprising, the roots of discontent are many and long established. The debate about the performance of British managers, the way managers are educated and trained, and the extent to which shortcomings in both these areas have contributed to our economic decline, has been running for several decades.

Until recently, this debate had been marked by periods of frenetic activity-stimulated by some report or enquiry and perhaps ending in some new initiatives or policy changes – followed by relatively long periods of comparative calm. But the underlying causes for concern persisted. Basically, the majority of managers in the UK appeared to have little or no training for their role, certainly far less than their counterparts in our major competitor nations. And there was concern about the nature, style and appropriateness of the management education and training that was available.

The catalyst for this latest revolution came in late 1986 and early 1987, when three major reports reopened the whole issue. The 1987 reports were *The Making of British Managers* by John Constable and Roger McCormick, carried out for the British Institute of Management and the CBI, and *The Making of Managers* by Charles Handy, carried out for the (then) Manpower Services Commission, National Economic Development Office and British Institute of Management. The 1986 report, which often receives less recognition than it deserves as a key contribution to the recent changes, was *Management Training: context and process* by Iain Mangham and Mick Silver, carried out for the Economic and Social Research Council and the Department of Trade and Industry.

It is not the place to review in detail what the reports said. Indeed, they and their consequences are discussed in several places in this series of books. But essentially they confirmed that:

- British managers were undertrained by comparison with their counterparts internationally.
- The majority of employers invested far too little in training and developing their managers.
- Many employers found it difficult to specify with any degree of detail just what it was that they required successful managers to be able to do.

The Constable/McCormick and Handy reports advanced various recommendations for addressing these problems, involving an expansion of management education and development, a reformed structure of qualifications and a commitment from employers to a code of practice for management development. While this analysis was not new, and had echoes of much that had been said in earlier debates, this time a few leading individuals determined that the response should be both radical and permanent. The response was coordinated by the newly established Council for Management Education and Development (now the National Forum for Management Education and Development (NFMED)) under the energetic and visionary leadership of Bob (now Sir Bob) Reid, then of Shell UK and subsequently chairman of the British Railways Board.

Under the umbrella of NFMED a series of employer-led working parties tackled the problem of defining what it was that managers should be able to do, and how this differed for people at different levels in their organizations; how this satisfactory ability to perform might be verified; and how an appropriate structure of management qualifications could be put in place. This work drew upon the methods used to specify vocational standards in industry and commerce, and led to the development and introduction of competence-based management standards and qualifications. In this context, competence is defined as the ability to perform the activities within an occupation or function to the standards expected in employment.

It is this competence-based approach that is new in our thinking about the manager's capabilities. It is also what is new about this series of books, in that they are designed to support both this new structure of management standards, and of development activities based on it. The series was originally commissioned to support the Institute of Management's Certificate and Diploma qualifications, which were one of the first to be based on the new standards. However, these books are equally appropriate to any university, college or indeed company course leading to a certificate in management or diploma in management studies.

The standards were specified through an extensive process of consultation with a large number of managers in organizations of many different types and sizes. They are therefore employment based and employer supported. And they fill the gap that Mangham and Silver identified – now we do have a language to describe what it is employers want their managers to be able to do – at least in part.

If you are engaged in any form of management development leading to a certificate or diploma qualification conforming to the national management standards, then you are probably already familiar with most of the key ideas on which the standards are based. To achieve their key purpose, which is defined as achieving the organization's objectives and continuously improving its performance, managers need to perform four key roles: managing operations, managing finance, managing people and managing information. Each of these key roles has a sub-structure of units and elements, each with associated performance and assessment criteria.

The reason for the qualification 'in part' is that organizations are different, and jobs within them are different. Thus the generic management standards probably do not cover all the management competences that you may need to possess in your job. There are almost certainly additional things, specific to your own situation in your own organization, that you need to be able to do. The standards are necessary, but almost certainly not sufficient. Only you, in discussion with your boss, will be able to decide what other capabilities you need to possess. But the standards are a place to start, a basis on which to build. Once you have demonstrated your proficiency against the standards, it will stand you in good stead as you progress through your organization, or change jobs.

So how do the new standards change the process by which you develop yourself as a manager? They change the process of development, or of gaining a management qualification, quite a lot. It is no longer a question of acquiring information and facts, perhaps by being 'taught' in some classroom environment, and then being tested to see what you can recall. It involves demonstrating, in a quite specific way, that you can do certain things to a particular standard of performance. And because of this, it puts a much greater onus on you to manage your own development, to decide how you can demonstrate any particular competence, what evidence you need to present, and how you can collect it. Of course, there will always be people to advise and guide you in this, if you need help.

But there is another dimension, and it is to this that this series of books is addressed. While the standards stress ability to perform, they do not ignore the traditional knowledge base that has been associated with 'management studies'. Rather, they set this in a different context. The standards are supported by 'underpinning knowledge and understanding' which has three components:

- Purpose and context, which is knowledge and understanding of the manager's objectives, and of the relevant organizational and environmental influences, opportunities and values.
- Principles and methods, which is knowledge and understanding of the theories, models, principles, methods and techniques that provide the basis of competent managerial performance.
- Data, which is knowledge and understanding of specific facts likely to be important to meeting the standards.

Possession of the relevant knowledge and understanding underpinning the standards is needed to support competent managerial performance as specified in the standards. It also has an important role in supporting the transferability of management capabilities. It helps to ensure that you have done more than learned 'the way we do things around here' in your own organization. It indicates a recognition of the wider things which underpin competence, and that you will be able to change jobs or organizations and still be able to perform effectively.

These books cover the knowledge and understanding underpinning the management standards, most specifically in the category of principles and methods. But their coverage is not limited to the minimum required by the standards, and extends in both depth and breadth in many areas. The authors have tried to approach these underlying principles and methods in a practical way. They use many short cases and examples which we hope will demonstrate how, in practice, the principles and methods, and knowledge of purpose and context plus data, support the ability to perform as required by the management standards. In particular we hope that this type of presentation will enable you to identify and learn from similar examples in your own managerial work.

You will already have noticed that one consequence of this new focus on the standards is that the traditional 'functional' packages of knowledge and theory do not appear. The standard textbook titles such as 'quantitative methods', 'production management', 'organizational behaviour', etc. disappear. Instead, principles and methods have been collected together in clusters that more closely match the key roles within the standards. You will also find a small degree of overlap in some of the volumes, because some principles and methods support several of the individual units within the standards. We hope you will find this useful reinforcement.

Having described the positive aspects of standards-based management development, it would be wrong to finish without a few cautionary remarks. The developments described above may seem simple, logical and uncontroversial. It did not always seem that way in the years of work which led up to the introduction of the standards. To revert to the revolution analogy, the process has been marked by ideological conflict and battles over sovereignty and territory. It has sometimes been unclear which side various parties are on – and indeed how many sides there are! The revolution, if well advanced, is not at an end. Guerrilla warfare continues in parts of the territory.

Perhaps the best way of describing this is to say that, while competence-based standards are widely recognized as at least a major part of the answer to improving managerial performance, they are not the whole answer. There is still some debate about the way competences are defined, and whether those in the standards are the most appropriate on which to base assessment of managerial performance. There are other models of management competences than those in the standards.

There is also a danger in separating management performance into a set of discrete components. The whole is, and needs to be, more than the sum of the parts. Just like bowling an off-break in cricket, practising a golf swing or forehand drive in tennis, you have to combine all the separate movements into a smooth, flowing action. How you combine the competences, and build on them, will mark your own individual style as a manager.

We should also be careful not to see the standards as set in stone. They determine what today's managers need to be able to do. As the arena in which managers operate changes, then so will the standards. The lesson for all of us as managers is that we need to go on learning and developing, acquiring new skills or refining existing ones. Obtaining your certificate or diploma is like passing a mile post, not crossing the finishing line.

All the changes and developments of recent years have brought management qualifications, and the processes by which they are gained, much closer to your job as a manager. We hope these books support this process by providing bridges between your own experience and the underlying principles and methods which will help you to demonstrate your competence. Already, there is a lot of evidence that managers enjoy the challenge of demonstrating competence, and find immediate benefits in their jobs from the programmes based on these new-style qualifications. We hope you do too. Good luck in your career development.

Paul Jervis

Preface

This book is written for 'first-line' and 'middle' managers and although these are not precise definitions we believe that people working in industrial, commercial and public service organizations will have a high degree of common understanding of what they mean.

However, it may help you, the reader, if we say here what we believe to be the essential characteristics of these groups of people.

As managers, they will be 'responsible' for achieving business or organizational objectives by producing goods or services for a client or customer. In order to do this they will have to work through others and will be 'accountable' for the resources of people, money and facilities and/or plant and equipment.

Within limits, they will have 'discretion' in the way that they manage their resources. They will have some authority in the selection of staff, in the way work is organized and allocated, in the way money is spent and resources are provided and utilized.

If discretion does not exist within a job, and the individual cannot take decisions in non-standard situations, then, whatever the job title, it is most likely a supervisory and not a managerial job. The 'first line' manager is the first level at which discretionary decision-making takes place. The 'middle manager' is the manager who operates through other managers – a manager of managers.

In very many situations, managers will find that the limits of their discretion are not very well defined and therefore in exercising that discretion and making decisions they will need to exercise sound 'judgement' of the situation. Sometimes, because of ambiguities concerning what they may or may not do, managers will also need 'independence' to make up their own minds and 'courage' to create precedents.

To be effective, organizations need effective managers who act decisively to get things done. This is not an argument for giving managers complete licence, for they will always need to work within a framework of policy advice and guidance from peers and bosses as well as staff. It is, however, a statement of belief that, in order to deliver a product or service of the right quality at the right time, managers have to be decisive. This is particularly true for managers in their operational role when they are delivering goods or services to customers and when decisive action is required to produce timely action. This will mean that they cannot please all of the people all of the time and if the essential objective is to please the customer, then other involved people within the organization will find their interests being subordinated to those of the marketplace.

The book is written as a companion to the national occupational standards for managers and as a support for managers working towards the National Vocational Qualifications (NVQ) at level 4 and level 5. The national standards, compiled by MCI (Management Charter Initiative), are, however, simply a basic description of the job of the manager; as such, what we have written will be relevant to all managers, whether or not they are aiming for NVQs.

This book is specifically concerned with the units and elements of competence which fall within the role of managing operations. We are not writing about what is classically understood as 'operations management', although a number of principles and issues will be drawn from this area. What we are concerned with is how managers control whatever 'operation' is at the core of their responsibility. Thus, the production manager in a manufacturing organization makes a physical product; the depot manager in a transport company organizes a fleet of vehicles to carry goods to their destination; the retail store manager ensures a stock of goods to sell to the customer; the nursing manager provides an appropriate and adequate level of nursing care to the patients; finance managers of large organizations collect, analyse and interpret data – they probably also pay suppliers, obtain payment from customers and pay the wages of the workforce.

It is these key activities, which are central to the manager's job, which we mean when we refer to 'managing your operation'.

We believe that the MCI standards provide an excellent checklist against which managers can examine their own jobs in order to see how they can be done better. At the same time they provide an agenda for examining the organizational framework in which they work. We also believe that, out of this examination, there can be developed a constructive dialogue which will improve performance through improved organization as well as through better trained managers.

If organizations are going to encourage effective and decisive managers, they must ensure that they create the conditions which encourage managers to be effective. This means setting out clear objectives for the manager's job; it means setting out clear organizational policies and procedures for such things as capital expenditure, staff development, information technology or procurement. It also means ensuring that such procedures act as a support to the manager's task rather than a hindrance to action. We hope that this book will not only help managers perform their operational tasks more effectively but also help them to influence and effect the continual organizational change required to bring about continuous improvement.

We believe that the majority of our audience will be managers of a department or perhaps more than one department, and probably working in medium-to-large organizations. However, we are sure that what we say will be just as relevant for managers in small organizations, although the structure in which they work will be somewhat different.

Our own backgrounds are in industrial and commercial organizations and therefore it is inevitable that something of this experience comes through. We feel, though, that rather than pretend that we understand the operational requirements of every kind of organization, be it heavy engineering, coal mining, banking or the Health Service, we should write from our own understanding and assume that our readers are better qualified than we are to translate principles into their own particular operating situation. What we do believe is that there are principles which can be applied across a very broad spectrum of management jobs, and our aim throughout is to provide practical observations and advice which is directly applicable to the reality of managing an operation.

There are, too, within the MCI units and elements of competence concerned with 'managing operations' certain broad themes:

- maintaining high quality standards;
- managing resources and suppliers;
- looking for continuous improvement; and
- effecting changes required for improvement.

These themes are the underlying themes of this book.

1 What business are you in – and does your operation match it?

Introduction

For most of our managerial lives we are asked to take custody of a 'running' operation – i.e. the operating unit, group or department was already in existence before we took responsibility for it and it will continue after we have moved on. Ours is a custodial role, to manage it for a period of time. We take over systems designed by other people; routines chosen by predecessors to suit their way of doing things. The equipment for which we become responsible may have been in place some time, selected then, we trust, to suit the business needs as someone at that time saw them. Our staff were chosen – recruited, promoted, trained – by former managers and organized in a way to suit their (the previous managers') way of working. All these aspects of the operation for which we are now responsible would have been influenced by the financial state of the company when all these former decisions were made. Lean times usually mean low-cost decisions, richer times maybe more expansive but possibly less considered solutions. Sometimes corporate policies would have ruled – 'this organization will standardize on XYZ company's computer equipment, or US Inc's advertising services'.

A whole host of influences impacted, controlled, guided, forced our predecessors to make decisions for the operation for which we have now been made responsible. It is highly unlikely we will know of all these influences, even if we've been in the company or department before. Maybe no one individual does know all the history and the rationale for the selections that have been made. But whether we know that history or not, we are now responsible for the results of all those decisions – namely the operation itself. Our job now is to keep it all running smoothly. Or is it? We think it is worth checking a few things about the structure and organization of an operation, and in this chapter we aim to help you do that.

This chapter is concerned with:

- assessing the need for change;
- achieving focus;
- key tasks and determining customer needs;
- strategy alignment and team work;
- aligning the sales operation;
- internal and external customers; and
- responsiveness.

The chapter relates to the MCI standards as follows:

- M1/1.1: Maintain operations to meet quality standards.
- M1/1.2: Create and maintain the necessary conditions for productive work.
- M2/1.1: Identify opportunities for improvement in services, products and systems.
- M2/2.2: Establish and agree customer requirements.

Assessing the need for change

Keeping things running smoothly is essential and there is always a strong temptation to avoid unnecessary disturbance. Such an attitude is understandable and obviously stems from the need to ensure that the operation does its best to support the business. However, our concern is that it probably leads to managers continuing to run operations in the way they were running when they took them over, without due consideration for whether or not that is the right thing to do. On day one of the 'new ownership' there is really no other way. The operation runs and you are new – you do not know enough to change anything even if

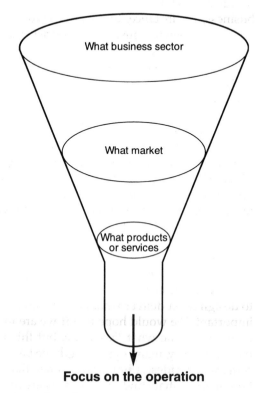

Focus on the operation

Figure 1.1 The focus funnel

you wanted to. It is highly likely instant changes would cause things to grind to a halt because you and your people need time to adjust to one another. Anyway, who said anything needs changing at all? If the operation is running, why this talk of change?

Indeed, things may well be fine. The operation may be well chosen, the result of sound decisions which collectively provide for an efficient and effective unit; one that is supporting the business to its maximum capability. However, the manager needs to know how to judge these issues for him- or herself as the essential precursor to deciding if any change is required. So how might you go about this assessment?

To try to provide some answers we would like you to consider a situation few of us are lucky enough to experience, namely that of the new or 'green field' operation. In such a situation there is no operation to take over; we have to design it and we need a framework to help us.

Figure 1.1 illustrates a process which can begin to help us to think through the design of an operation in such a 'green field' situation.

Achieving focus

In a 'green field' situation, the first task for the management is to decide the sector of the market on which it is going to focus. For a hotel business, for instance, this would involve decisions such as whether the aim is towards business or tourist trade; short-term or long-term clientele, high quality or low cost. For a manufacturing business, it would involve such aspects as commodity or niche markets, high or low volumes, single or multiple products.

Having made our decision about the market sector in which we are going to operate, we are then in a position to decide on the essential features of the products or services which we are going to offer.

As an example, if we were setting up a 'business' hotel we would need to consider the services that business clients would expect, such as late check-in, early check-out, communication systems (telephone, fax, business video conferencing), secretarial services, conferencing/ meeting facilities. This thinking process then leads us to consider the type of operation that has to deliver those products or services. We are attempting to 'focus' our minds upon the essentials of the deliverables from the operation. Although it is our own minds we are trying to focus, we are actually making an attempt to put ourselves in someone else's mind, namely that of our customer. The operation we are going to design must deliver what our customer values, not what *we* think is important. We would hope that if we are in tune with our customer(s) *we* would value what *they* value, but this is certainly not universally the case. Many, many operations have been set up to provide what the company decides is important rather than what its customers need. Low market share and low margins are almost always the result and, in severe cases of mismatch, eventual failure of that operation if not the company. This phase of focusing minds, therefore, should not be rushed, as everything flows from the results of these crucial decisions, and it usually takes time to research and understand what customers really value. Our aim is to deliver on these customer-valued aspects better than any of our competitors, and our operation must be set up to do this. Focus is the vital first step in this process – that is why we have called Figure 1.1 'The focus funnel'.

Box 1.1

The UK business press reported on a trend in volume hotel operations within the UK. This is the provision of low-cost commodity type hotel accommodation aimed primarily at the business traveller. The major chains, such as Trust House Forte and Granada, are introducing these new hotels as rapidly as they can. Location is vital, and they are always sited at strategic road travel points, excellent access by car being crucial. Accommodation is standard, and satisfies the majority of overnight needs; it includes families, so as not to eliminate an important section of the market. Running such an operation as this particular type of hotel requires specialized systems and staff; twenty-four hour coverage is essential for very late arrivals and very early departures; simple, fast billing; straightforward restaurants, not 'a la carte' are required here. And so on – the whole operation geared to the market need. Its success shows it is just that.

At this point, let us revert to the more common situation of managers – maybe you, who are running a longstanding operation rather than our 'green field' hypothesis. If you are in this situation, are you clear about the focus of the organization and your own operation? What market have you chosen to operate in? Is it one clear market segment or several? Does your own operation serve more than one market through the products and services you provide? And are you clear about the inference behind this latter point, namely, just what *are* the products and/or services your own operation is in place to provide? We think it is more difficult to be clear about these issues when the business has a long history because the original focus may well have become blurred to the managers now running the operation. This is why we are using the green field example as people often find this a simpler concept.

Try to project your current business into a green field situation and focus in on these vital aspects of your current products or services. You may need to talk to others in your business to get at this information – obvious choices would be marketing, sales, your boss, the MD, design, product managers, branch managers, and customer service groups. Indeed, many departments have a contribution to this discussion and you will be surprised, if not confused, by some of the views expressed. You may find they differ widely and this will not make it easy to produce the focus you need. Persist – it is vital for your successful contribution to the business through your operation that you succeed in this search. Indeed, your probing questions may promote a business and management team discussion that will help everyone through better business focus. Remember, you are not out to be provocative – you are simply trying to give a better service from your operation. We will return to this issue later as the whole picture becomes clearer; but before moving on, try completing Box 1.2.

Box 1.2
1 Our chosen market sector is:

2 The products/services I provide are:

3 My customers are:

Key tasks and determining customer needs

Returning to Figure 1.1, we have so far considered the market focus of the business or organization and how this helps us to understand what we are trying to achieve. We now need to carry out a further check on the quality of this focus – is it sharp enough? To do this we can use some thinking expounded in the West by Professor Wickham Skinner from the USA, who has provided much food for thought to those employed in the field of operational management. In this particular area of focus for the operation, Skinner uses the idea of the 'key task', and we will spend a few minutes explaining this useful concept.

Skinner believes that in any operation there is one single critical performance factor which can make or break the business. Concentrating on this activity ensures the success of the operation and the business. The key task is identified in relation to customer need.

If we consider the customers served by the operation, we must be clear about their needs if we are to serve them well. If we are not clear about this, our business performance owes as much to luck as to any planning we might do. We *must* be clear on this issue if we are to improve our operation's ability to serve the market well and from that to improve customer service levels and, eventually, our market share. These are the aspects of our total business we need to improve for survival and growth, and the improvements must target the areas the customers truly value.

It is essential to 'know your customer and your customer's needs' before setting about the design of an effective operation. We address this topic in more depth later when we look at quality and performance assessment. Right-minded management teams constantly seek to learn more about their customers' needs and how they are changing. This is a fast-moving age, and assumptions that we understand our customers, markets, products and services without a regular process of updating could lead us into business dead-ends.

So in this quest for our customers' needs, we will produce, from whatever source, a list of product and service characteristics which could be seen as benefits. These would include:

- high quality;
- reliability of products and services;
- meeting promises;
- courtesy;
- low prices;
- after-sales service;
- regional/national/international coverage;
- leading-edge technology;
- respected image;
- wide range of products or services;
- 'one-stop' shopping – 'we meet all your needs';
- twenty-four-hour coverage; and
- fastest, i.e. shortest timescales.

The list, while not comprehensive, is reasonably long, embracing – as we are trying to – any and every type of business. For your individual business it will still be long, and the wider the range of services, products and customers served by your operation, the longer the list will be. (Usually, this occurs with older, established businesses and operations where the business has expanded to absorb and take advantage of new business opportunities as they have arisen.)

Does a long list matter? Surely all it shows is that all customers have become much more demanding? They want everything! And we must provide it if we are to survive and win their business. To a certain degree this is correct. However, even if all things are equal, some things are more equal than others! Not all items in the needs list are equally important and this brings us back to Wickham Skinner's thinking process. He challenges us to be clear about the really important items in the list or, for him and his model, the really important single item. His basic premise is that, in order to retain customers, markets and market share, we must excel at supplying customer needs, but no operation can excel – be the world's best – on all fronts. It cannot be the lowest cost, most flexible, highest specification, most responsive. They are conflicting characteristics for a single operation, and anyone trying to achieve this multi-purpose target will simply compromise performance on all fronts; it will be unexceptional at everything and outstanding at nothing. In his eyes, this is what has happened to many Western businesses and we have lost the advantage of focus. This focus must be on the 'most important item' as perceived by the customer, and we must become outstanding at that aspect. This, then, is what Skinner refers to as the 'key operations task'. If we are working to his model, no decisions we make would ever jeopardize or compromise outstanding (market leading) performance in this key task.

It may help to illustrate this approach by considering a true commodity market, one for product or services where there is a standard offering made by many suppliers and not differentiated by quality or service. The long-term winner in a true commodity market will be the lowest cost producer. Hence the key task in a true commodity market is to achieve low, or lowest cost. This is the performance characteristic that must never be compromised by ill thought-through decisions.

Box 1.3
Price is a marketing or business decision. A high-cost producer can take a contract at a low price by squeezing margins or 'buying' into a market, i.e. taking no profit. But this can never be a long-term strategy – to be successful, businesses must make money! So over the long haul the winner will be the lowest cost producer.

In this demanding world customers do expect good performance on all fronts, but not necessarily outstanding, world-class performance on all fronts. This is, however, what they expect in the area of the key task. That is what makes it the key task!

The most usual starting point when establishing your operation's key task is to question your senior management and your sales and marketing departments. If they respond to your questions by asking for excellence on all fronts, be wary. They, you and your business, may be on the slippery slope towards a general purpose operation that satisfies no-one. Dangerous! You may need to educate them along the way that you need more guidance than they are providing.

We do have some reservations about Skinner's idea of the single key task. Although it is a very valuable concept in channelling debate, leading to focus for us and our operation, we think it needs refining for most operations. It is probably too simplistic to think of an operation having only one key task. Most operations do have to serve several if not many customers and their differing needs do mean we have differing demands placed on those operations. As many operations service diverse customer bases, we should consider an expansion to maybe two key tasks and, in some special cases, three. If you highlight more than this you are really in the field of the general operation full of compromises, and better-targeted competitors will almost always out-perform you in your selected markets. Steer clear of long lists of key operation tasks because you are unlikely to be able to deliver outstanding performance on all those fronts simultaneously. Prune the list severely (but carefully, like a valued rose bush) to one, two or at most three performance aspects that count (Box 1.4). Now you have a direction for continued efforts to enable your business to succeed in the marketplace through sharper-focused operations.

Box 1.4
The key task(s) of my operation are:

No. 1

No. 2

(Sometimes) No. 3

Strategy alignment and team work

We have been talking here about the focus of *your* operation but undoubtedly your operation is only a part of the whole. Other managers – your peers? – are responsible for their own operations. Together, all your separate operations or functions will combine to make the organization. In some organizations this act of combining is well managed, and in others not so well managed. When departments work well together, it will be because their 'key task' is aligned to the overall strategy of the organization. If all operating units of the organization are pursuing the same key task or tasks, you give yourself a better chance of succeeding in the market. When the salesforce is out there selling high-performance products or services *and* 'operations' are targeting above all else to deliver high-performance products, then you stand a good chance of satisfying your customers. When the sales force is selling high performance while operations are straining to achieve lowest cost, you have a mismatch and customers are likely to be disappointed. Remember that sweet-talking sales staff and impressive PR may well get you the first order. After that, the customer sees your company through the performance of the operation. Operating performance wins or loses you follow-on business! When the key tasks of all the different parts of the organization line up behind the overall strategy, we say that we have 'strategic alignment'.

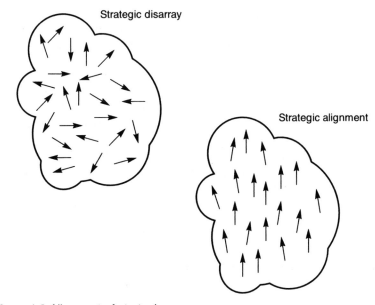

Figure 1.2 Alignment of strategies

Figure 1.2 gives a representation of this, each arrow depicting strategic direction and decisions for separate parts of the operation. Alignment does not mean slavish adherence to central policy. It *does* mean adherence and support for a general direction.

Sometimes, perhaps in order to improve performance in a specific area, a particular part of the organization may need to deviate from the alignment. This could be to achieve a valuable step-change in a performance element valued by an important part of the market, say an important customer. An example of this might be a print room buying a new copying machine because it provides higher quality printing, when the whole organization is pursuing a policy of speedier market response. This would be a legitimate one-off decision if the print room manager had evidence to say they were falling behind market standards or that adverse customer comments had been received. However, most decisions should support the speedier response drive.

Such minor deviations apart, the informed observer will be able to see how all decisions and initiatives fall into alignment across the various departments and operations of a well-organized business. This alignment identifies a robust organization to the outside world and is particularly powerful in relation to customers and competitors.

Strategic alignment can be likened to the cohesion of a tug-of-war team. Watching a high-class competition between very accomplished teams really illustrates the value of working together in every sense of the phrase. Each team is made up of very big, powerful individuals, but it is unusual to be able to pick out the winners before the pulling starts. All teams look much the same when assessed for individual size and fitness. However, once the competition, the pulling, starts, the major factor affecting the outcome is the way the team pulls together. Timing is everything and the team which wins is the one which achieves split-second timing throughout the event. They know when to keep a steady pull on the rope – taking the strain to resist the other team's best efforts – and when to exert that extra effort themselves to pull the other team off-balance and have them slithering forward to defeat. Top teams at national or international level are a revelation and it is clear what great efforts go into achieving this split-second timing. To ensure success during the pull, they have an organizer, a team leader, to produce this result. In their case the key task is getting the right timing.

This simple case can be parallelled in the business world. If the key task is too important to be left to chance in tug-of-war, and needs a dedicated team leader, the same is surely true of business. In the absence of anyone else doing it, you must first seek out and develop your operation's ability to deliver on the key tasks and then try to ensure your peers do the same. We are not advocating interference in other managers' affairs but a concerned enquiry to ensure that all team members know 'in which direction we are pulling', i.e. the key task discussion again; having established that, then to ensure, as in a tug-of-war, that all parts of the operation are co-ordinated. You may not have formal responsibility for this, but as an aware manager you can demonstrate both the negative impact of disparate efforts and the positive effects of alignment. In so doing, you can seek to guide events through the exertion of influence.

Aligning the sales operation

The relationship between the sales operation and the rest of the operating departments is critical. Too many times in our experience there is a major difference, not only of opinion on the strategy or key tasks, but also in the execution. Too many times sales staff accept orders that the organization cannot deliver; there is no greater cause of internal wrangling, mistrust, even hatred in our experience, than this continual self-inflicted problem. If it is that common, why is it not better understood and then avoided? Why do seemingly intelligent people keep making these mistakes?

The answer is not too difficult to find and is usually explained by differing objectives and differing pressures or constraints placed on both parties. To take sales first, they are operating in the cauldron of the marketplace. Very rarely do they have the comfort of a seller's market, where they can sell on their own terms. More usually, the need to match and/or beat the efforts of competitors, whether real or perceived, together with a genuine desire to give the customer what he or she wants, leads sales people to agree to things that the other operations simply cannot achieve. The inevitable problems then arise internally (arguments, disputes, accusations, constant progress chasing) and externally (apologies, failed deliveries of products or services, upset customers). These instances eat into margins, cause losses and exacerbate the problems.

However, we have only looked at the sales side for the causes. What about our own operating area? The issue is this: if the market is really demanding the performance the sales team had to agree to and the rest of the organization cannot achieve it, ask yourself why, and what the likely outcome of this will be. The answer to the first part of this question may be that your operation is out of touch with its market and that as you have not addressed this problem you cannot satisfactorily serve your customers. Sales have a right to expect more from you. Clearly, the likely outcome if this situation continues is a decline in, or loss of, business; an unattractive proposition. You must resolve it positively and we aim to provide help in our chapters on matching resources to demand, quality and improvement.

But why does an organization lose touch with its customers in the first place, if it is so important? The answer is often to be found when we look at the objectives and performance measures placed on most operations. It is usually the case that most operations are given internally-oriented objectives – operating or unit costs, efficiency, meeting budgets, waste or scrap levels, headcount, material costs. The big drawback of such objectives is that they do not of themselves impact on the customers of the operation. To adopt a customer or market focus and hence keep ourselves ahead of market requirements we need different types of objectives. These will be customer-oriented objectives – such things as delivery performance, lead times, product reliability, defect rates – and will be in addition to some of the more important 'good housekeeping' type of objectives highlighted above. Meeting and improving on these outward-looking objectives will keep us more in tune with what our customers want. Chapter 8 goes into this in more detail.

The internal and the external customer

Much of what we have been saying has been centred on the external customer, those people or bodies who use or buy the product or service from the total organization.

To any organization these are the most important type of customers because without enough of them we go out of business. In a non-business organization our services are withdrawn because on-one wants them. But for many of us, particularly those of us in operational management, there is another type of customer, the internal customer, who is usually *our* customer. In the past, traditional thinking has not recognized the internal clients we serve as 'customers', with the implied need to give them the sort of service that we would expect to give an external customer. Obvious and universal examples of this are purchasing operations and research and development. Neither is supplying the external customers of the organization, but is providing services and goods to other departments to enable them to do so. Less obvious examples are probably finance operations and personnel operations. In our experience, too often these functions are run as fiefdoms by their managers, over-concerned with technical issues of their particular specialism. In the 'internal customer' model these managers need to be asking 'who are my customers and how can I serve them better, so that they can better serve the external customer?'.

Where is your operation situated in this model? Do you have external or internal customers, or both? You may provide several products or services to several different customers and some may be external and some internal. The important thing here is to be clear about who your customers are. Write them down, particularly if they are internal, as this is the type of customer we most easily overlook or take for granted. We will be looking at ways of ensuring good contact and communication with your customers as they hold the key to focusing improvement plans. Their feedback will be the priming pump of these improvements.

Responsiveness

What you decide about your customers' needs and the key tasks suitable for your purposes will depend on your type of operation. One area of operating performance which is common to all operations, is responsiveness to the market. As competition becomes tougher and markets faster-moving, our customers are making it more an essential feature of all successful operations. More and more organizations and businesses are finding it essential to be flexible in their operations as customers demand more of their own way. We are all demanding more ourselves as customers, in restaurants, on aircraft, in hotels, as buyers in shops. When suppliers cannot or will not respond, we are upset and may indeed take our business elsewhere – if not now, in the future. Responsiveness is what we expect as customers and these are features we must be better able to deliver as suppliers. Are you and your operation treating this area of performance seriously enough? How often do you tell your customers, internal or external, 'I'm sorry, we can't do that'? If it is too often, your operation is preventing you meeting customer needs, with inevitable long-term results.

Summary

When taking over an existing operation, particularly if it is of long standing, it is important to question whether it is (still) organized to match the business you are in. Start by reviewing the focus of the business or operation on the market you are serving. Focus can be sharpened by establishing your key task or key tasks against a well-researched list of customer needs. It is essential to keep key tasks to a minimum – ideally one, three at the most. Within an organization it is essential that key tasks for different parts are aligned to deliver the overall strategy. Ensure that the sales team does not offer more than the other operating departments can deliver. Recognize internal customers as such and give them the best possible service as a means of serving your external customers. Responsiveness to both the market and customers' needs is an essential common feature for all operations.

Management checklist

- How was your operation set up to fulfil its function? Has there been a review since? How could you improve it?
- How well do you understand your customers' requirements? Where do you get this information from? Are you satisfied that it reflects what they really want?
- List the qualities your customers seek from your operation.
- Having identified your Key Tasks, what do you need to do to secure outstanding performance?
- How would you score your company's strategic alignment on a scale of 1–10? Are there any parts of the organization operating to their own private agenda? What can you do to correct any failings?
- Do you have internal customers? Do you treat them like external customers? List the ways in which you could improve your service to them.
- Check your own responsiveness using Box 1.6.

Box 1.6
Responsiveness and your operation

When did a customer ask for something on which you could not deliver? Who was it? What was requested? What constrained you?

The instance	Who made request?	What was it?	What constrained you?
1.			
2.			
3.			

On a scale of 1–10, how would you vote yourself? Are you satisfied with your rating?

2 Get your operation in context

Introduction

We assume that most readers will be managers, running departments or sections within larger organizations. Many of you will be responsible for several departments with first-line managers reporting to them. In smaller organizations you may be at, or near, the top of your business and this will mean that the problems you have will not all be quite the same. However, the basic frameworks and the messages will be relevant to all these varied operations. You will need to make the connections which make them relevant to your specific job.

One of the major problems in organizations is to ensure that all departments are working together to fulfil the overall mission of the organization, and we have already explored this problem in Chapter 1. The converse of this is the problem of department managers who frequently feel that other departments are working against them and not with them, or that they are not clear enough about the overall strategy of the organization to be able to make departmental decisions which properly support that strategy. When this is the case, managers will make decisions in a way which will suit their department and not necessarily the departments with which they interface, nor the organization as a whole.

When strategy is clear you can see how decisions made in different parts of the organization line-up to support that strategy.

> Box 2.1
>
> If your strategy includes a high level of customer service you will find the marketing and customer service departments devoting resources to investigating what the customer really wants; employees at all levels and in all departments fully aware of the customers' needs; information to all employees about customer success stories and customer complaints; training to incorporate customer service values and processes for achieving them; investigation and analysis of business processes and a willingness to alter established systems to give better service; investment in stock management or computer systems or improved vehicles or brochures; upgrading of staff with customer contact and recruitment of a better type of staff – all those things, in fact, which distinguish 'smile campaigns' from a genuine attempt to give better service. Most people within an organization, and particularly managers, can recognize the signs.

Often middle managers make decisions which are sensible for their departments but which do not make sense for the organization as a whole, which indicates a lack of understanding of the objectives of the organization as a whole. Sometimes lack of understanding of strategy is simply a lack of information. This is not necessarily because senior managers are unwilling, for whatever reason, to impart that information, although this is occasionally true. Often it is because senior managers just don't realise what middle- and first-line managers need to know and don't know. Sometimes information systems are not geared to supply first-line and middle-managers with information concerning the overall performance of the organization which would help them run their own departments. Sometimes organizational needs and structures change, without a change in the information systems to reflect this.

This can be particularly true with the trend towards 'delayering' – the removal of a whole layer of management within an organization. The idea behind this is that too many layers of management have been allowed to build up between the policy makers on the 'Board' and the 'sharp-end' managers who have to deal with the operations and the customer. It is argued that these intermediate layers form an unnecessary and costly barrier to information flows both up and down the organization. This in turn creates delays in decision-making, both by those dealing with the customer and by the 'Board' in making tactical and strategic decisions.

Removing a whole level of management, as sometimes happens, obviously has significant effects on the way an organization runs and, with the best will in the world, it is not always possible to anticipate every effect. Each level of management fulfils a positive purpose: filtering information upwards so that senior management does not get swamped, interpreting information downwards or acting as a safety net. Removing one level of management empowers those at the next level down, but may at the same time remove a source of knowledge and advice.

With flatter organizations with fewer intermediate management levels between the policy makers and the 'sharp-end' operators, it is even more important that first-line and middle-managers have a good understanding of the organization's overall policies and objectives. This is essential to ensure that operational decisions can be made which are in accordance with the overall objectives of the organization. This chapter will examine the issues which can help operating managers to understand the organization's overall strategy, and in particular will discuss:

- the 'business plan';
- departmental budgets;
- the 'value chain';
- the operations role;

- the contribution of specialist support services; and
- accountability and authority.

The chapter has a general application to the MCI units concerned with the key role of 'Managing Operations'.

The 'business plan'

The term 'business plan' may not seem entirely appropriate for all organizations, but increasingly it is being used by non-commercial organizations such as government departments and charities, and it has acquired a common currency. There are a number of different terms used to describe the planning processes of organizations, although there are few definitions which will mean precisely the same thing from one organization to another. Check carefully the exact definition of planning terms within your organization.

At the corporate level, we have statements of 'vision' and 'mission' which are more like articles of faith than planning statements. Sometimes it is difficult to distinguish what is 'vision' and what is 'mission' and the debate can become somewhat academic.

Box 2.2

Vision and mission statements contain very broad and philosophical statements of intent such as:

- serving our customer to the highest quality standards;
- providing industry leadership; or
- developing a public reputation as a good corporate citizen.

Often they describe what the organization is striving to become.

These statements are sometimes expanded and relate to the values held by the organization and the sort of behaviour employees need to demonstrate in order to uphold those values. Such statements can be useful in guiding managers as to how the company expects them to behave, but are not specific enough to indicate what are the goals of their job.

With corporate strategy we begin to get on firmer ground and this will be concerned with such things as: which markets will be attacked or withdrawn from; how expansion will be achieved; how much research will be undertaken and in which areas; how much funding will be needed and how to raise it.

In a *Harvard Business Review* in 1989, Hamel and Prahalad separated the idea of 'strategic intent' from 'strategic planning'. Strategic intent is very long-term and beyond the scope of planning – it may be as grand as 'global leadership', or it may be as specific as Honda starting out by building little motor cycles with the intent of ultimately challenging the Ford Motor Company. Strategic planning is about how you create the steps to achieve the intent.

Strategies may then be set out in a long-range business plan which might cover a period of 3–5 years, setting out how those strategies will be implemented: which parts of the business will expand; which parts will change products; how new plant and equipment will be funded and installed; where and how new staff will be recruited and trained.

In the immediate future, over the ensuing year, these measures will be described in greater detail and will be the basis for setting the budgets for the whole organization. This is a rolling process as each year creates changes and updating in all the plans.

Most organizations have their own terms for the business planning process, but a typical model might look like that in Figure 2.1. Business plans are necessarily confidential documents as, in the case of commercial enterprises, they will contain information which would be of vital interest to a competitor, perhaps about new products or processes or perhaps about the intention to attack a new market sector. They will contain financial information which could influence tendering by suppliers or they could contain information, like the intended closure of a facility, which requires special and careful handling in a controlled manner.

For these reasons business plans need to be kept secure and sometimes this means that within an organization managers are not well informed about the overall objectives nor about the objectives of

		Timescale
Vision/mission	Philosophical statements of what the organization would like to be in both business and social terms.	10 years (approx.)
Strategy and strategic plan	Statement of long-term business aims and the milestones for achieving them.	5–10 years
Long-range business plan	Statement of medium-term business goals and how to achieve them.	3–5 years
Annual business plan	Statement of current year's business goals and how to achieve them.	0–1 year
Annual budget	Detailed (month by month) plan of current year's incomes, expenditure and cash flow.	0–1 year

Not all organizations will have longer-term planning programmes. Some will be thinking ten years ahead, others no more than five – and indeed some no more than to the end of this year!

Figure 2.1 Business planning model

other departments. While this is understandable, it is in the best interest of the organization for responsible managers to have as much information as possible; how else do they know how to focus their efforts? If it is not made available, they should be pro-active in seeking it. In advising you to do this there are two issues which should be borne in mind.

Firstly, the security of the business plan must be acknowledged, and measures need to be taken to safeguard very sensitive information. This means that an edited version may have to be produced which eliminates that information which is ultra-confidential. To release such information too early, and not fully planned, is irresponsible.

Secondly, if managers are going to perform to the best interests of the organization, they need as much information as possible. For their part, they, the managers, must provide the other half of the equation and keep safe this sensitive information. This requires a strong element of trust between managers and their seniors.

It is sometimes the case that senior managers assume that because they know certain things, other managers will also know. In addition, when organizations change, sources of information sometimes disappear, as when levels of management are removed from the structure. It is generally agreed that people at all levels should be fully informed if they are to perform well. This does not mean that everyone needs to know everything but that everyone gets the information they need in order to do a consistently good and improving job. You, as a manager, must seek out the information you need to do your operating job, and use it wisely.

Sometimes strategic information is not passed on because that is the way it was always done in the past. Some senior managers still keep people in the dark deliberately, and we have no easy solutions to that problem; we can only counsel well-thought-out arguments against this practice and repeating them as persistently as may be considered sensible.

Department budgets

The MCI management standards at M1 (NVQ4) and M2 (NVQ5) define the financial responsibilities which managers have when working at these levels. Thus we are writing for people who are responsible for operating their own budgets. At M2 level there is likely to be greater responsibility for the overall preparation and negotiation of budgets. It is not the intention here to discuss the technicalities of budgets and budgeting as this has already been done comprehensively in this series in *Managing Financial Resources* by Broadbent and Cullen (1993), but to look at some of the issues involved in preparing and using budgets.

The preparation of budgets usually involves several weeks, perhaps months, of intense activity, driven by organizational needs and to organizational timetables which cannot have too much regard for the individual departmental concerns. Much of the process is usually conducted by accountants who have to ensure that timetables are adhered to and the Chief Executive gets the necessary information on time. Departmental managers find this process a chore and a distraction, and are sometimes tempted to leave as much as possible to the accountants. Setting the budget is, however, the departmental manager's main opportunity for setting his or her own agenda for the coming year, and should be grasped energetically. The budget obviously derives from the organization's business plan and as such gives a fundamental pointer to the organization's expectations for the inputs and outputs for at least the next twelve months. The discussions around the budget therefore give you a good opportunity to gain a thorough understanding of the big picture regarding the whole of your organization, as well as more detailed information about how related departments will be operating. Get involved!

You will hear old hands talk about budgets being 'tablets of stone' or 'set in concrete' and certainly, once budgets are fixed, in most organizations it becomes very difficult to make alterations in mid-year. The experienced manager therefore ensures that every likely contingency is considered and a view taken. This requires consultation with all the key players who could affect your operation. Within the organization the overall objectives come from the business plan, but it is worthwhile consulting other colleagues in relevant departments such as marketing, purchasing or personnel for their views on how events may develop in the coming year. Additionally, external sources such as suppliers and customers are vital to the process and, while it may not be your direct responsibility to deal with these people, you should consult those for whom it is.

Finally, it is also important to bring into the process as many of your own team as is relevant. The first reason is in order to ensure that no potential happenings or issues are overlooked. Every member of your team is likely to be more expert in their own field than you are, and for that reason have a specialist or expert contribution to make. The second reason is that you will only be able to fulfil your department plan by working through them and, in our experience, one of the best ways to achieve their commitment is to involve them from the outset. Here is the opportunity.

Broadbent and Cullen (1993) make the point that '... budgeting within organizations can be fraught with difficulties. These difficulties are mainly of a behavioural nature.' Most systems in organizations are less than perfect and frequently this is so because they are called on to serve more than one purpose. People can work constructively to make things work and when that happens they usually do. The reverse can also be true and it is your job as a manager to ensure that everyone is pulling together to overcome problems rather than look for imperfections in the system as excuses for failure. First-line and middle-managers have to work within systems laid down in the organization but the need is constantly to look for competitive advantage; to seek it by obtaining better data and by liberating managers from internal cost-system constraints. This choice is making people look for better ways of operating departments as an integral part of a business. This is the basis of what has become known as 'business process re-engineering', in which organizations re-design ways of working and reshape business and organizational systems. The aim is to eliminate old, wasteful methods which lead to high cost and sluggishness. In the budgeting areas we have the ideas of 'zero-based budgeting' as a means of challenging the necessity of operational activities, and 'activity-based budgeting' as an attempt to identify the true cost of products and services. These are both means of getting away from taking last year's budget and updating it by inflation – a widespread practice. Another concept aimed at improving competitive advantage is that of the 'value chain', which is a particularly useful model for managing operations and which we will describe in more detail.

The 'value chain'

Michael Porter in his *Competitive Advantage* (1989) describes the concept of the value chain as a method of separating out the strategically important activities of a business, and of showing how they interact.

All of us carry in our heads a model of how our organization works. This model is usually of the type of the traditional organization chart, and will be influenced by the reporting relationships involved, – i.e. which functions report to different Board members. These reporting relationships may not always be totally logical from a functional point of view, and may reflect historical quirks from the way the organization has evolved over time. In commercial organizations there may also be reflections of the costing structure, particularly in relation to 'direct' and 'indirect' functions.

Box 2.3

Most managers are familiar with the idea of 'direct' activities, those which relate directly to the product or service – and 'indirect' activities which support the direct activities. One of the behavioural problems which result from these definitions is the antagonism which can generate when indirect staff are viewed as superfluous by direct staff and indirect staff feel resentful because their efforts are unrecognized and unappreciated.

A modern phenomenon with high-tech automated systems in all types of business is the declining numbers of direct staff. Traditional assumptions built into costing systems can cause unnecessary weaknesses in systems.

Unfortunately, these traditional functional models or structures really do not help staff understand how the business works and the operations interrelate. The Porter value chain approach can help in this regard. The value chain analyses the structure of the organization in a way which relates activities in a strictly logical operational way. Figure 2.2 shows a generalized model of the chain.

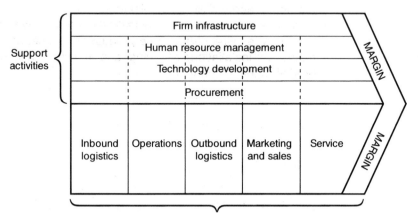

Figure 2.2 The generic value chain (Source: Porter, 1985, reprinted with the permission of The Free Press, a division of Simon & Schuster Inc. Copyright © 1985 by Michael E. Porter)

Porter's model analyses the organization of the business in two categories. 'Primary value activities' consist of the chain of operations which are directly concerned with producing the goods or service and getting them to the customer. 'Support activities' consist of specialist services which contribute to and support the whole range of primary value activities.

One significant difference in the model is the way in which it breaks down primary value activities into functional groups. This analysis puts an emphasis on the contribution of inbound logistics, outbound logistics and service which does not feature in more conventional systems.

Another difference is in the way it seeks to relate support services to the primary value activities. This helps to overcome the weaknesses of systems which imply that 'indirect' or 'overhead' activities do not contribute to the main purpose of the business.

Brief definitions of Porter's terms are as follows:

- Inbound logistics – concerned with receiving and storing raw materials and components, materials handling, warehousing, internal distribution, inventory control and scheduling, i.e. all incoming goods and services needed to run the operation.

- Operations – concerned with transforming raw materials and components into final products or services.
- Outbound logistics – concerned with collecting, storing, warehousing and distributing the finished product or service, i.e. getting it to the customer.
- Marketing and sales – concerned with making the product or service available to buyers and persuading them to buy through advertising, promotion and a selling organization.
- Service – concerned with providing the services which maintain or improve the value of the prime product or service, and covers such things as installation, servicing and maintenance, updating and product enhancement and training.

The support value activities can usually be divided into:

- Procurement – concerns the whole of the function of purchasing materials, components, machinery and equipment, buildings and maintenance services. Procurement is often one of the most diffuse activities within an organization. Purchasing departments often are only concerned with major significant items such as raw materials, plant and equipment, vehicles, oil, gas and electricity, while departmental managers are engaged every day in purchasing a host of (apparently) minor items and sub-contracted services. These in aggregate can amount to a very significant expenditure and yet frequently do not receive the professional scrutiny which they probably warrant. We refer to this more fully in Chapter 5.
- Technology development – concerns the range of activities connected with improving the product *and* the whole process of producing it, such as information technology and office or warehouse automation, product design, research and development (R & D) and production engineering.
- Human resource management – concerns all aspects of ensuring the supply of the right people at all levels and their continuing development. The function is highly significant throughout the whole of the value chain but, as Porter says, it is probably the one whose interaction with the business is least well understood. It is also the function in which there are the most inconsistencies of action, often due to the tension which can exist between operating managers, who are jealous of their relationships with their people, and the perceived impersonality of human resource policies.
- Firm infrastructure – concerns those activities which support the whole of the value chain, and not individual activities, and how they are integrated throughout the organizational structure; examples are finance, secretarial and legal, quality management, stationery and printing. These things are sometimes seen as pure overhead but can also be a source of competitive advantage.

As the manager of a department or departments, you will have a place in your organization's value chain, but the use of this form of analysis does not stop at your own organization. You will be dependent upon suppliers and how their outbound logistics relate directly to your inbound logistics, just as your outbound logistics will relate to the inbound logistics of your customers.

Most managers, whether in the manufacturing sector or not, are aware of the revolution which took place in the motor industry with 'Just-In-Time' (JIT) supply of components and the similar thinking which applies to the supply of products to the large food retail stores. Just-In-Time delivery results in significant cost reductions in warehousing and in work-in-progress inventory; in order to achieve this, however, the supplier has to achieve very high standards of operational efficiency and quality control. In this way the supplier's competitive advantage translates itself into competitive advantage for the customer by reducing the cost of production, and improving flexibility and responsiveness. Additionally, your distribution network and your customer will have their own value chain, which could also influence the attractiveness of your product or service to the customer.

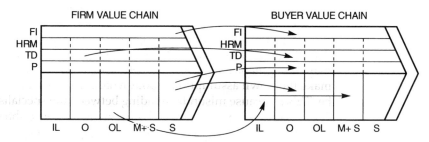

Figure 2.3 Representative linkages between the firm and the buyer's value chain (Source: *Competitive Advantage*, Porter)

Figure 2.3 models how this can be shown.

The value chain analysis can also be extended to your competitors so that not only do you understand your own sources or potential sources of competitive advantage, you are also able to understand those of your competitors.

The contribution of specialist support services

Department managers do not manage in isolation; they are part of a management team which works together to fulfil the organization's objectives, and the more cohesive the team, the more effective the total organization. Very often, however, departments within an organization are supplied by other departments within that same organization, and have customers who are also in the same organization. Creating and maintaining effective working relationships between internal customer and internal supplier needs to be carried out with as much attention as though they were external. Unfortunately, in many organizations this sometimes takes more effort than managing external relationships. This is explored more fully in Chapter 9.

In addition to these working relationships there is the equally important task of managing the working relationship between your department and its specialist support services. The purpose of this section is to examine some of the issues involved in order to encourage you, if that is appropriate, to get better value from your specialists. The main specialist functions that we have in mind are:

- finance;
- human resource;
- research and development;
- purchasing; and
- information technology.

You may well be managing one of these areas; what follows will be just as useful for you as for those who operate in direct line management.

The first issue is that of the terms of reference of specialist departments. These are often not too closely specified, with the result that other managers – and sometimes the specialists themselves – make their own assumptions about what the terms of reference should be. This can cause misunderstanding between the specialists and other departments. It can be argued that terms of reference should therefore be tightly specified but there is usually some reluctance to do this. Organizations are dynamic social systems; they have a need to be constantly evolving to meet the evolving needs of the marketplace in which they operate. The core operating departments of organizations evolve in response to changing customer need but the support services do not have the external customer interface to stimulate change. If they are too restricted in the way they can operate they become rigid and out of touch with the way the organization is changing in response to changes in the external environment. This can make them a hindrance rather than a help, and can make operating departments seek to sub-contract services outside in order to achieve improvement. This is not the most effective way to run an organization. If it applies to your operation, beware! An effective approach, therefore, is not to make assumptions but to ensure that you know how specialists perceive their function and what it is they believe that they should be doing. In many cases, not only does this clarify the relationship but it also helps to shape the specialist function itself. If you manage such a specialism, make sure you and your internal customers have a sound and close understanding.

The second issue concerns the overall function of specialists. Effectively, they have two sets of objectives – one is to provide specialist services to individual parts of the organization on an *ad hoc* basis, and the other is to provide a continuous service to the organization as a whole. In the latter role they may be the guardians of company policy and sometimes of the law of the land. In these capacities they can sometimes be seen as negative – a constraint on a manager's need to get things done.

Box 2.3

It can happen that a manager believes that there is a good cause for dismissing an employee, only to find that the personnel manager insists on the required application of a lengthy formal procedure. Managers should know that such procedures are absolutely necessary but still believe that it is the personnel manager's job to 'fix' such situations. It is the personnel manager's job to ensure that such managers have the right expectations, and the knowledge and understanding to apply the correct procedures.

Thirdly, specialists in their corporate capacity can create extra work for the manager which does not directly further the department's objectives. Frequently this is in the form of a request for non-standard information or data which cannot be produced from the normal data-gathering, or it could be concerned with corporate involvement in some governmental or quasi-governmental initiative such as 'work experience'. For these reasons, functional specialists can become unpopular with other managers, who are struggling to meet business objectives.

Fourthly, functional specialists can set their own agendas for action under the guise of corporate need, but in reality in the interest of increasing their own importance within the organization. Sometimes such motives are not obvious at first but once recognized will result in mistrust and obvious lack of co-operation. Even with good relations, managers themselves can perceive legitimate specialist intervention as a threat and/or restriction to their own personal authority and so they will exclude the specialist as much as possible.

Organizations cannot afford to employ specialist functions in order to contribute to overall corporate effectiveness, if they are only used on a 'take it or leave it' basis. They represent too costly an investment. The managers of specialist functions, then, must ensure that their operations provide real value as seen by their own customers. They must be responsive and innovative – others must *want to use them*. To obtain real benefit, however, requires team work of a high order. As effective team-working between managers often involves issues of authority and accountability and such issues are central to the job of managing effectively, we will conclude this chapter with a brief look at some of the things which are involved.

Accountability and authority

Sometimes some of the toughest situations which managers have to handle are concerned with the issues of accountability and authority. We use the word 'accountability' rather than 'responsibility' because it carries with it the idea of 'answerability'. As a manager, you are not only 'responsible' but you have to 'answer' to someone for what you do.

Accountability and authority should be in balance – the amount of authority you have is exactly the amount required to fulfil the responsibilities which you hold. There is, of course, no golden rule for achieving that balance and we shall not be attempting to find one. For one thing, authority cannot be fully given. You will carry a certain amount of authority by virtue of the position you hold – the 'status' of the job. Some authority can be conferred or removed by the actions of your superior or superiors. If you have their trust and support, it will be apparent to the rest of the organization. If their actions undermine yours it will be equally apparent and will weaken your authority. However, the most important part of your authority as a manager within your own sphere of accountability will come from your own actions. Figure 2.4 offers a simple analysis of the three sources of authority which you will exercise, not only as a manager but in any sort of situation.

All three sources of authority are equally useful to us but there is a subtle difference between structural authority and the other two sources. Every manager should understand this difference. Whereas structural authority is given to us by the organization when we are

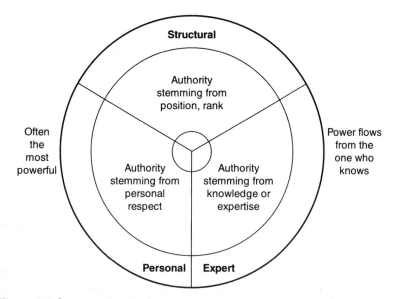

Figure 2.4 Sources of authority

placed in the job, the other two are not. So who gives them to us? When asked this question, managers usually reply 'I do – I give them to myself', but it is not the case. We must do a lot to earn them but we cannot claim them as a right. Our peers, staff and others give us that authority. Unless they see you as an expert, your word has no expert authority with them. The same is true with personal authority. Understanding this will help keep your feet on the ground. Ensure you are not claiming or assuming with others authority you do not have.

Structural authority

Structural authority is the authority conferred by the status of the job, the job title and the company structure. In broad terms, authority will stem from accountability. If you are expected to produce 5,000 meals a week from a hotel kitchen, it is obvious that you will need the authority to decide the programming of the work through the kitchen, the purchase of everyday materials, the scheduling, training and replacement of operating staff – anything, in fact, which affects the day-to-day operation of that unit. This authority, arising from the need to operate effectively, is usually implicit and seldom written down, except in the broadest of terms. In day-to-day working there is a constant need, too, for non-routine decisions and actions which are always slightly different; it would be impossible to describe every potential situation and lay down rules to cover them.

Expert authority

This is the authority we exercise that stems from some area of expertise that we possess. Most managers start their working lives as a specialist in some discipline that begins with a university or vocational education, perhaps as an engineer. After some years practising as working engineers they are promoted to manage others, usually other engineers. For a while they are still as expert as their colleagues, and more so than most in the field of engineering. However, the management role takes them away from full-time practice as an engineer and their expertise wanes. It *must* be replaced by some other expertise, otherwise they are losing a major source of authority. For most of them, that expertise becomes management expertise – to organize, to plan, to co-ordinate, to problem solve, to counsel, to delegate – all those diverse management skills. If they are successful, people will invite them in as experts who are good value to have around.

Personal authority

Personal authority stems from the respect in which you are held and the value which is placed upon your opinions. This may result from your experience, knowledge, intellectual capacity and judgement. It will also reflect the strength of character and personality which you project and the energy and commitment which you bring to any situation.

Managing upwards

In the final analysis, your boss is responsible for everything you do and your authority is delegated by him or her. Delegated authority can be operated at three levels:

- Those things which you do without reference to your boss;
- Those things which you need to inform your boss about, after the event; and
- Those things for which you need to get your boss's approval before proceeding, or your boss specifically asks or gives you to do on his or her behalf.

Defining the boundaries between these levels is something which needs attention. Good managers and good bosses understand this, but we are dealing now with the interaction between two human beings with all the subtleties that this implies. Some bosses like to get more involved than others, and what may seem like legitimate involvement to the boss may seem like interference to you. For you to run your day-to-day operation, you must develop a clear understanding here with your boss. This may take time but it is essential. Work at it!

You may lack confidence and try to get your boss's approval for everything – in which case you are not managing. Getting the balance right is an important part of the manager's job and the management standards define this in the element entitled 'Establish and maintain the trust of one's immediate manager'. More succinctly it is known as 'managing upwards'.

The manager and specialist functions

The issues of accountability and authority between the manager and specialist functions are rather different in that we are not dealing with 'delegated responsibility' but with 'shared responsibility'.

Problems arise for a number of reasons; sometimes when there is not sufficient understanding of the nature of each other's responsibility; sometimes because of individuals pursuing their personal objectives; sometimes because one personality is stronger than the other. Mutual trust, team working and giving credit where it is due is essential to get the best results.

Box 2.4
A purchasing manager finds a cheaper source of raw material for the machine shop but the tolerances are inconsistent and cause stoppages. In any case the machine shop manager has a good relationship with the existing suppliers and knows that they can be relied on to provide emergency deliveries in times of crisis. A 'stand off' between the two of them could result from the purchasing manager thinking that the machine shop manager is in the pocket of the present supplier and the machine shop manager assuming that the purchasing manager was not interested in the ultimate cost and quality of the product, only in demonstrating the lower price.

The machine shop manager is the one accountable for the quality and the cost of the product. He or she should therefore have the authority to make the decision about raw materials. The purchasing manager also is accountable, however; the responsibilities may not be so precisely defined as those of the machine shop manager, but will be concerned with providing a proper supply of the best possible materials at the best possible price. Although the machine shop manager may have the final say in a particular case, he or she is not entitled to disregard the views of the purchasing manager – because of the purchasing manager's overall accountability and specialized knowledge he or she, too, has authority and the machine shop manager must take any proposal very seriously indeed. Obviously in this case, the two must work together with the various suppliers to see if quality could not be improved with the one, and price with the other.

In different organizations the nature of accountability and authority will differ. We have just referred to the role of purchasing manager in a manufacturing organization where it is a question of supplying a raw material to an operator. In that same organization the purchasing manager may have an entirely different accountability and authority when it comes to buying bulk diesel fuel for the company pumps or negotiating tariffs for electricity or gas. Similarly, in a supermarket chain the roles of purchasing manager and store manager may well be reversed. With central buying of the large quantities of goods required to fill the shelves of a national chain of stores, the purchasing function will operate with a great deal more authority and the store manager may have a very limited choice of what has to be stocked.

A factor which can help managers to define their authority – both in regard to delegated authority and to shared authority – is that of the timescale of the operation or of the issue. Where line managers in production or service departments, perhaps dealing directly with external customers, need to make decisions, there is frequently little time for delay. This in itself makes it clear that the authority for those decisions has to be with the appropriate manager, otherwise business will come to a halt. Similarly, in exceptional circumstances where decisions should be made with the approval of the boss or in consultation with a specialist, time pressure may make it imperative that the line manager acts alone. In order to ensure that these situations are resolved in the best interests of the organization, however, mutual trust has to be established.

There is always likely to be a difference in outlook between line managers and specialist managers because of the timescale factor. Line managers usually work to short timescales, producing results today so that the organization can live on to operate tomorrow. Some specialist managers are closely integrated with the main operating process and are bound up in the short-term situation. Others, such as research and development or human resources, have a significant long-term element built into the function.

The long-term element easily becomes converted in the minds of line managers to the 'ivory tower' element – a perception of the personnel manager or the researcher as no doubt very clever but divorced from reality. Reality is, of course, the need to produce results *today*. Conversely, concentration on the short-term can be seen by the specialist as an abdication of responsibility for the long term health of the business. The good manager understands these forces pulling in different directions and the need to create a sensible balance between the long term and the short term. This is not, however, an easy matter and probably represents the biggest test of managerial mettle. In general terms, as seniority grows so does the need to be able to take the long-term view while meeting short-term needs.

In times of crisis, in the scramble for survival, it is easy enough to justify concentrating on the present and ignoring the longer term. The problem is that management at the sharp-end sometimes feel that they are in perpetual crisis and disregarding the longer term can become a habit. Good managers understand this danger and attempt to create the conditions in which a sensible balance can be achieved. If managers are not devoting time to planning the future of their particular operation, who is? If someone else is planning the future of your operation, then may have far less knowledge and understanding than you have – and far less concern about how you will fit in!

Specialist managers have to ensure that they are not perceived as being so dedicated to the long term, or to their particular function, that they fail to understand the daily issues which confront their colleagues in line management.

A further factor which can help to define limits of authority is the 'knock-on' effect of decisions and actions. Where decisions are taken which only affect your area of responsibility, the authority is rightly yours. Where decisions affect a wider area, either within the organization or outside it, then authority has to be shared in some way or another. Where the 'knock-on' has impact indicates who the responsibility has to be shared with – and therefore the action to take in making decisions.

Understanding the accountabilities and pressures which drive various colleagues in the management team helps to give appropriate weighting to those issues in which there is shared responsibility. Building up trust between colleagues in the management team means that people spend less time protecting their 'turf' and leads to swifter and more confident action. This in turn leads to a more responsive and effective organization. One of the key factors in achieving competitive advantage is the responsiveness of management action, which comes from managers being clear about what they can or cannot do, and having confidence when meeting new situations.

The effectiveness of a manager in maintaining the momentum of the operation will often depend on the ability to steer a decisive course through these sometimes unclear corporate waters. This ability, in turn, will depend partly on 'expert' authority but more on 'personal' authority. Managers must know their business. This is not an argument for the manager to know more about every aspect of the operation than anyone else, but to know and understand everything he or she needs to know as a manager. A managerial strength can lie in deferring to the superior knowledge of a particular expert who is expected to know more about his or her specialist subject. Managers, however, must have 'expert' knowledge of their own which other employees will respect.

More important, though, is the personal respect in which the manager is held. In the long term this is the greatest source of a manager's authority. Structural authority has a short-term power, but in the long term it is the way that the manager uses that power which will determine how he or she is respected by subordinates, colleagues and superiors. If managers lose that respect it will not only weaken their ability to get things done, it will eventually destroy it.

Summary

Managers need to understand the strategy and the business plan of their organization, otherwise they cannot make departmental decisions which effectively support the aims of the organization.

The preparation of departmental budgets offers the opportunity for managers to influence their own activity and ensure that it is properly integrated with strategy.

Porter's 'value chain' offers a different way of looking at an organization which is based on linking all activities into a coherent chain which serves the customer. Integrating specialist support functions into the value chain can be difficult and create internal frictions and inefficiency.

Managers need to work hard at understanding the full range of their accountability and authority in order to be effective. They need to understand how to work with others in order to optimize the use of the talents of the various members of the management team.

Management checklist

- Does your organization have a statement of vision and/or mission? Write out how they affect the way in which you do your job. What is the one major issue for you personally to support the mission?
- Is there a medium- to long-term strategy for your organization, together with an immediate business plan? Do you have copies? If not, could you start to produce what you think they should look like? Have a go!
  - What is your role in the budgeting process?
  - Are you satisfied with this role? If not, what causes dissatisfaction?
  - Write an action plan for improving your budgeting process.
- Apply the value chain model to your operation. Does it suggest that you might organize your own operation any differently? Would this mean getting other departments to organize themselves differently? How can you set about doing this?
  - Do you have competitors?
  - How does their value chain differ from yours?
  - Write down the key specialist departments which you deal with.
  - Do you understand their objectives?
  - List any problems which you perceive with each department and decide how you can improve your working together.
- Write down the accountabilities of your job. At the side of each write down which of the three types of authority you use to achieve results in that area. Are there any which are not in balance? If so, what will you do to get them into balance?

3 Matching resources to demand

Introduction

To ensure your operation provides a full contribution to the success of the organization, you need to consider two fundamental aspects in the way it is organized. The first is its 'focus', dealt with in Chapter 1. The second is its 'operational capability' and it is the combination of these two which determines whether your operation fully helps or hinders the total organization's pursuit of its goals.

Operational capability is about making sure that you have the optimum match of resources – people, facilities, systems, materials – to the demands which your customers are likely to make of you. In discussing these issues we shall be drawing heavily upon ideas which come from the area of 'classic' operations management. These ideas are often expressed in 'production' or 'manufacturing' terms but we shall attempt to draw parallels with other types of organization. We believe that the principles apply to every sort of operation in some way or another and that you will be able to make the necessary connections.

The chapter will deal with:

- identifying areas for improvement;
- process choice;
- people within the operation;
- machines facilities and equipment;
- organization;
- systems; and
- supplier/customer Links.

It relates principally to the MCI elements of competence as follows:

- M1/1.1: Maintain operations to meet quality standards.
- M2/1.1: Identify opportunities or improvement in services, products and systems.
- M2/1.2: Evaluate proposed changes for benefits and disadvantages.
- M2/2.3: Maintain and improve operations against quality and functional specifications.

Identifying areas for improvement

In matching resources to demand our aim must always be to maintain the perfect balance between our operational resources and the demands being made on us. In reality we may not always succeed in this aim, but we must always strive to achieve it.

Your operational capability will have limits or boundaries to the performance it can deliver in different sets of circumstances – when operating normally, or when operating under pressure. These performance boundaries define the total capability. Total capability is the sum of a number of different contributory operating factors, such as the type of process we use, the skills of the staff, or the type of equipment we have. Your performance in all of these factors may not be as good as the best among your competitors or in the market you are supplying. In some you may be poor, others average and others outstanding. It is very important to recognize and understand the quality of our performance in the varying operating factors because this enables us to target our areas for improvement. In some cases it may be most beneficial to concentrate on improving the weak areas. In others it may be better to concentrate on improving even further those areas in which we are strongest. Only judgement in individual circumstances can decide.

However, in order to decide the areas to target when seeking operating improvements there is a simple principle which can be applied – that is, the principle of constraining the customer. If, at any time, we are forced to deny the customer what is needed, because the operating capability cannot deliver, then we have an indicator of where to look for operating improvements. If our customers are internal, operating constraints will simply make that internal customer's operation less efficient with a 'knock-on' effect through the whole business. If your operation is at the end of the value chain, operating constraints can lead to dissatisfaction for the external or ultimate customer and hence to loss of business.

Box 3.1

In most hotels there is a morning check-out or departure time – 10.00 is a common requirement. Similarly there is a time before which, on checking-in you cannot occupy the room – commonly 14.00. All of us have experienced the annoyance of these constraints when wanting to use our hotel room beyond or before these times. This is typical of the type of constraint placed on customers by the operation. We all know that the 10.00 until 14.00 period is for the operation to clean/change rooms but this knowledge does not reduce our annoyance when it happens to us. A customer-oriented hotel will ask what departure time you need or would like and will arrange its cleaning routines to suit. It will require some special arrangements by the housekeeping teams but leads to a happier customer and gives the hotel competitive advantage.

Recently, Ford in the UK conducted a pilot scheme to produce cars to order, rather than deliver from stock, with dealers placing orders directly on the manufacturing system. The objective is to deliver a car to the customer's precise specification and colour, within fifteen days of the order being placed. Customers will be able to choose the colour of their car only two days before delivery. Not only will this improve customer service, it will also make enormous savings through stock reductions and in the need for discounting models which have been made in unpopular colours.

This is a very far cry from the famous Henry Ford principle, which was that customers could have any colour they wanted ... provided, it was black, and demonstrates how 'value chain' thinking can revolutionize an industry. In this case it is the application of technology to outbound logistics (stocks), together with a flexible manufacturing system, which will radically improve customer service. In the process it will also radically change the manufacturing organization.

Analysing the operation – the Ishikawa Fishbone

The operational capability, the performance limits and the constraints all stem from the actual operation itself. How it is set up, staffed, organized and supplied will all impact on these crucial performance aspects and we need to be aware of that fact. This means that choices we make for the design of the operation are really vital in dictating how well we are able to 'serve' our customers, internal or external. So these choices are important and we must understand their impact fully.

As an aid to understanding we suggest you use the analytical techniques for problem solving called the Ishikawa Fishbone, after its Japanese originator, Dr Kaoru Ishikawa.

The Fishbone enables you, in a simple and practical way, to break your operation down into its various components, so that you can identify the impact of each component part upon the total operation.

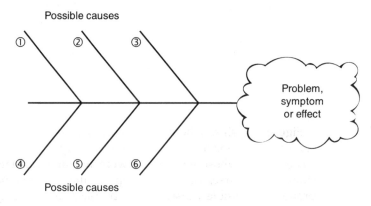

Figure 3.1 Fishbone diagram

Figure 3.1 shows how the Fishbone is used in general problem solving. The problem or the effect is entered on the right side of the figure and then we move in a structured way 'upstream', as it were, to explore possible causes. By having several prescribed headings on the various 'bones', we concentrate our minds on each topic in turn and focus on seeking possible causes for the problem under that heading.

When we are using the Fishbone to analyse operational matters there are two sets of classifications which are used to identify the principal components of an operating organization. Both of these models use terms which are already related to manufacturing operations. With a little thought, however, they can also be related to any type of operating unit. These two models are called the 4M (Figure 3.2) and the PEM/PEM (Figure 3.3) models.

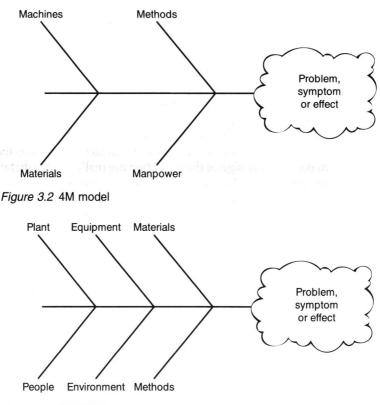

Figure 3.2 4M model

Figure 3.3 PEM/PEM model

Figure 3.4 shows how we might use the Ishikawa Fishbone to analyse the problem faced by a domestic appliance service company, 20 per cent of whose service calls were over one hour late. The diagram shows, of course, only one step in the process, namely that of proposing possible causes to the problem and logging them on the diagram. The next steps would involve obtaining the information

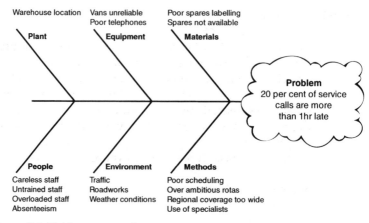

Figure 3.4 Fishbone example

necessary to establish which of these possible causes are the main contributors and then tackling those issues. If studies showed that the most common causes are say, road works and poor telephones, we need a plan to resolve both issues.

The foregoing shows how the Fishbone diagram is used in the context of general problem-solving. To use it specifically to analyse operational capability we use a model which is concerned with:

- process   Pro. ⎫
- people   P   ⎪
- machines and facilities   M ⎬ ProPMOSS
- organization   O ⎪
- systems   S ⎪
- suppliers.   S ⎭

Figure 3.5 shows the ProPMOSS diagram.

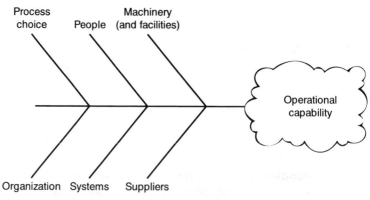

Figure 3.5 The ProPMOSS model

We will discuss each of the six ProPMOSS components in more detail.

1 Process choice

This is the most fundamental of the six and it will greatly influence – if not dictate, the characteristics of the operation and its performance. The choice of process type needs to match the market needs and enable you to deliver your chosen products or service in the best way. It is greatly influenced by the nature of your products and services (discussed in Chapter 1) and we will return to this later in the chapter.

The three basic types of process are:

- project or jobbing;
- batch; and
- continuous/assembly line.

Most of the studies into process types have been conducted in the manufacturing sector and the terms used reflect this. While terms such as 'jobbing' or 'batch' may not be used in service sectors, the principles can be applied just as well.

Figure 3.6 shows how these three types of processes are best fitted to different types of product or service.

Process type	Project basis or jobbing shop	Batch process	Assembly/flow Line or continuous process
Product/service	Low volume High variety	Medium volume Medium variety	High volume Low variety

Figure 3.6 The process fit

Project or jobbing shop

The first category shown in this table is for low volume, high variety products or services. If you are supplying low volume products/ services to customers, whether internal or external, and most items you supply are different (i.e. you only supply a few of that type before you need to change), then you will need an operational process along the lines of a project system or a jobbing shop. This process type can handle variety with ease – it is its greatest strength – and the customer is really buying your operation's capability in the general areas in which it trades. Often the customer does not know exactly what he or she wants and the early stages of any transaction or contract may be a phase where you and your customer are 'designing' or specifying the solution. There is rarely a standard product or service in a jobbing operation – it is the supply of a bespoke or tailored service unique to that particular customer and that particular requirement.

The bespoke, or made-to-measure tailor is a good example of this type of operation. Here the customer with an individual requirement makes a series of choices against a range of options to produce a unique specification. Although the range is not infinite it is very wide, embracing options on materials, lining, pocket types, style, finishes, sizes, fit. This range of options will virtually guarantee that no two products are the same, unlike the mass-produced ready-to-wear equivalent.

The operation must be able to deliver on these needs, and it obviously takes a particular set-up or process to do so – namely, a jobbing shop. We would normally imagine these operations to be small, with only a few people engaged within them such as the small-owner tailors. However, in the large fashion houses, the bespoke element encourages people to pay high prices for unique products, although in these cases, exclusive products are produced by large teams of people.

Jobbing shop operations, then, are not always small, although the low volume aspect of their services means they tend to be.

The characteristic the jobbing shop must deliver is the flexibility to handle variety. (This is the first reference we have made to flexibility; there will be many more as it is one of the major issues in operational capability.) If ever a jobbing shop operation fails in this regard or puts too many constraints upon its customers it will jeopardize its own survival. Flexibility and variety are at the heart of this type of operation and must represent a major capability. If you manage such an operation you must constantly be asking how you can maintain and improve this capability. It is not, however, the only area of performance you need to look to. The other major aspect of your capability should be your operation's command of its 'technology'. Whatever business area you are in, your customers come to you for (external), or need from you (internal), the best 'technical' performance they can get. A jobbing shop or, bespoke operation needs to provide it. It is unlikely that they come to you because you are fast or low cost – jobbing shops are usually the reverse! They come to you for your expertise and to get exactly what they want for their unique needs. This then is the essence of a jobbing shop type of operation. These performance characteristics are all impacted by the other five contributing factors in the ProPMOSS model which we shall continue to explore later.

Batch processes

Referring back to Figure 3.6, we move on to look at the broad area of medium volume and variety products/services. In this area of activity work is done by the operation in larger quantities or batches. The use of batch processing is often dictated by the nature of the work to be done, such as processing the passengers for an aircraft flight. A Boeing

747 can take in excess of 400 passengers. All have to be security-checked, ticketed, moved about the airport, boarded, seated, fed, disembarked, within prescribed times. The passengers are being handled as a batch of 400 or so. When that aircraft has left the staff prepare themselves for the next batch.

Our earlier example of the hotel room cleaning process is another case of a batch operation. For efficiency purposes it is best if the hotel staff can clean all rooms on one floor one after another, i.e. within the same block of time. Hence the formal, but often inflexible, check-out and room availability times. We can see it makes sense for the operation to work in this way but it may not serve every customer's need – an example of the operation 'constraining' the service offered in the interests of efficiency. This is a topic we will explore further, particularly in Chapter 9.

Many manufacturing operations and their support units use batch processes where items are made in lots of so many units at a time. These units can be in numbers, weight, in volume, in production time – whatever measure fits the products being supplied. The concept of the batch of 'a thousand off' of an item, say a batch of 1,000 cases of whisky from a distillery bottling plant, leads us to one of the key commercial aspects of a batch process. This is the reset, or set-up time between batches.

When one batch ends, the operation has to be reset to produce a different product, or a variation of the product. This will mean resetting the operation in one way or another. It may mean loading it with different raw materials or components, and putting in train another process schedule. In the distillery bottling plant, for example, after the 1,000 cases of one type of whisky, the schedule may call for 5,000 cases of another type, say six to a case rather than twelve, in litre bottles rather than 70 cl and a different mix or blend. This would demand different labelling and packaging, the whole operating line needing to be re-supplied and reset before the next batch can be produced. The time taken to set-up, from completion of one batch, to the start of the next batch is a vital element in the profitability of a batch process.

This set-up time is all lost time. The operation is producing nothing of value during this activity and is a drain on the business. Setting up itself does not 'add value'. The operation is only of value to the business when it is producing. Many managers do not realize this and as a result not enough attention is paid to reducing the set-up time in operations. When the set-up time is long, we are forced into long runs or large batches to off-set the effect of that lost time. For instance, if a set-up took two hours, we could not afford to run a batch of only two hours. The effect would be 50 per cent efficiency at best and few operations can afford such a low figure. However, to improve productivity we might be forced to run longer batches even though the customer or the schedule would prefer shorter ones. For example, if we run for six hours, we are running for six of the eight hours in the cycle, i.e. 75 per cent productivity. On the face of it this sounds good, but it takes no account of the customers' needs. It may mean we are producing two or three times as much as we want at that time and we must stock the excess hoping to deliver or sell it in the future. Its costs may never be recovered.

A much better way of improving efficiency of the process is to reduce set-up time. In our earlier case of a two-hour batch run with a process taking two hours to reset we talked of increasing the size of the batch run. Why not reduce the setting up time? If we were able to reduce to, say, half an hour for the same two-hour batches, our efficiency rises to 80 per cent. Through this strategy we may be able to reduce the size of the batches and so be able to respond to smaller orders. This is one of the aims of every batch process because it increases its ability to be responsive and flexible to customers' needs. We will therefore return to this question of set-up reduction in our chapter on improvements.

We have referred to batch and set-up examples mainly in production or manufacturing processes. In fact in service businesses there are many examples of batch-type operations with their attendant advantages and disadvantages. Restaurants needing to serve groups of six or eight people to a meal are using the batch process and must ensure that all meals are ready on time even when individuals can select separate menus. The process must cope with batch delivery yet handle the variety of choice. When batches become larger, such as at Christmas, many restaurants have to limit variety by having pre-determined holiday menus to reduce choice. The operation cannot cope with large batches and very great variety and this trade-off always has to be made in a batch process. Managers have to decide on this trade-off. A solution in our restaurant might be to limit table sizes to, say, ten guests. This effectively limits the maximum batch size to ten which could enable the full meal choice to be re-introduced. A kitchen's capability to produce meals simultaneously is taxed somewhat less by a group of ten than by one of thirty! This decision would give them a better chance of performing well in the eyes of the customers. However, this solution does bring us back to the issue of constraints. If a group of thirty want Christmas lunch together, they may not be prepared to sit at three tables of ten. Our solution to the service problem may lose us some customers. Managers must make these decisions for their operation; but at least make them with their eyes open.

Another potential disadvantage of batch operations is in items waiting in a queue resulting in inventory build-up. This may sound like three or four issues but it is really only one. By the very nature of a batch operation, items are waiting at some stage of the operation to be handled as a group. This means some waiting for all items. In a post-room operation, mail will be gathered until there is sufficient to warrant a delivery. Until then, items already received wait. A local office, say an insurance broker, may gather several customer enquiries together before forwarding them to either its HQ or out to the insurance companies. This could be a day or two, or even a week; delay, again.

In a production operation where the operation might be making several hundred items in a batch, the whole batch will move through the process together, often in a crate or some suitable transportable container. The first item into that container will wait until the last item is made and put in. This could take some time – days. These items represent work-in-progress and become valuable or costly inventory. They are made from raw material that has been bought and has been processed using labour that must be paid, on machinery that was an investment which will produce no return until they are delivered and paid for. Waiting around is the last thing we want them to be doing. Yet batch processes inevitably lead to this.

The most effective attack on this phenomena is the small batch. For instance if we have a batch of one, there would be no delay. The batch would move on as soon as the item is completed. There is another spin-off from this 'batch of one' idea. In almost all markets today customers are wanting more flexibility, more tailoring to their instant needs, and faster response. They want to order later, in smaller quantities and yet get faster deliveries. If your operation can handle very small batches effectively (and profitably) you can offer customers what they dream about. We have already said that a key to reducing batch size was set-up reduction. Great business benefits result from the ability to handle small batches, which provides yet further justification for set-up reduction.

Continuous processes

Our final process type from the table in Figure 3.6 is for high volume/low variety operations. Here we have continuous processes which include 'assembly' or 'flow-line' operations. The terms used will depend on the product type – as they originate from manufacturing use – but this process choice exists for many service operations.

In this type of operation, the volumes are so large that the operation runs for very long periods delivering the same products or services. Variety, therefore, is very low or, in truly continuous operations, non-existent. Examples of this might be the production units of large chemical plants, food stuffs and utility supplies such as water, gas and electricity. Although there may be cyclic changes in demand, such as day and night or summer and winter for energy supplies, the plants producing them cannot be easily shut down. They are genuinely continuous in operation.

Assembly or flow lines are less continuous in many instances and although they may work on only one product they will usually be closed down, at the end of the shift or day or week, and remain shut down for a period. Start up needs to be simple and swift, so that efficient productive operation results as soon as possible from the operation becoming 'live'.

In production situations these operations exist when demand becomes so high that it warrants a dedicated operation to supply the volume. This usually results in a large investment by the organization to put that dedicated operation in place – equipment, people, facilities, organization, systems. One of the results expected from such an operation is significant reduction in unit cost; the classic search for 'economies of scale'. To achieve it, companies will often combine several small operations producing the same or similar products at different times through batch processing into one large operation, geared up for highly productive results running on a dedicated, continuous basis.

The motor industry, and many other high volume sectors, have followed this pattern; globally we have seen small operations closed in a country such as the UK to be replaced by one large plant which might even be in another country. The cost effectiveness of such operations has been seen as overwhelming to date and therefore has proved an irresistible strategy to many manufacturers.

It is not all good news, however. In more recent years a major drawback of such operations has been the issue of flexibility. These large operations have been very good at low cost, high volume operations. They have not been good at changing over effectively to make or deliver different products. As markets have become more demanding and more volatile, product changes and product flexibilty have to be introduced more rapidly and many large operators have been found wanting. Expensive resetting is required for product changes and many large organizations have been too cumbersome to respond quickly enough to these requirements. It is not surprising. They were never designed to do so!

The result is that efficiency drops through long change-overs and costs rise, ruining the very rationale for such processes – normally low unit production cost. Now we have the worst of all worlds – a slow, cumbersome, inflexible plant, designed for long runs, but trying to operate in short runs. It cannot effectively serve the market and its market share will fall.

This is one of the undoubted challenges to managers of such operations, now and in the future; the need to make the operation more flexible without losing the low unit cost performance. We address this issue in Chapter 9.

There are also examples of operations having to deal with high volumes in the service sectors. They also operate on the same principles as flow line or continuous process.

We can think of such examples as postal services, ticketing and toll collection, fast food operations, some banking or financial services and twenty-four hour operations such as airports or hotels. In all these areas of business activity, just as in high volume manufacturing, the whole operation is geared to producing the same result repeatedly, hour by hour and day by day. It is about producing predictability in response to standard (or almost standard) requirements. Just as in our manufacturing examples, variety is low and the operation is designed for high volume at low cost.

Figure 3.7 summarizes the discussion of the three basic types of process used in operating characteristics.

Process type	Best suited to:
Jobbing type	Low volumes Wide variety of products or services High unit cost Small volume orders (but each might be high value) Bespoke nature Little repetition Many changes or modifications
Batch type	Medium volumes and variety of products or services Higher volume orders Low to medium unit cost Mostly standard products/services Products/services often repeated Some changes/modifications
Continuous process; Assembly to flow line	High volumes Low variety Higher volume orders Low unit cost Standard products/services Extensive repetition – if not continuous Infrequent changes/modifications

Figure 3.7 Process uses and characteristics

Our illustrations have, however, all been concerned with the operation of total organizations whereas the majority of our readers will be concerned with departments or clients which are part of a total organization. In order to understand fully one's own operation it is, of course, essential to understand the nature of the whole organization and the type of processes being used. Often organizations are not restricted to one type of process and more than one will be found within it. An airline, for example, will be processing passengers in a batch process but will want to give First Class passengers the impression that they are receiving individual treatment. Special facilities help to do this, but so does information technology and staff training. In First Class, therefore, they try to operate as a jobbing-shop.

As far as your particular operation is concerned, it is most likely that you will have inherited a process with some history behind it. Analysing the process is probably the most valuable thing you can do in looking for opportunities for improvement. Changing the process is probably the most fundamental thing you can do and therefore needs approaching with a great deal of care. Part of that care will consist of discussion with, and seeking views from, colleagues, your boss and also the members of your team. Making changes of a fundamental type not only needs careful examination to ensure that it is well-founded, but also needs support in order to make it work. It is in these circumstances, too, that it is important to reconsider your position in the 'value chain' and how process changes may affect other links in the chain. Do not make fundamental changes lightly – you need to be absolutely certain the change will lead to improvement, so extensive consideration is always to be recommended.

Choosing the right process type

The development of these different processes and process choice is usually attributed to the Industrial Revolution, as the industrial owners of the time strove to find better ways to supply their fast developing world markets. Over the hundred or so years from around 1870 to around 1970, these processes and their applications within organizations followed traditional patterns, with the broad performance characteristics shown in Figure 3.7 found almost universally in the applications of the processes. There is of course an overall rationale for the process choice, and most businesses and organizations will have used that rationale at some time in the past to make their process selection to match their markets. However, with process type there are some advantages and some disadvantages and we need to understand which is which. The disadvantages are significant because they represent opportunities. If we can overcome them we can better the competition, but sometimes making the decision about which process type is the best for a particular operation is not always straightforward. One of the most difficult decisions for managers to make is when the volumes required are such that they are in the margin between jobbing and batch or between batch and continuous. Figure 3.8 shows the relationships of unit cost and flexibility to the different types of process and also how they can overlap in effectiveness at points A and B.

The advantage of the jobbing process is its high flexibility with the disadvantage of high unit cost. The continuous process with high volumes of throughput has low unit cost but low flexibility. Making decisions on process at either end of the volume spectrum is not difficult. The difficulties arise when managers are dealing with volumes at points A and B, where the choices could be for either one or another process. What can you do, then, to help to make the right choice?

Few problems of this type can be solved mathematically, so that you could be virtually guaranteed a 'correct' solution. In the final analysis such decisions are taken by using judgement. What managers have to do is to support their judgement with as much factual and rational

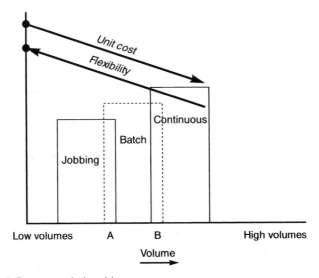

Figure 3.8 Process relationships

evidence as possible. We believe that there are three approaches which can help in this case.

The most important evidence relates to the trend of the volume of business. If volume is decreasing or increasing, it is obvious that this will influence your choice of process. Increasing volumes will move you to the right on the chart, decreasing volumes to the left.

Secondly, once you have completed this chapter and the whole of your 'Fishbone' analysis, using the ProPMOSS model, you will have more evidence which will undoubtedly help where process choice is not obvious.

Finally, we suggest a rather unscientific method which needs handling with care. If you cannot be certain of the likely volume shift, or it appears static, we suggest that you have to make a choice by preference. Managers who are experienced in a particular situation will accumulate a knowledge and understanding of the operation which is difficult to express in an analytical way. It will, however, tell them what feels 'right' in certain circumstances and if it feels right to an individual they will probably make it work. It is, however, difficult to be convincing about the correctness of such intuitive decision-making and it is best used to support a judgement which relies on other positive factors as well.

2 People

Returning to Figure 3.5 and the ProPMOSS model for analysing operating capability, we now propose to examine the remaining five factors and of these the first to be examined will be the role of people.

All operations use people. Even the most automated, robotic, computerized, mechanical systems cannot perform without some human interaction; designing them, building them, loading them, adjusting them, cleaning them, reconfiguring them. People are key to the capability of operations and their management is in all respects an important part of the operational manager's job.

Each operation needs particular types of people to work in, and run it. Each individual is not suited to every type of operation – far from it. As far as jobs go, 'one man's meat may be another man's poison'. Jobs may be disliked for many reasons and what appeals to one person may repel another. Let us use the process types to look at this issue. At the high volume, assembly line type of operation, we are looking for people who are comfortable with a regular, routine-based approach. They will be systematic people. We want predictable performance in the main, as the output of their efforts must produce the same result again and again. Cleaning those hotel bedrooms we referred to earlier demands the same daily approach, the same checklists, the same result over and over. Each person may clean twenty to thirty rooms in a day and we are looking for the same results every time. Two tablets of soap, one shampoo, one shower gel, one bath towel, two hand towels, one bathmat and one shower cap in every bathroom. Every time. The sheets folded the same way – housestyle. We need people who are prepared to work in this systematic way, paying meticulous attention to detail. Cleaners cannot be allowed to use discretion in the way they service a room, depending, perhaps, on whether they approve or not of the way that the guest leaves it. To some this 'sameness' or predictability in a job would be boring, while to others it provides a sense of security. They like knowing exactly what is required of them and will take a pride in doing it well every time. These are the type of people who will do well in the high volume, low variety types of process.

At the other end of the spectrum, in the jobbing types of process, the work tends to be different every day, in a significant sense. Because the essence of this type of operation is variety, with each job or each customer demanding something unique to them, this ensures a wider variety of demand on the people within that operation. Managing changes is the very essence of this type of work and we need people who can cope with that. In their own sphere, they need to be entrepreneurs. Such operations are really selling this entrepreneurial capability above all else; the ability to turn their hands to whatever the customer needs. No standard product for them: that would be boring. So if that's what the operation needs most, they are the type of people we must employ.

In the middle ground, the batch type of operation, we probably need people who can handle a little of each. They need to be able to make changes efficiently when asked to do so and maybe handle several jobs along the way (multi-skilled, multi-disciplined people). When the batch-to-batch change is over they need to be able to settle down to a

Box 3.2

One of us once worked in a defence supply company at the inception of a company-wide quality improvement programme – a 'total quality' initiative. Up to this point this particular well respected company had been earning substantial revenue from the on-going repair of its own equipment supplied to the Ministry of Defence. It was recognized that by increasing the reliability of the product the company would reduce the revenue from the repair business. It was felt, however, that this potential loss would be more than offset by the increased business to be achieved through improved reliability.

One old-hand, a contracts manager, actively worked against this policy in the belief that Defence business had always been like this and the company would be cutting off valuable business by such a policy. His experience of one way of working precluded or prevented him from seeing the danger of his approach in a modern business world. However; he was influential enough to slow the whole initiative down by almost subversive means. He did eventually accept the new approach but only after coming within a hair's breadth of dismissal.

A second example of mismatch involved a gateaux supplier to a major supermarket chain at the time of the shift from frozen to chilled cakes and pastries. The company had supplied frozen cakes for a considerable time to the supermarket chains when the market shifted towards chilled rather than frozen products. The supermarket gave over a year's notice to the supplier of this change of requirement to give them plenty of time to prepare, which they attempted to do.

One of the business features they had to adapt to was very much shorter lead times. Frozen product shelf-life is measured in weeks if not months while chilled equivalents have a life of just a few days. The organization put in all the systems to enable them to meet this new demand and new investment was made where needed.

Even after substantial investment and extended preparation for the change, they failed to satisfy the new requirements and eventually lost the contract.

In the post-mortem on the affair, senior management concluded that one of the main reasons for the failure lay in the operation's management and staff inability to accept and adapt to the new short timescales. After years of operating in a weeks/months environment, they just could not adapt to an hours/days requirement.

routine for a while and produce predictable results for the duration of the batch. They will be reasonably happy to be asked fairly regularly to learn something new and to add a routine to their capability. However, there will be clear limitations to what they can be asked to do and in the main they will be employed on similar tasks within their own discipline.

So we have three types of people described here; the systematic type, the multi-skilled and the entrepreneur. The operational manager must be clear about the need to match the people to the operation, process and task. When it is not right conflicts can occur (see Box 3.2).

3 Machines and facilities

Just as people are a vital element in every operation, so is the equipment we provide for them to operate. We call them here 'machines' but we use the term to cover all equipment, whether 'hand tools', powered equipment and machines, and we include all facilities and buildings.

When we observe different operations we usually find recurring themes in the machines and equipment area. In the jobbing, low volume, processes we find high grade, flexible equipment capable of handling wide variations of task. This is a necessity to provide that bespoke end of the market. Equipment is usually selected for a combination of high operational specification and flexibility, not for speed of operation, although speed of adjustments is important to handle the many changes.

In batch type operations the equipment is selected for its ability to operate not only at high speed but also to be adjustable to a number of products or services. Resetting ability is important, or, more accurately, fast resetting ability is important. This is necessary in a batch type operation because, as illustrated earlier, resetting between batches results in lost time and therefore lost revenue. Unfortunately, particularly in older plants, we often find that resetting takes too long.

In an assembly-line type operation we find highly focused, dedicated equipment and machines. Limited flexibility is usually found and the equipment and systems have been selected and tuned to perform mainly one function for a single or limited range of products. A major problem that we are finding more and more today, as we work with many companies with this type of operation, is the changing nature of the marketplace. These operations are finding that they are being forced to operate more as a batch process with smaller orders, shorter lead-times, more product variety and less standardization. Traditional assembly lines were not designed for frequent changes and each one takes a great deal of time leading to low productivity and low efficiency.

Finally we would like to mention, briefly, the role of the computer in process capability. Most people are aware of the differing ways in which the computer is used across the spectrum of operating units. It might be in a Computer Aided Design (CAD) application in the project/jobbing field, or for scheduling and computer controlled manufacturing in batch processes. Control of the process itself or assembly using robots are applications often found in high volume assembly lines.

However, in spite of the general awareness that exists of the computer impact on every type of operation, we still find traditional businesses failing to use them to full advantage. We do stress the need to be alert to the opportunities and to exploit them for the good of the operation and, of course, your customers. This is not advice to use computers for the sake of it – too many businesses have done and are still doing that – but to do so intelligently for the benefits they can provide.

4 Organization

The way your operation is organized will be the result of either positive decisions made earlier or of a chain of events over a period of years. In the first instance you will have a structure that has been thought out, presumably to enable the operation to perform well. In the latter situation this may not be the case, as on many occasions the structure that exists is the result of a series of decisions, moves to accommodate particular people, adaptations to adopt new company systems, any number of unco-ordinated events which can affect an organization. What we would like to do now is to offer some ideas about how different organizations suit different processes.

The varied nature of the work in the jobbing, low volume type of operation results in many new situations over short periods, and although the staff we employ have initiative they will need regular guidance. Hence these operations work best with fairly narrow spans of control for each manager. This tends to produce 'tall' structures with a number of layers of management. No manager should be responsible for too many 'direct reports' – the classic view of 'no more than seven or eight direct reports' might apply. This is because each person needs ready access to his or her boss for guidance, agreement, or decisions.

At the other end of the scale, the high volume, continuous, or assembly line process, where tasks are much less diverse, we find much flatter structures with supervisors and managers having a great many 'direct reports'. In some major manufacturing applications, and the large back offices of financial institutions, we are seeing one supervisor/manager to many tens of operators. This is possible because of the repetitive nature of the work. Operators face far fewer new situations on a day-to-day basis, so less management guidance is required. Because much more of this guidance can be built into formal procedures used by the operation's staff, on-the-spot guidance and decision-making by managers is required infrequently.

Where organizations have to cope with a complex 'batch' type of process the 'matrix' structure is often used. A good manufacturing example is in the production of flight simulators for aircrew training. The production cycle for these very complex capital items can be from twelve to eighteen months and there could be anything from eight to twelve simulators being produced at any one time, all at different stages of completion. Each one of these items has to be produced by production facilities common to all. The matrix structure tackles the problem by allocating responsibility to a project manager who is dedicated to one single item. Other staff, such as designers and assembly teams, may be assigned as and when they are required, but the key role is that of project manager who drives his or her project across a functional structure. This in turn has to balance the demands of different projects or products in order to optimize the use of resources against the requirements of all the customers. Figure 3.9 represents how the structure appears.

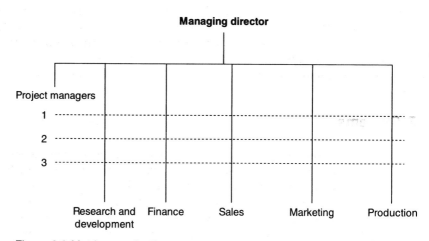

Figure 3.9 Matrix organization

People working in this sort of matrix structure have to become accustomed to working for two bosses. As part of a function they have a permanent boss who will be responsible for the general administration. At any one time, however, they may be working for a different person – or maybe more than one – who is responsible for their work output.

Matrix structure, or project management structures, come in different forms; producers for the retail industry have sales teams dedicated to a single product or range of products – say a brand of jam – which places orders on a common manufacturing facility. Hospitals have teams dedicated to particular specializations, such as kidney transplants, which have to operate within the general facilities of the hospital.

This sort of cross-functional team-working is now being used more as a means of breaking down the parochialism of the functional organization. However, such systems have their own problems of how to deal with conflicting demands on common facilities. There are those who believe that the truly successful organization of the future will be those which can harness project management most effectively.

In the West, all three of these basic structures have been subject to great stress in the 1990s, as each organization has driven for efficiency and cost-cutting, following recessionary pressures. This has resulted in delayering, removing whole tiers of management. We already referred to this and some of the pressures it produces in Chapter 2. It must be said, of course, that there is substantial evidence that most long-standing organizations do develop unnecessary and costly management jobs. This is partly due to the natural tendency for individuals to expand their roles and 'build empires' and partly to the reluctance to remove management jobs once the need for them has passed.

Senior managements are now much more aware of these dangers in times of rapid change but this has created an uneasy feeling of uncertainty among managers. Because we recognize that the idea of a (managerial) job for life has now gone, organizations have to work out how they retain and motivate their managers. Managers have to work out how to develop a career.

5 Systems

We need systems in place to enable those who work within the operation, including the manager, to control the work that must be done. These systems may be helpful to us – well-designed and user-friendly – or they may not. They may feel like systems being used for their own sake, where we have to fill in forms, or enter information via keyboards, which we cannot see is of benefit to anyone. In these challenging competitive times there is no place for such wasteful activities. These systems need killing. What we want are simple, effective, easy-to-use systems that will help us achieve the operation's objective, to serve the customer, by the efficient production of output, products or services.

This area of managing operations comes under some scrutiny in Chapter 6, but as it forms part of our model we will cover the fundamental needs of the process types here. The system needs of each is quite different.

In jobbing situations we are most interested in monitoring and controlling the key features of design, design changes, modifications, progress, staff, project milestones, work-in-progress (WIP) and cost. We need a good uncluttered way of gathering information on all these activities and providing it to all who may need it. You will notice that we have not highlighted raw materials, finished goods or stock as needing particularly good information or control systems. This is because in these jobbing, low volume type of operations, raw materials are not usually large items of cost. Finished goods are not held in stock (to be lost, if we are not careful!) but are immediately delivered. If we are working efficiently we have the products or services ready just when they are needed. We are not saying that no systems are needed for raw materials or stock, but that in jobbing operations they are less important requirements when compared to others.

In high volume continuous operations we have quite different system needs. Raw material usage is high and we have considerable investment to keep track of. The operation or process itself is usually fast, i.e. not a major part of the whole operation's elapsed time or lead time, therefore we have little need for a work-in-progress system. However, finished goods or services are completed in high volumes and in many operations are not delivered immediately. Therefore a good finished product record and control system is essential. There is usually little need for a control system based on hours worked by staff. We do need to know broadly that people are there, but beyond that little detail is required, because it is not of major value to us!

Some measure of the system's efficiency is of great value. When volumes and throughput are high the efficiency being achieved is really vital. If we can improve by, say, 1 per cent, on a high throughput process this is a significant improvement and would be financially valuable. Conversely if we lose 1 per cent on efficiency, that too is significant. If we know, through the system we are using, then we can tackle the efficiency loss, and we hope restore it. With no system the 1 per cent reduction would exist for a long time before we saw the results through the business profitability figures.

Batch system requirements are more similar to high volume assembly line processes than to jobbing. In addition, however, they need to be supplemented with information for batch control and batch traceability. Staff use and development is also necessary as labour becomes a more significant cost element.

This, together with batch to batch changeover and processing times, is the sort of information required to compute economic batch quantities (EBQ). In manufacturing text books much has been written on the topic of EBQs. However, in a climate of smaller orders, shorter lead times and higher product and service variety requirements, the demand is towards smaller and smaller batches. The ultimate, as we have mentioned elsewhere, would be the 'batch of one'. If yours is a batch type of operation, you should be aiming in this direction.

In most operations these information and control systems employ computers – screens are everywhere. Every day extra software capability is added to the market. You need to keep close to these developments either directly or through your IT or computer department, to ensure that you are obtaining advantage for the operation.

An area not yet mentioned, to which we devote Chapter 4, is quality. Every operation must have systems for controlling quality and gathering the information necessary to target quality improvement work. Does your operation have such a system? Are you clear what the system is measuring or controlling, and are they the correct things?

6 Suppliers and customer links

Chapter 5 deals with supplier management in some detail. In this section we will restrict ourselves to outlining the key elements.

The usual situation with linkages is to find them on an almost personal level in jobbing/project processes. This is necessary to handle effectively the many changes and the variety which exists in this type of operation. The relationships thus formed help to overcome what would otherwise be recurring difficulties. This is true whether suppliers and customer are internal or external. Relationship building by managers and staff brings real rewards over the longer timescale but they must devote time to it.

As more and more organizations are using the benefits of specialized sub-contracting – or outsourcing as it is also called – to supplement their own core competences, this need for close supplier and customer links is important across all three types of operation. However, the close personal relationship is not as frequently found at the batch and higher volume continuous type of operation. Here we usually find more formal links existing, a greater reliance placed on scheduled orders, perhaps with call-off rates. However, whether you are operating a jobbing, batch or continuous process operation, there is no substitute for close links and strong relationships with key suppliers and customers. This is the key to finding ways of improved working to provide better service to one another with shorter timescales and lower costs. You should all be working towards it and Chapter 5 will help you focus on it.

These then are the elements contributing to the capability of your operation as outlined in our ProPMOSS model. By addressing each element in turn you should be better able to evaluate the performance of your own operation and to spot areas where there may be scope for improvement drives.

Summary

We have looked at the basic process types that most operations are based upon. This should enable you to establish which of the process types – project/jobbing, batch or assembly line/continuous – most closely matches your own operation.

Then, through the use of the ProPMOSS analysis tool we have studied the elements that contribute to an operation's capability. It is every manager's responsibility to improve that capability continuously, and this structured analysis is helpful in highlighting areas for possible improvement.

Management checklist

- Does the organization of your operation impose any constraints upon your customers? What is the effect of these constraints?
- What is the principal process operated by your organization as a whole?
- Are there different business areas using different or secondary process choices? List the main areas of difference.
- What process does your own operation resemble?
- Does your operation have enough flexibility to offer more customer choice/service?
- Apply the ProPMOSS analysis to your own operation. Do you think that your process type is the most suitable for your requirement?
- Do the other characteristics of your operation match the process type? i.e.:
  - suitable people;
  - appropriate machinery, equipment and facilities;
  - suitable organization;
  - relevant systems; and
  - good supplier and customer linkages.

4 Quality, and how to maintain it

Introduction

In this chapter we look at what is actually meant by quality and offer a business definition. Quality is contrasted with standards or specification and we try to clear up any misconceptions in this area.

The business climate in the 1990s is highly competitive and quality standards are ever-increasing, but who is setting these standards and what is the role of the manager of an operation in this? We extend this question of role or responsibility beyond just setting standards and explore who is responsible for what in the quality chase.

One of the recent quality issues has been the explosion that has occurred with organizations seeking quality accreditation through systems such as BS5750 and ISO 9000. We explain what these systems entail and how most organizations adopt them outlining some of the advantages and the pitfalls.

Another long-standing quality drive has been 'total quality management' (TQM) and we cover what is usually meant by the term and outline how the most successful organizations to use the approach have gone about it. We also look at the interaction between BS/ISO systems and the TQM approach in an attempt to avoid misunderstandings about the role of each in quality.

At the heart of every organization's drive for quality are the systems designed to deliver it. These systems are described together with an approach to ensure they are as good and useful as they can be. We explore the value and methods of involving in these systems your staff, suppliers and customers. How that involvement is arranged is important and we provide some advice.

We describe setting targets and monitoring performance against those targets and indicate the value and methodology of sharing that information with everyone through open displays within the operating environment.

We conclude with a brief look at the part new technology plays in quality and quality improvement.

This chapter relates to the following MCI Management Standards.

- M1/1.1: Maintain operations to meet quality standards.
- M2/1.1: Identify opportunities for improvement in services products and systems.
- M2/1.5: Introduce, develop and evaluate quality assurance systems.
- M2/2.2: Establish and agree customer requirements.
- M2/2.3: Maintain and improve operations against quality and functional specifications.

What is 'quality'?

The Oxford dictionary says quality is 'degree of excellence'. While this may be fine in a casual context, as a definition against which we can run our operation it lacks some depth and detail. What you consider to be a 'quality' item or performance may be greatly different to the views of others. When these differing views are held by you and the people your operation serves (your customers) trouble can result. Your output, of which you might be pleased and proud, may be unsatisfactory to your customers if their expectations are either higher, or just different.

Box 4.1
In a busy restaurant, the waiters are constantly on the move between tables and the kitchen. They welcome customers, seat them, take orders, they deliver meals, they clear the tables, and they handle payment. As the menu provides a wide and varied choice, customers often take quite a time deciding on courses and the minutes tick by, with waiters trying to encourage and advise on choice, without ever being seen to hustle or hurry customers. Overall, customers are rarely kept waiting between courses more than ten minutes and this is fine and acceptable to most groups on an evening out. A few customers, however, may be on a tighter schedule – for the theatre, for instance – and a ten minute wait is less acceptable to them. So the same operational performance can please some and annoy others. Both parties would see the quality standards as differing markedly. Yet it is the same service level.

Since the 1960s, the topic of quality has probably had a wider press, particularly in business and managerial journals, than any other managerial issue. The 'best operators in the world', mainly from Japan, have forced managers and leaders to view the subject as critical and now all serious businesses and organizations have a keen awareness of the topic. Sad to say, not all know how to deliver it, and in our experience too many are still not prepared to change old, traditional approaches to quality in their operations. The definition of quality for business and operations use is at the very heart of the understanding we all need in order even to stand a change of delivering it.

A working definition

The definition most widely used in the 1990s is that 'Quality is conformance to requirements'. We understand if your first reaction to this definition is negative, as the words sound typical of remote gurus, experts or consultants. They do not sound like everyday words used by most of the people who staff day-to-day operations, and indeed they are not! However, they are so precise and helpful when everyone does understand them that the definition is worth persisting with. Managers have to take on the task of explaining it to others and ensure that its significance and not just its meaning is conveyed.

Let us clarify what is so special about 'conformance to requirements' as a definition. 'Requirements' means the requirements of that particular transaction or operation. For continued customer satisfaction, the operation must be clear about what the customer regards as 'the requirement' and then it can set about satisfying it, or 'conforming' to it. When we, therefore, 'conform to the requirements' we are supplying a quality product or service.

Understanding the requirement is vital – we cannot over emphasize this. So 'quality' operations go to great lengths to ensure that they have clear contracts, or service level agreements, or specified service times, or specification data sheets – the actual stated requirement can take a variety of forms. When the requirement is clear and agreed with the customer the provider must then go to great lengths to ensure that everyone engaged in the operation is clear about it. We address how this communication phase is achieved later in this chapter.

We might have made this vital phase of getting the requirement agreed sound easier than it often is. It is a source of great misunderstanding and disagreement in many situations. If you think now of the last time you had a disagreement with your customer, could it have been that muddled requirements contributed? It may take many discussions, meetings and communications to get this early stage completed but it is worth it in the end. There is a real advantage to be gained from insisting on the requirement existing in written form. While this may sound obvious, it is not always done. We would even say that in most instances, the requirements placed on operations are *not* written down. The reason? Because most operations are serving an internal customer, which are other parts of their own organization. No contract exists, and no real attempt is ever made to produce any form of written requirement against which everyone in the operation can strive, measure, monitor and target their efforts.

This is now changing in some forward-thinking organizations where inter-departmental service level agreements are being drawn up. These provide just such a clear set of requirements for all parts of the organization, not just the externally facing operations where contracts or publicly claimed service levels provide written requirement which operating units must meet.

As the manager of your operation, is this something that you are clear about? Do you and your staff know what the requirements are that you have to meet? Have your customers agreed? Are they written down? Do your staff understand them? Being able to answer these questions positively is the first real step towards running a quality operation, producing good quality results.

Box 4.2

Our earlier example of the busy restaurant illustrated the frustration of misunderstandings when customers need a faster service than the norm.

Possible solutions to this dilemma may require action by both the operation and the customer. Maybe the restaurant could declare publicly, in the menu or discreetly on each table, the average time taken for a three-course meal for a party of two. It might be an hour and a half. The onus is then placed on the customers to declare if this is a problem for them. If they only have an hour, say, there might be savings in time in choosing certain dishes. The waiter can advise. Or skipping a course can obviously help. Maybe ordering all courses at the outset. There are a number of options that, within the scope of the operation, enable the requirement to be met. Correctly handled, then, both parties can feel satisfied that a good result was obtained – a win/win outcome.

The definition is 'conformance to requirements', and we have covered the word 'requirements', so what about this word 'conformance'? At its simplest level it means 'meeting' the requirement but we think this conveys a one-dimensional view and quality demands more depth. A requirement to 'deliver on Thursday' can be met by a wide variety of service. Delivery up to one second before midnight on Thursday will 'meet the requirement' in actuality, but maybe not in spirit. 'Conformance' has a three-dimensional quality; the dictionary talks about 'shape' in its definition. 'Conformance to requirements', then, better conveys this feeling of providing satisfaction 'in the round'. If the customer took as read delivery in the normal working day, a midnight delivery is likely to displease, not please. In order to conform, we really must be clear about all aspects of the requirement – we need to satisfy on every level, every nuance, in the customer's eyes.

'Conforming to requirements' – or exceeding them?

You will hear people talking about the need to 'delight customers'. This is one of the messages emerging from many customer care programmes and we do not take issue with what is intended. The problem can be that people do not know *how* to delight the customer. Does it mean giving him or her much more than promised? 'Delight' sounds more than just a little better than hoped for in service or product performance, so how much better do we have to be? With no answers to this question forthcoming, staff can be confused, and deliver much more than promised. But there is a limit to what the operation (and the business) can afford. To use a well-known phrase, we cannot afford to provide a Rolls-Royce when a Mini is needed.

Customer delight is an interesting phenomenon. In our experience it does not need a great deal more than that promised to achieve it. Many customers will be truly delighted by consistently reliable service and products, particularly in a sea of mediocre performance from your competitors. The icing on the cake for them may be the occasional 'extra' in an area they really value, thus showing true empathy and understanding of their needs.

Box 4.3

The management of an American hotel decided to change its approach to customer complaints. As an experiment they gave their staff the authority to give customers whatever they asked for to compensate them for anything they regarded as poor service. When customers complained about something, staff responded by apologizing first of all and then asking what the hotel could do to make it up to the customer. At the end of the experimental period, analysis showed that the most frequently requested item was nothing more than a free drink at the bar. The overall impression was that they, the customers, were taken aback at the initial apology – words like 'I'm so sorry madam. We try to avoid those sort of mistakes. I will report it and have it attended to straight away' – rather than the oft received 'aggressive' defence of the situation. So when asked 'Is there anything we can do to make it up to you?' they did not ask for excessive items. A drink at the bar was adequate because the sympathetic response was valued much more.

Non-conformances

In this quality 'jargon', the use of the word 'conformance' has another advantage. When we do not meet the requirement we can use the term 'non-conformance' rather than 'failure'. 'Failure' somehow sounds critical and could produce defensive responses, where 'non-conformance' has a more neutral connotation. 'This is a non-conformance' is a less emotive statement than 'we have a failure'. In such an event we want to be able to focus people's minds on facts not emotions. That way we can analyse with a clear head! This seems to us another tangible benefit of using the rather cumbersome 'conformance to requirements' definition.

'Quality' and 'standards'

Before we leave the subject of the definition of quality, we would like to recheck the understanding. This can be a difficult concept to grasp for some of us so clarification of the difference between quality and standards warrants some space.

Consider what might happen if you arrive at a company reception desk fifteen minutes early for an appointment. The receptionist establishes that the person you are seeing is actually busy until the appointment time. The receptionist then asks if you'd like a coffee, which you accept. The result might then be one of many:

- You may be told where to find the coffee machine.
- You may be brought vending machine coffee in a plastic cup.
- You may be brought coffee in a cup and saucer.
- You may be brought a pot of coffee with cream and sugar in good china.

Here we are talking about standards, or specifications, not quality. Some of these offerings are being made against higher standards than others. However, even though the offerings are against higher standards, their quality could still be in doubt. If the coffee in the china pot is cold or bitter, it deserves the label of low quality. If the machine coffee is exactly as specified by the supplier it deserves to be regarded as meeting its own quality specification. It can, of course, never match a 'bone-china' coffee offering because it is designed to different standards.

We would urge you to ensure you and your staff are clear on the definitions we have covered so far. Quality can only be provided by our operation if all those employed in, and supporting it, understand what it means.

You and the quality department

In the 1970s in the West, everyone knew that quality was the responsibility of those employed to deliver it – namely the Quality Department. Or Quality Assurance, Inspection, Quality Control – anyone with quality in their title. Indeed, most organizations set themselves up in ways that encouraged this thinking. Quality managers signed off procedures, inspectors signed off products and services. Processes stopped until quality control said it was OK to continue. *They,* the quality people, controlled the flows so *they* must be responsible for the quality.

Today most organizations recognize that this cannot be the case. Quality and the operation are inseparable. You are responsible for the quality of the output from your operation. When your operation is 'conforming to requirements' it is satisfying all its output aspects; schedule, throughput, lead-time, costs, defect rates, service levels. There is no aspect for which you are not responsible, and when you achieve all you can claim to run a quality operation.

So, you might ask, if you're doing all this what are the 'quality people' responsible for? Most organizations still have people with 'quality' in their title so what do they do in this new world? Their role in the main is that of the specialist department providing the operating departments with advice and guidance on how to manage the quality of their operation. Additionally they almost always provide an audit function and sometimes a monitoring function. They should on one hand be developing company standards, and on the other the skills necessary to advise on quality issues. These will involve such things as the way processes are designed to ensure quality output, the way measurements are made and how the results are analysed so that quality improvement efforts are correctly targeted. You, as an operational manager, should be working with them. They are an ally not an adversary, because they are one of the resources available to you, as manager of the operation.

Have you and the organization established the correct relationships between you, the operating department, and your specialist quality departments? Does anything need a rethink here, either structurally, which might be outside your responsibilities, or personally with the way you have been thinking of, or addressing, the issue of quality accountability?

Setting the standards

For your operation, you have a major role in agreeing the standards that you and your teams will work to achieve. However, in more junior roles, we are often given these standards either by others – our customers – or by more senior managers – our bosses. Even in these situations you must make sure you have clearly understood, because there will be times when you are forced to challenge the setting of unrealistic standards. This is part of the argument we made in the opening chapters, concerning the operating departments' roles in supporting the corporate strategy. In the area of standards this is equally the case. If standards are set too high for the current operational capability, you must alert others. Either standards must be adjusted or the operational capability must be changed. This is the manager's responsibility, then, and cannot be avoided. We will be looking at how to improve capability in Chapter 9.

The management of any organization will decide the standards to be met by that organization and by the individual operations within it. However, in the long term, standards are set, if not dictated, by the market. In turn, the market responds to the 'best in class' in any market sector. So, effectively, your competitors are setting some of the standards you have to meet. This is particularly true when organizations become complacent and fail to raise their standards over any time period – they will fall behind.

Box 4.4

An example of standards being set by the 'best in class' occurred in the USA when Federal Express offered a new parcels delivery service. Many parcels services existed in the USA and they exchanged market positions on a regular basis as they traded the various service elements one against another. Then Federal Express broke the mould by offering a unique standard of performance when they were the first to offer 24-hour delivery across a wide geographic spread in the USA. Their operations were designed to deliver this service reliably, and they stole a march on their competitors by so doing. Overnight the market realized this was an achievable service standard and could give them, the customers, competitive edge. They queued up for the service and competitors were forced to copy.

Once the standards have been set for your operation your job is to meet them – every time. Nothing else is good enough. As an advertisement for the products of an international computer company once said, 'if your defect rate is one in a million, what do you say to that customer?' The aim is for 100 per cent conformance at all times, and world class operations take this very, very seriously. Every part of the operation needs clearly specified standards so that the people doing the work know exactly what is expected and required of them. These standards will cover such things as accuracy limits, error rates, performance times and work rates and there is an almost limitless list of the standards used in different types of organization. Your task is to see that standards do indeed exist in all parts of your operation and that they are sensible and selected to ensure overall achievement by your total team. If an area of the operation is letting you down, are new standards required, or do staff need more guidance in meeting those standards? Remember, as we were at some pains to explain earlier, such things as standards must be written down. It is a major factor in people's understanding of them, as is the subject of simplicity. Do ensure that standards are simple to understand. This is not an area where we should demand that our staff should have a command of higher mathematics or *Roget's Thesaurus* to interpret the standards. Simple statements and simple numerical data are invaluable in avoiding confusion. Your staff will be grateful for this and the output of the operation will be enhanced.

The part BS and ISO systems play

In recent years, BS5750 and ISO 9000 quality systems have grown in use throughout every type of operation. We have recently adopted the ISO 9000 system and achieved accreditation within the management centre with which we are both associated. It was rare then for academic-based service businesses to follow such practices, but month by month it is becoming more widespread within every business sector.

The BS and ISO quality accreditation schemes were introduced in the 1980s in an effort to raise quality standards in British industry and commerce. The British Standards Institution (BSI) designed these systems and there are standards for many types of organization. The standards outline the key processes within the business which must be controlled for the business to receive accreditation. Accreditation enables a prospective customer to have more confidence in a supplier's ability to deliver quality products or services. What it indicates is simply that an independent third party, the assurance authority, has audited the systems of the supplier and found that they comply with good quality practices. It is not a guarantee of good quality but should be a strong indicator of quality performance.

The way these systems work is as follows. An organization wishing to become accredited must obtain the standards for their type of operation. Using these as a guide, the management must decide which of their operations and processes must be controlled by procedures. Procedures must then be written and established within the organization. After a period when the procedures have been in use, typically three months, an approved accrediting body such as BSI or Lloyds, visits the organization for an assessment. They first check that the procedures adequately cover key processes and meet the requirements of the standards. Secondly they check that the staff understand and use the procedures on a continuous basis in their day-to-day work. Important failings on either part of the assessment can lead to a failure to meet the accreditation standard, and approval will be withheld.

A successful assessment will result in accreditation and the organization can use the BS5750 or ISO 9000 mark on their company paperwork. Repeat assessments and/or audits take place on a regular basis and again failure to meet the requirements will result in withdrawal of accreditation.

If your organization is one of those accredited to either scheme, your operation will have approved procedures for quality performance and it is your responsibility to see that they are adhered to. Do not complain about bureaucracy as quality always demands some discipline. If you consider your procedures are overly onerous, talk to your BS or ISO systems people, or your boss. Maybe they can (and should) be simplified. These BS/ISO systems should not need complex procedures – that defeats the very BS/ISO objective of procedures helping people achieve quality performance.

'Total Quality Management' and 'Continuous Improvement'

One of the most prevalent management initiatives in recent years, spanning every type of business activity, is Total Quality Management

(TQM). Its praises have been sung world-wide as a technique for ensuring the quality of results indicated in this chapter.

The subject of TQM is a big one and has been written about extensively. The key figures of the approach are in the USA (Deming, Juran) and Japan (Taguchi, Ishikawa). The idea came out of the USA during the Second World War but lay dormant until the Japanese adopted it, with help from the USA, as part of their post-war economic recovery. The rest, as they say, is history, as Japanese businesses grew on the platform of stunning quality levels.

TQM involves a number of principles and attitudes to work. Put simply, it is the adoption of a belief *across the whole organization* that quality must be built into *every* operation. It cannot be inserted by the inspection function at the end of the operation. A second principle is the belief of everyone that tomorrow's performance can, and must, be better than today's for continued business success. So everyone in the business is continually looking for ways to make improvements in their own work. This is the 'many small steps' approach which the Japanese call 'Kaizen' and is referred to as 'Continuous Improvement' (CI). This seems to us a much more appropriate title than TQM.

When a TQM or CI approach is adopted by an organization, it usually means a shift in emphasis by everyone. In many traditional organizations quality has been 'assured' by inspection and defect correction routines. With a TQM approach much more attention is paid to defect prevention by having mistake-proof processes. If these types of processes existed throughout we would not need inspection, but they rarely do, so there is almost always a need for some inspection. In the best organizations this usually takes the form of auditing, both targeted and random.

The TQM approach is very useful in raising quality standards and we expand on that issue in Chapter 9. However, the main elements of any TQM or CI approach are as follows:

- top management commitment;
- education for all in the organization;
- measurement of current performance, setting targets to focus improvement efforts;
- creation of plans and implementation;
- problem definition/root cause; and
- using teams to solve problems.

The two last elements should use teams from the workplace. TQM and CI are covered widely in business books and journals; for greater detail, you should refer to those publications. Figure 4.1 lists against each of the six elements those factors which in our experience are most important.

One of the most frequent reasons for the failure of a TQM initiative to deliver what it should in terms of improvement is because part way through an initiative, top management either lose interest or fail to

● Top management commitment	– Essential, but must be real.
	– Deeds, not just words.
	– Messages need continued delivery and reinforcement.
	– Must extend to supporting staff spending time on the subject
● Education for all	– Allocate a budget.
	– Takes time and money – rolling programme.
	– Train in the techniques such as team working for front line staff.
	– Everyone needs it; managers up to ten days, operators maybe fifteen hours.
	– Staff cannot implement until trained.
● Measure current performance and set targets to focus improvement efforts	– Measurement is key.
	– Today's performance sets the datum.
	– Set challenging but achievable targets.
	– Focus is vital to avoid dispersed efforts.
	– Ensure targets are known and understood.
● Make plans and implement	– Prioritize – everything cannot be improved at once.
	– Plans need to be clear and communicated.
	– A volunteer to try the approach is invaluable.
	– Seek early success – do not tackle intractable problems first.
● Problem definition and root cause analysis	– Identify problems, not symptoms.
	– Define these problems.
	– Analyse to get at root cause (technique training needed).
	– Use the working teams to do this.
● Problem solving	– Use new creative problem-solving techniques.
	– Working teams as in the point above.
	– May need authorization to make changes.
	– Monitor effect of actions – has the problem been solved?
	– Continuous review of results.

Figure 4.1 Main elements of a TQM or CI approach

recognize the importance of taking an active part. As a result, the staff reporting to them do the same, because they are responding to what the top management declares interest in – this is only human nature. Hence all managers cease to be interested in TQM and therefore so does everyone else. The initiative dies.

Figure 4.2 shows the traditional organizational pyramid. If you are in an organization pursuing TQM and the top management loses interest you can still keep your department's initiative work going. Consider yourself to be 'top management' as indeed you are for your operation. So keep your own commitment live and visible and make improvements happen.

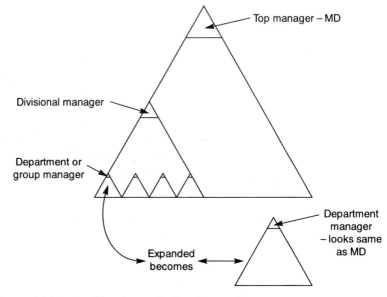

Figure 4.2 The traditional organizational pyramid

Figure 4.3 shows how the two approaches, of TQM and BS or ISO systems, can be effectively used together. Initially the BS/ISO procedures establish a quality standard at point A. At point B, the company launches a TQM or CI process and many small-step improvements are made. The BS/ISO procedures need regularly updating to lock-in the new standards, e.g. as at point C on the 'steps' equating to point D on the vertical axis.

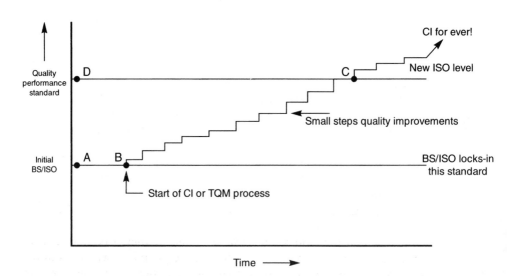

Figure 4.3 TQM and ISO systems working together

Box 4.5
A story we like on this subject of top management commitment, involves a major UK airline. They introduced a TQM-style 'customer service improvement' programme and everyone in the airline was trained in new beliefs, priorities and methods.

Soon after the training programmes, one check-in clerk found herself with a problem at passenger check-in for a London to Paris flight when the computer failed. Her check-in line was delayed and two business people missed their flight to Paris. They complained bitterly that through no fault of their own they would now miss an important evening meeting in Paris.

Recognizing the airline's responsibility for this and with the 'customer service' training fresh in her mind, this entrepreneurial clerk decided to resolve the issue. She immediately called a friend who worked in a small executive airline and arranged an executive jet to fly the two business people to their meeting, at no cost to them. They, needless to say, were delighted.

The story went around the airline's staff like wildfire and everyone waited to see what the management would do. To their eternal credit they behaved in exemplary fashion, or in TQM fashion. They made her 'employee of the month' – front page of the airline's newsletter. In addition, they sent her on a one-day training programme to give her further insight into the ten other avenues she might have explored that would have satisfied her passengers and avoided additional costs of many thousands of pounds.

This did more to establish, in everyone's eyes, that the management were indeed committed to this programme than any pre-planned 'flag-waving' ceremony.

Box 4.6
BS and ISO systems are mainly concerned with 'locking-in' a certain quality performance through procedural control of processes. Although there is scope and indeed demand for methods to overcome any failures or faults that occur, quality improvement is *not* the main aim, while locking-in the quality standards is. TQM and continuous improvement, however, are all about finding improvements – a never-ending process.

If your organization has BS/ISO systems, are they used in this way? If not is there anything you can do to raise people's awareness of the issue? In this way you can maximize the advantage your operation and your business obtains from these systems.

Systems for achieving quality

In the simplest of operations, such as the one-person business, it is quite feasible to consider the operation running effectively without the use of formal systems. One person can carry the system information in their heads – or can they? Even these simple operations will be using some systems to enable them to provide quality service to their customers. It could be as simple as a card-based customer name, address and order information system. Or a system for keeping supplier information readily to hand so that they can quickly and correctly respond to an enquiry. As operations increase in complexity, so does the need for formal systems. They are a means of ensuring consistent performance from the people working within the operation; indeed in multi-disciplined, multi-person operations, people cannot function at all without formal systems.

These systems normally fall into two categories. Firstly, those that guide people in what they should be doing within the process; we can refer to these as control procedures. Secondly, there are systems or procedures to measure how the operation is doing, or the effectiveness of the operation to deliver quality output. We can call these quality monitoring procedures. Both of these procedural systems play a major part in helping the operation to produce consistent quality output. We will look at these two categories separately.

Control systems

These are the systems we need to run the process of the operation. They must be designed to help ensure everything is done in the most efficient and effective way and will produce quality output. A useful way of considering these systems is to try to look at the operation through the eyes of a new recruit. What are the activities that must be done correctly to ensure quality? What systems or procedures do you need to help a new entrant to learn to handle these activities? This analysis can help you to establish the systems that the operation needs, to control the key processes. It must include the complete operation taking account of suppliers and links with your customers, internal or external (Porter's Value Chain model at work again). At the heart will be the systems for controlling the operation itself, i.e. the operation for which you are responsible. These systems will control how people go about doing the work they are employed to do. In this way you are trying to ensure consistency of quality in their output. This overall objective is important and we should keep it in mind continually as it is your main guide to what the system should control tightly, and what can be left to discretion. In our experience failure to stick to control procedures often results from the staff's belief that they are left no discretion even in areas where they can and should be allowed to choose methods or approaches. Rebellion against over-control in those areas can produce rebellion against other procedures so that even essential systems are ignored or bypassed. Quality becomes a hit and miss affair in those circumstances.

Once you have established which areas of the operation need control systems, you need to establish what key elements need to be covered by each procedure. Previously in this book we have used the cleaning of hotel bedrooms as an example of an operation of which most readers would be aware. If we think of the system needed for the cleaning staff to ensure consistency of quality in room preparation, we could start to formulate a checklist of the work to be done during a room service.

Box 4.7
Room service checklist

Attend to bed	● change sheets
	● change pillow-cases
	● make bed – house style
Check laundry	● collect left laundry
	● leave bags if required (min. 2)
Clean bathroom	● clean wash basin ⎫ using special
	● clean bath/shower ⎬ cleaning fluid 'X'
	● clean toilet ⎭
	● wipe down all tiles/floor
	● change towels – bath
	● change flannels – face
	– hand
	● empty waste bin
	● replace soaps/shampoos/toiletries
	● check tissues/toilet rolls
	● neatly arrange room
	● finally, ensure bathroom looks attractive
Check wardrobes	● hang up dressing-gown etc.
	● arrange shoes neatly
Replenish fruit bowl	● five pieces of different fruit
	● replace plate/knife/napkin
Dust all surfaces	● arrange any papers neatly
	● do *not* remove/discard any item

Clean telephone with hygienic fluid

Vacuum carpets throughout

Visual check of room for anything needing cleaning or other attention

---

Box 4.7 is an example of a checklist. It is not a procedure – it does not dictate *how* the work is to be done but *what* is to be done. In some areas it does come close to doing that in that it dictates the cleaning fluid to be used for bathroom cleaning. This is necessary to ensure those quality standards we need to maintain. Where you can leave things to your staff's discretion you should do so. For instance, it is unlikely that we need to dictate whether or not the vacuuming is carried out in long straight lines, as in ploughing, or in short fan-like movement. Either done well will give the quality results we need. Control only what you truly have to, leaving the rest to the judgement and training of your staff.

Although we said our example was a checklist it could actually be a little more than that. It is quite possible to see that such a list of work to be done, could benefit from a 'best sequence' approach. If it had been found by experience or study that making the bed after vacuuming the carpets resulted in the carpet looking dusty again, then we would want to advise or even dictate that the sequence of cleaning had bed-making before vacuuming, as they appear in our checklist. So the list could become a procedure if we felt it a necessary move to ensure quality. However, remember, the less you allow staff to work to their own methods, the less they are able to use their brains at work. They become automatons and may end up not thinking at all because you have over-controlled them. The result of this is, that when they encounter something the management has not considered, they have no capacity to react sensibly. It is not their fault; it is the result of over-control.

Box 4.8

One of us spent several years as general manager of a defence-related business. The product was high-reliability instrumentation systems and the Royal Navy was a principal customer. The business was visited annually by the Controller of the Navy, a position filled by an officer with the rank of Admiral.

During one of the visits, as we moved into quality control, it was said 'Admiral, to prove that you are at one of the country's highest quality suppliers to the Navy, let me show you our fifty-three highly qualified inspectors.' He was impressed and we had, as we always did, an excellent visit.

A few years later, when we had learnt of the TQM approach and of prevention rather than detection/correction, those words were recalled with some guilt. If we had truly been a quality company why did we need fifty-three inspectors? We were good by the standards of the day, but they were wrong! You cannot build in quality afterwards. It must be built into the work as it progresses. Nothing else will do.

What we are trying to do with control systems is to *prevent* errors or failures occurring during the operations. While this has always been the case, this need has been greatly emphasized in the 1990s. Previously, quality was mainly achieved through the mechanism of inspecting after the work was done and then carrying out remedial work to correct any defects. This meant as much emphasis being placed on inspection (or detection) and correction as on prevention. This approach built into the minds of operating staff the idea that errors were expected because quality is difficult to achieve – otherwise why were those inspectors needed? Staff are now being trained to believe that work can be done without mistakes and the control procedures we have been describing are a major subscriber to achieving that quality goal. Fewer inspectors are found today.

Quality monitoring systems

In order to ensure that the systems and procedures you use do deliver quality through the efforts of your operation, you need to check that quality regularly. The simplest quality monitoring systems would be used to check at the 'output' or delivery stage of the operation. Two types of system can achieve this. One involves the operation itself running regular checks on its own output; the other involves asking the customer for that feedback. The latter is a much less commonly found method, but is the most effective for providing really valuable evidence of quality. It is much more important to see how you perform against the customer's measures of your quality standard than it is to get an internal opinion. This is not to say 'the customer is always right', as right and wrong are not really important in the end. What is important is to learn what the customer thinks of your quality against the agreed specification or requirements. If your quality is seen as poor, you need to know because you need to correct it. An unhappy customer does not stay a customer for long!

Output checks should make measurement of all the important criteria as seen by the customer. They usually include timeliness, completeness of service or product delivery, and defect or failure rate. An increasingly used measure is that of 'On time, in full' (or OTIF), to assess an operation's overall performance. Was the delivery (service or product) on time and in full (or complete)? For this measure to be taken seriously, 'in full' must mean what it says and the measure must be rigorously applied. This is an area where the target must be 100 per cent success, because it is simply a case of keeping all your promises or commitments to customers. The reputation of your operation will grow as your OTIF performance improves.

Measuring at the end of an operation is all very well and is the ultimate measure of your performance, but it is not all you should be doing to keep good control of your quality standards. Every operation consists of a sequence of events, all of which have a contribution to make to the whole. A good system of measurement will include checks or measurements made at several points along the sequence. The aim is to ensure that further work is not carried out after a defective action, e.g. it is pointless binding a report for despatch if the printing on the pages is faulty. So your aim should be to put in checks at these key points in the operation to ensure that the procedures upstream of that point are working and producing the level of quality you need. In this way you are trying to achieve several things:

- to avoid wasted work on already defective items;
- to discover faults earlier – this assists fault cause tracking;
- to correct those faults at an earlier stage;
- to raise overall quality standards;
- to lower costs through reduced waste; and
- to improve customer service.

Your approach should be to have these checks made by the operator and not by an independent inspector. The self-inspection aspect of these measurements is a vital element in making operations staff more aware of quality as their responsibility. They become their own quality assurance manager.

You need to decide at which points to make these checks and what to measure at each point. This is best done with the people who know the work best, namely the operations staff. They are well aware of the areas of failing that can lead to output being lost or faulty – these are the areas that must be covered, and the measurements must be designed to locate those failures that occur most regularly. You should, of course, be consulting others in this process as well, such as design, quality assurance and customer services staff, but we emphasize the role of the operations team as we find they are often excluded in the process. Do not fall into that trap; they are your best source of information.

What we are recording as a result of these systematic checks is usually the extent to which the operation fails to be 100 per cent successful. This involves how often and to what degree non-conformances occur. If it is a simple 'pass' or 'fail' procedure then that is straightforward, but more often some measurement of degree is involved. It is valid to check whether a service call is late or not. Measuring 'how late' is a measure of degree and provides additional useful information. In this case you should be recording both.

Regular measurement provides very useful data but it is only a stepping-stone to something more important. When it indicates a performance level less than 100 per cent, you need to understand why the shortfall has occurred; what problem existed that prevented the operation performing correctly; and, finally, the root cause of that problem. Once this is established target your efforts to ensure that the problem does not recur, i.e. solve the problem for ever. This is the cornerstone of quality and quality improvement. Very rarely is a problem due to a random cause. The overwhelming evidence is that the vast majority of problems occur over and over again because the root cause is not established or eradicated.

Box 4.9

For many years, the whole computer industry was plagued with poor reliability from cables and connectors. It was probably a decade before this problem was taken seriously and improvement made, but even in the 1990s the reliability of these components falls sadly behind that of the electronic components in the system.

Some problems seem so obvious they are never properly addressed. Do you have any glaringly obvious 'root causes' not being dealt with? This could be a good time to tackle them, or one of them at least. Make a start!

Involve the people

Throughout this chapter we have referred to the people who work in the operation and emphasized their importance in sustaining and improving quality. No manager can achieve this without the staff and we will outline here the key issues to be pursued.

Staff attitude

You have the responsibility of ensuring that your staff take quality seriously. You will not achieve this by just telling them to do so – they may or may not listen to you. Their belief will grow as they see you (and the organization) taking quality seriously on a regular basis. The real test comes when you and the organization is under pressure. The moment they hear you say something like 'we're too busy for all those quality routines just now – just send it out!' they know how important you really consider quality to be. So do not fall into this trap with your team because it takes a lot to recover lost positive attitude.

Education

Your staff will need educating into exactly what quality is, because, as we outlined, it is not a straightforward issue. They need to understand what the organization expects from them, and how they 'deliver' quality through their own work. We have, too frequently, come across organizations that change or raise the quality requirements from their staff but fail to explain the new needs adequately. People cannot deliver what they do not understand. Understanding is the first step on the ladder of changing attitudes and you need to ensure that your staff have it.

We have discussed involving staff in setting up control and measurement procedures. This not only produces better procedures as a result of their detailed knowledge of the work, but is also essential if you want to build any ownership of the procedures. If they help to produce or develop them, the systems and procedures become their own. They are much more likely to use them in that situation, than if management produce and impose them. An additional benefit is that it continues to build the correct attitude towards quality that we need them to develop.

Be your own 'quality manager'

A third area of involvement is in the application of the quality measurements to the operations. Instead of someone else, such as quality control people, coming in to run these checks, the operation's staff should do them themselves. That idea of being one's own 'quality manager' comes to the fore here. If members of staff measure their own performance or output and find problems, they are likely to be able to get to the cause more quickly than anyone else. They probably know or suspect it anyway. They can then fix the problem at source, or at least flag it up to you, the manager, if it is beyond their own capability to resolve.

Teamwork and partnership

Most operations run with people operating as individuals on one hand, and as a member of a team on the other. Both activities improve through involvement in all aspects of the work. When it comes to teamwork, your staff may need some help and guidance. If you want them to work as a team, they will need some development in such things as running meetings, sharing information, and team decision-making. You need to arrange for them to receive this help through training or your coaching or both (we will return to the issue of training shortly).

The aim is for manager and team to work together as one in a complementary way. In the past, particularly in the West, organizations believed that all decision-making and problem-solving was the responsibility of management, leaving the workforce to do as they were told. Enlightened managements recognize the weakness of that thinking. Any management still pursuing this thinking is probably only using a fraction of the brain power available to them, and history shows managers are not necessarily the best people to design systems on their own.

Box 4.10
Surveys have shown that over 90 per cent of all quality problems are caused by the management systems in use.

If shortcomings in management systems are causing problems, managers should welcome the opportunity to get their staff to help overcome these shortcomings. We experience far too many occasions when management are not prepared to consider this. This may be because they are still unaware of the developments which have occurred in involving staff in decision-making – and the benefits which have been achieved. It may also be that, although aware of potential benefits, they do not know how to go about achieving them.

The most potent factor in improving quality standards lies in the close involvement of the workforce in helping to design the system. With this sort of involvement, the management will benefit, the staff will benefit and the business will benefit.

Box 4.11

At Sundridge Park we use high reality business simulations as part of our general management courses. One of these simulations involves three teams of managers, Groups A, B and C, producing business plans for a manufacturing business. The product is a complex three-dimensional cardboard assembly. It is a difficult product to assemble quickly, particularly if high quality standards are set. Later in the simulation, after the plans have been entered, each of the groups in turn takes the role of a manufacturing workforce trying to meet the business plan that has been set by one of the other groups. They also work to the other group's manufacturing system. Almost always, they have difficulty meeting the quality standards at the production rate set. What usually happens is that the workers point out the quality problems to the managers, only to be told (a) not to complain (b) not to be rebellious (c) not to be careless and (d) to get on with it. Almost always observers can see that the problems rest with the managers' design of the process and/or the procedures, but this is almost never acknowledged by the management team. They defend the system, closing their eyes and ears to the problems. Later, in review, they invariably blame the workforce for the shortcomings, who themselves are shocked and hurt to be blamed. Their view, mostly borne out by observers, is that they are trying their hardest to make an inadequate system work.

Both parties go through a period of blaming each other. In our simulations we use this experience as a learning vehicle and negative feelings are soon overcome. In real life such feelings grow unless management take the initiative and recognize the dangers of this situation. Management need to be enlightened and staff will follow their lead.

Performance on display

It is critical to keep everyone informed of how any quality initiative is performing. Such information is a logical consequence of involving the staff in the first place and an essential requirement in maintaining commitment and motivation. This means that in the design of the system, decisions have to be made about the use of performance data for promotional purposes as well as for analysing and solving problems. Charts of results should be publicly displayed so that the whole team can see if quality is improving. If correctly designed, these result charts show people immediately how things are, whether they are meeting targets, and whether things are getting better or worse.

Charts should be clear so that they can be easily marked up by the staff themselves, and easily understood by others. They need to be absolutely up-to-date. Out-of-date charts are a sure sign that the management are not really interested in quality.

The key parameters and outputs you are checking through the quality measurement checks should all be charted. We show some examples of formats in Figure 4.4 but there are no fixed ways of doing this. We strongly advise charts rather than tables of figures because people are much more likely to see trends and targets not met, or indeed exceeded, in a chart form. To do that with tables of figures comparing actuals with plan or target, is far harder and has less impact.

Display all the parameters being measured, but be aware that it is easy to get into overload on this type of information display. Display too much, and the staff do not know what is important.

Box 4.12
The palletizing section of a major bottling plant displayed by each workstation excellent charts of the quality performance of the palletizing group. There were a great many on display and the display wall was a mass of coloured charts, all very neatly drawn and each one very clear. The problem was that with so many charts, no-one knew the story that they were telling.

We need to provide highly focused information so that the team can see the overall performance at a glance. Be careful what you display and how you display it; take time to get it right. Finally, ensure that everyone understands the charts and is clear what messages are being conveyed by them.

In some cases you may be reluctant to post your quality performance on the wall for all to see. What if customers see it? They will see that you do not always achieve 100 per cent and won't that work against your interests? In our experience, this is not the case. Customers are pleased to see that you are taking quality seriously and are involving everyone in it. Of course, if the charts show an abysmal

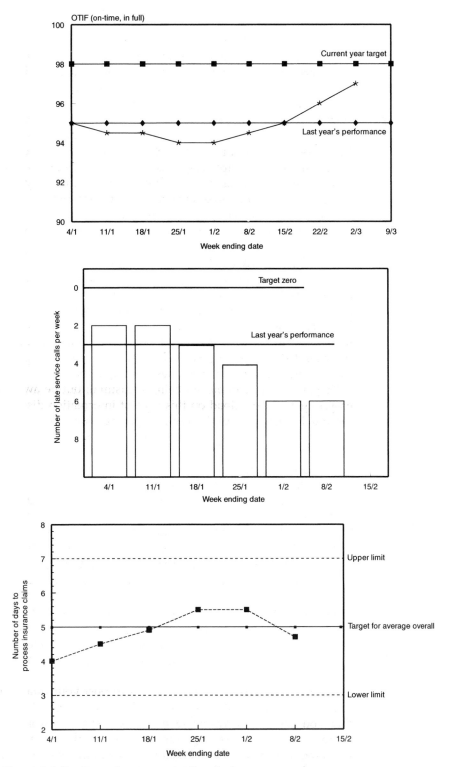

Figure 4.4 Quality performance charting designs

performance you *will* get customer concern. Similarly, if the charts show declining performance and you are not acting to stop that, their confidence will be shaken. Charting performance is not a substitute for good performance; it is a useful tool to enable you to achieve better performance. Customers will appreciate that too.

Training your people

People cannot produce quality work if they do not know how to. Although this seems very obvious it is surprising how often people are asked to do this. Our guess is that most of you reading this were asked to manage staff with very little guidance as to how to do it! We receive extensive training to be, say, an accountant, an engineer, or a chef but virtually no training to do one of the most difficult tasks around, namely that of managing others.

One of the critical quality systems you need in your operation is a training plan to cover all the people and all the tasks and processes to be performed within that operation. Over a period of time all your staff must be trained and developed to do as much of the work within the operation as is both sensible and possible. Not everyone is capable of doing everything, but we should provide as many as we can with multiple skills. This will give them greater confidence, capability, and job satisfaction and provide us with staff flexibility and cover in the event of absences or losses. These training plans can again be displayed as a detailed programme, so that everyone knows what is in store for them as individuals and for the team as a whole.

Many of the formal quality assurance systems, such as the BS and ISO systems, demand plans and records of training achievement as part of formal systems. It is management's job to arrange and provide training. It is an absolute prerequisite to the involvement of people in the quality process.

Box 4.13
A supplier of components to the Ford Motor Company displays the most comprehensive training charts on the wall beside each operation. This was demanded by Ford's own highly developed quality system to which every one of their suppliers has to adhere. It displayed in detail each individual's developmental plans and progress. In this way Ford seeks to ensure that quality problems do not arise due to staff not having the necessary skills to work the operation.

Suppliers and customers

No system designed to guarantee quality can exclude the 'input' and 'output' stages. We explore the supplier side in Chapter 5 and the customer figures prominently throughout this book, so you should be in no doubt of the need to involve them in your quality systems. However, as they are a key element in this quality equation we will summarize the main points here.

Firstly, involve them in your plans and systems. If their attitude is the correct one they will want to be involved. The best operations are regularly inviting suppliers and customers to join them in working and social sessions, to help build relationships and understanding.

Secondly, measure the effectiveness of your suppliers as you would your own. Remember to include regular checks of the quality of your suppliers' performance. With the right approach, you can get them to self-check – the equivalent of the self-checking operations staff – and furnish you with the results. Such arrangements can become part of the contract.

Thirdly, measure your own performance at the interface with your customers and supply them with the results. If they are also measuring you, as is likely these days, ask if you can see those results and compare the two. Arrange discussions with them to clear up discrepancies or disagreements and to find ways of improving your performance in the future.

Fourthly, check your customers' input to your operation. Record the completeness and correctness of the information supplied to you against which you are trying to perform. Are there problems there that they should know about and could rectify? For instance, orders that are illegible or ambiguous help no-one. If that situation exists you should tackle it. You do, of course, need to be careful here; if you do find this situation exists, treat the discussions carefully. Suppliers cannot afford to give any impression of arrogance or superiority in these discussions. What you must convey is the idea that you are looking within your system for causes of poor quality in your own performance. If error is found to have been influenced by the way the customer has specified you need to work together to eliminate it. Correctly handled, customers will be impressed that you are leaving no stone unturned in your pursuit of quality. You will be better received in this campaign if their short-comings are just one in a list of several things you are pursuing.

Finally, treat your suppliers and customers as if they truly are part of your own organization; you will improve communication enormously. Involve them in, and inform them of, your current and future plans (as far as is practicable) and keep in constant touch with them. As most problems stem from misunderstandings and poor communication, this one move alone will pave the way for improvement between you.

Robotics, automation and new technology

New, high technology systems can contribute greatly to both meeting and improving quality. There is a belief that automation is used to speed things up and, while that is to some extent true, as big a contribution to productivity is made through the raising of quality standards which results from automating. Every manager of every operation, should be constantly looking for improved ways to do things. New technology can provide major advances.

What you should be trying to do through your systems is to ensure that people working in your operation work to the standards you require, and make as few mistakes as possible – that ultimate target of 'zero defects'. Most managers still cherish the opinion that this goal is unreasonable and have not really understood the concept of zero defects as the target to aim for. However, in robots and automation, we find the capability to perform day in, day out to a zero defects target. Correctly set up and maintained, automated systems do not have lapses of concentration, hangovers or 'bad days' – the situations that can lead to human error.

'Automation does not only cover the big, expensive machines made famous by countless television programmes on volume production methods. It also includes 'new technology' which can be of greater importance for many managers. In our hotel bedroom cleaning example, this would embrace considering the latest vacuum cleaners, or wash and vacuum machines combined and, when the hotel is refurbished, the inclusion of a built-in vacuum 'grid' system through-out the hotel, with access points in each room, thus avoiding the need to move machines around.

Box 4.14

In the print-room where we are based, great strides in quality resulted from the purchase of the latest 'intelligent' copying machine. The operators can now correct quality errors through the machine, and because this is easy to do, more errors are cleared. Before, they sometimes accepted small errors because of the loss of time and the hassle of going back to the originator.

You should constantly be on the lookout for advances being made and seek to take advantage of them where appropriate. Of course, investment in any new technology must show improvements, but if improvements will result, these investments can be self-funding. Learn how to evaluate them for the 'pay-back' that every accountant looks for and then be prepared to fight the business case. Your operation and your staff need the best equipment if they are to deliver high quality. It is your responsibility to get it!

Summary

Quality is 'conformance to requirements'. Ensure you understand what the customer requires in order to achieve 'conformance'. Internal customers need to be dealt with in similar ways to external customers. High standards do not necessarily mean high 'quality'. Quality departments provide the framework; operational departments ensure 'quality' results. Standards must be within the capability of the operation, but ultimately, the market dictates what is acceptable: in turn the market is influenced by the standards set by the competition. Staff must be helped to understand what your standards are.

British Standards and International Standards systems consolidate standards required; total quality management systems are concerned with achieving continuous improvement. Maintaining commitment to continuous improvement is probably the most difficult thing to achieve.

Quality performance cannot be achieved without systems to control and to monitor. Systems should be more concerned with 'prevention' than 'detection'.

Involving staff in design and measurement of quality standards helps to achieve the right attitudes and ownership of the process. Operators and management need to be in partnership. Charting performance helps maintain focus and motivation. Training plans are indispensable.

Suppliers and customers need to be involved in the determination of quality systems. Technology offers many opportunities for improving the process.

Management checklist

- Do you think your staff are clear about the difference between quality and standards? How could you clarify this for them?
- Have you a good understanding of your responsibilities for quality? Do they dovetail with those of the quality department?
- Can/does your operation continuously meet the standards required? What are the three weakest areas:

  1 . . . .

  2 . . . .

  3 . . . .

- Are all your major requirements:
  - clear?
  - understood?
  - written down?
  - User friendly?
- Are your procedures designed to *prevent* defects or non-conformances?
- Do you use OTIF as a measure? If 'yes', what is your performance level, and is it good enough? If 'no', should you?

- Are there any recurring problems within your operation? What are the root causes? Which one will you tackle first?
- Are your staff involved in the quality procedures so that their views are incorporated?
- Do you display quality charts in the operation? Are they simple, clear, and up-to-date?
- Do you have a formal, declared staff training plan to ensure quality is maintained and improved?

5 Supplies and supplier management

Introduction

When explanations are being given to a customer who has been subjected to a failed delivery, faulty equipment or poor services, often heard excuses include 'I'm afraid one of our suppliers has let us down' or 'There's nothing we could have done; it's the supplier's fault'.

In these days of 'total quality' and heightened awareness of customer satisfaction, these excuses are not acceptable. They never were, of course, but customers didn't always realize it. Now more and more of them do, and they also realize that it is a vital part of a manager's job to be managing our suppliers effectively. If they (the suppliers) are the cause of us failing our own customers, why did we pick them in the first place? Why did we not spot the impending failure before it occurred? These would be valid questions in such circumstances so we must avoid the need for them to be asked by developing an excellent supplier base. When you fail a customer they will see and recall *you* as the cause, not your suppliers; and rightly so.

No operation, manufacturing or service, specialist or generalist, private or public, can function without a whole raft of suppliers. They will cover, for example, fuel and power, stationery products, raw materials, sometimes people (e.g. design services), distribution and delivery. For most operations the list is very long indeed and embraces a very wide range of 'services'. As the manager of the operation you must ensure that this activity is managed well. It may not always be your direct responsibility to manage the suppliers themselves, but it is your responsibility to see that your operation is never let down by suppliers. Even more emphasis is placed on this area when we realize that in most operations the costs of supplies and suppliers will amount to between 30 and 70 per cent of the total costs. This alone justifies a great deal of your attention. In this chapter we aim to provide you with some pointers and questions you should ask yourself and others about your supplies management approach and systems.

Most supplier management systems are designed around the external supplier, i.e. from another company or organization. However, many and in some cases all, of the suppliers to your operation will be internal. These will include such areas as maintenance, print room, personnel, sales, despatch and stores. The fact that they are internal rather than external should not materially alter your approach. We still need efficient, effective performance from them even if we do not have a rigorous contract with all of the 'small print' detail.

Additionally for many managers of operations, particularly with internal suppliers, the actual choice of suppliers is not theirs to make. We recognize this, but would recommend all sections of this chapter as providing sound principles against which to manage suppliers. At some stage in most managers' careers they will be required to select suppliers, so this basic awareness should prove valuable.

To help with the special case of managing the internal supplier we have included a separate section within the chapter. The chapter relates to the following MCI Management Standards:

- M1/1.1: Maintain operations to meet quality standards.
- M1/1.2: Create and maintain the necessary conditions for productive work.
- M2/1.1: Identify opportunities for improvement in services, products and systems.
- M2/1.2: Evaluate proposed changes for benefits and disadvantages.
- M2/2.1: Establish and maintain the supply of resources into the organization.
- M2/2.3: Maintain and improve operations against quality and functional specifications.

Supplier/buyer linkages

Chapter 2 outlined Porter's 'value chain' as a model for analysing our own operations and the linkages upstream and downstream. Here, we are concentrating on the upstream links from our own operations into (or from) our suppliers. This is shown in Figure 5.1 where the outbound logistics of our suppliers are interlinked with, or indeed become, our own inbound logistics. Other links which impact our own operations, such as service links and technology links, are shown between various functions of suppliers into our own business.

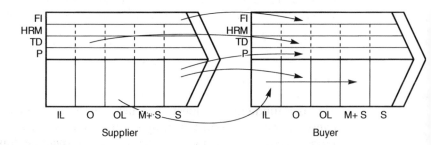

Figure 5.1 The business to business value chain (Source: Porter, 1985, reprinted with the permission of The Free Press, a division of Simon & Schuster Inc. Copyright © 1985 by Michael E. Porter)

These links are an important source of advantage for our operation if we seek improvements in the arrangements to minimize waste and unnecessary work. A simple but good example of these opportunities can be found in delivery arrangements. A supplier who will deliver exactly when you want, to suit your operation and in the form you require, is adding value to your business because you can run the operation without compromise. If these arrangements are not 'tuned' you are failing to get the best from your combined operations. The value chain provides a model to analyse these supplier/buyer linkages in our bid to find those opportunities for performance improvement.

We must be clear about the breadth of these opportunities. Adjustments or flexibility in paperwork systems to enable us, the buyer/user, to work more easily with a supplier have real value to us. They can mean less confusion, fewer errors, less time spent in paperwork or information handling. A natural follow-on to such improvements would be fewer staff tied up handling supplier interfaces, both purchasing and others. Fewer staff mean less cost or more business for the same number of staff. Whichever way it turns out, this means better productivity or business performance. And all this could come from relatively simple adjustments on the part of the supplier. However, the opportunity does need to be sought in the first place and we believe that responsibility rests with those who are managing the operation that is using the supplier. Once the question has been raised, best progress is made when joint discussions are held between supplier and user, with the clear objective of finding better ways of working.

There is a trap here and we must not fall into it. We have talked about suppliers changing *their* systems. It is just as effective if we adjust *our* own practices to suit an effective supplier system. It needs a mature mental approach on our behalf to even consider this. Traditionally, 'the customer is always right', leads us to believe the supplier must always change to suit us. It takes a balanced manager to look impartially at every situation. If the supplier's ideas are best, we should adjust our systems. What we are seeking is overall advantage between us – the source of the improvement or idea is not important. We cannot tolerate any 'Not invented here' thinking in this area of the operation.

What do you buy in?

This is a fundamental question which should constantly be asked in every operation within a healthy organization. It used to be believed by management that any and everything that *could* be done in-house, *should* be done in-house. This was seen as the best way of maximizing the use of assets and facilities and of maintaining control. Management consultants such as Tom Peters (and the Japanese) tore holes in this thinking, proposing that the best companies in the world only undertake in-house what they do better than anyone else. Other 'non-core activities', where specialist suppliers can out-perform our own in-house capabilities, should indeed be out-sourced.

Box 5.1

In an electronic manufacturing business for which one of us was responsible, we contracted to supply high volumes of a piece of equipment we had made in lower volumes for a few years. The volume increase, together with high pressure to keep costs down in a competitive tendering situation, encouraged us to look outside at comparative costings for every activity. The unit wiring harness had always been manufactured in-house. We were shocked and amazed to discover that we could have harnesses made in Mexico, to higher quality standards than we could achieve in our South London premises, on shorter delivery times, delivered to our factory in the UK and at lower cost! The Mexican operation did nothing but harnessing – they were true specialists operating at the leading edge and we could not match them. By using them, we improved our performance and lowered our costs. It spurred us to look at other areas and we found several where out-sourcing led to significant improvements.

For this strategy to be followed we must regularly assess all the activities within the operation. In a manufacturing operation this is the traditional 'make or buy' assessment. Similar decisions are needed throughout service operations. In order to make these decisions, therefore, it follows that those in charge of operating departments must be aware of the performance capability of other organizations in the marketplace – how else can we assess and judge our own operations to make the decision whether or not to sub-contract? It is no longer adequate to ask 'Can we do it in-house?'; we must now ask 'How well can we do it in-house?' and, 'Can it be done faster/with higher quality/at lower cost outside?'.

There are, of course, areas which need no decision. The first of these is that of the core operational competences on which the whole business is based. These are never sub-contracted. They are the operational areas we must handle better than anyone else – those critical success factors for the operation in supporting the business strategy. These areas are what Tom Peters refers to when he talks of 'sticking to the knitting'.

The second area is that of our own capabilities. If we cannot do it at all, we must buy it. Raw material supply, or specialist capabilities we just do not possess, are usually good examples.

Operations are *always* dependent on supplies and suppliers, and it is vital that those in operations management understand supplier management and have some guidelines to operate by. The rest of this chapter concentrates on these basic guidelines.

Choosing your suppliers

In many cases you have a choice of which supplier to use. Where the services or products you need can be provided by more than one organization, you need to decide who to use. So how do you decide? A simple step-by-step system can help.

Step 1: Decide how important this supply issue is. This is usually a combination of importance (critical items to the operation) and size or value of the supply (percentage this purchase represents of your total purchases). Where an item scores high on either or both of these criteria using, say, the Pareto 80/20 rule (e.g. 80 per cent of the value of total purchases is accounted for by 20 per cent of the items or suppliers) then we would apply the following steps in the procedure.

Step 2: Decide what performance criteria are important to you in this supply situation.

These would usually include items such as:
- specification or standards;
- lead time;
- price;
- reliability;
- responsiveness;
- delivery arrangements;
- flexibility; and
- quality system.

Step 3: Decide if all are of equal weighting or importance. If not, decide weighting.

Step 4: Assess each supplier rigorously against these criteria, using a 5-point scale.

Step 5: Calculate results – highest score wins unless something critical has emerged during assessment which overrides the result. However, do ensure you have more than just a 'hunch' if you are vetoing a result. A typical system is shown in Figure 5.2.

When referring to Figure 5.2, note that the top rating scoring of 5 is referred to as 'excellent'. 'Excellent' here means in relation to *your* requirement, not in relation to some hypothetical world scale, i.e. if your need is for 10 cm plus or minus 1 mm, *that* is what scores excellent results in the offerings of a would-be supplier. You should not overrate

Company name:			Superior Supplies Ltd.				
			Scoring				
	Poor		OK		Excellent	**Weighting**	**Result**
Criteria	1	2	3	4	5		
Specification			3			-	3
Leadtime		2				-	2
Price		2				x2	4
Reliability				4		-	4
Responsiveness				4		-	4
Delivery arrangements					5	x2	10
Flexibility				4		-	4
Quality systems			3			-	3
						Total score	34

Note: Best possible score here is 50.
Note: Price and delivery arrangements are deemed in this example to carry twice the importance of other elements in the table. This particular hypothetical company scores well on only one of these aspects.

Figure 5.2 Supplier assessment chart

plus or minus 0.1 mm because you may be overpaying for a tighter specification you truly do not need.

In Step 2 we have suggested a number of criteria with which to assess suppliers. Our list is not prescriptive or exhaustive: there are always a large number of factors and you should take time and care over their selection, consulting others who will be affected by the suppliers' performance.

If you are picking a supplier you have not used before, ensure you obtain a third-party view of their performance. Talk to some of their existing or previous customers, some they recommend and some out of their customer list that *you* select. You are not seeking to be underhand here, but to obtain genuine, honest experience from as independent a source as you can find. This is equivalent to carefully checking out references and previous employers when recruiting staff. Obtain the information and use it wisely.

We included an assessment of the importance of each purchase as Step 1 in the selection procedure. When an item does *not* qualify as important, the selection of supplier is not so critical as to demand the full rigour of the five-step procedure. However, it does provide the basis of a checklist for supplier choice without demanding significant managerial time. You should at least be clear about what is, or are, the critical performance criteria the supplier must meet for your operation to succeed, and then ensure your selection gives the best chance of achieving that performance.

Rating your supplier's performance

Having selected suppliers to 'feed' our operation, their continued performance must be monitored. It is surprising how few organizations formally do this. They rely on people's emotional assessments rather than facts and this can result in the continued use of a poorly performing supplier because someone in authority 'thinks they are OK'. What do the facts reveal? That is only known if the facts are gathered.

What facts, then, are important? There is a simple answer here, namely the performance related to the criteria established as important during selection, (step 2 in the selection process). If important during selection, those same criteria are what you are interested in during supply execution. If no criteria have ever been set you need to decide now what they are; these become the items to be monitored, on a regular basis – at least quarterly, and preferably monthly.

Two things can result from this data collection and its use in reviews. Performance can improve simply as a result of the interest and focus the monitoring generates in both supplier and customer organizations. In addition, there will be the obvious benefit of highlighting any actual shortcomings in performance.

Box 5.2
The first type of improvement is an example of the power of the phenomenon known as the Hawthorn Effect from experiments in the USA in the 1930s. The valuable lesson from the Hawthorn experiment showed that the performance of people who knew that they were part of a management experiment improved both when their working conditions were improved and when they were worsened. The conclusion was that people's performance was affected more by the attention it received from management than by their working conditions.

When shortcomings in supplier performance are shown up, it allows you to draw up a programme of improvements in addition to continuing the monitoring activity. When relationships and conditions are good, suppliers can be asked to monitor themselves and supply results regularly. This relieves the customer (you) of that duty and places responsibility where it should be – on the suppliers who should be interested in, and monitoring, their own performance. This is one step towards ensuring that they keep your business by continuously improving performance. Monitoring is the first essential step in this direction.

Chapter 4 referred to the concept of OTIF (On Time In Full) as a criterion for assessing your own delivery performance. The same concept obviously applies when you assess your own suppliers, and in monitoring their performance it is important to collect clear and factual data as a basis for dialogue with them.

How many suppliers?

This seems at first sight a rather stupid question. Once we have decided what we need to buy in, surely the number of suppliers results naturally? We use as many as we need. Although this sounds very simple, this thinking has led to most organizations using far too many suppliers. The main causes of this are:

- Poor supplier performance means you try elsewhere for repeat orders – this often leads to two or more suppliers being used for the same items at any time.
- The belief that having only one supplier (i.e. being single-sourced) is risky.
- The belief that having two or more suppliers competing for your business keeps prices down through healthy competition.
- Overload on suppliers during peak periods.

A proliferation of suppliers means that even quite small operations – say with turnover of less than £1m – can be utilizing as many as 600 suppliers. The downside of this is the sheer management task that goes with such a large supplier base. You *may* be reaping some benefit but the cost is in an immense organizational task. Purchasing becomes a paper chase of writing orders and amendments just to keep up. No time is available for actually talking to suppliers, monitoring and reviewing performance, solving problems and dealing with those other tasks vital to performance improvement. Purchasing becomes a clerical function.

It is important to your operation that you get away from this approach. You need to spend more time with your key suppliers to review problems and improvements. But with a great number of suppliers, how do you achieve that? The answer could be more staff in the purchasing department. This, however, flies in the face of today's cost-conscious operations. So if we cannot get more time per supplier by increasing staff, we must look to another aspect of supplier management. One of the fundamentals of total quality management, in relation to suppliers, is to use fewer of them.

Organizations such as Sony, IBM, Rolls-Royce, Boeing and Prudential have all declared programmes to produce drastic reductions in the number of suppliers used. In some instances these reductions are as high as 10:1 from, say, 3000 to 300 suppliers over a five-year period. These are major programmes and while smaller operations such as your own may not stretch to quite such lengths, the benefits of on-going supplier reduction programmes for all operations is universally recognized.

The ultimate in this regard is single-sourcing, the term used when an operation buys all its services or materials in an area from only one supplier. This used to be regarded as highly risky and avoided at all costs but today's world-class operators are actually setting up such arrangements for the benefits that result. These are mainly:

(a) lower cost of administration;
(b) more time available to manage each supplier;
(c) from (b), a greater understanding of the requirements;
(d) from (c), improved quality of performance;
(e) joint working parties on problems; and
(f) solving problems more quickly through better communication.

Box 5.3

A small (£20 m turnover) engineering company decided to buy all its tungsten tipped tools from a single source. These are the sort of tools used to cut metals on lathes in machine shops. Previously they had shopped around on an as required basis, placing many orders during a year. They selected one, their best, supplier and gave them all the business. To effect this they decided to 'pool' all their tools for each machine shop on a central table so all machinists were asked to use the table as a 'tool store'. The first benefit came to light – they had far more tools than they imagined because everyone had been keeping their own private stock. Secondly, when the tool supplier's representative came on a regular visit to see what was required by surveying this table, he would see damaged tools there. By talking to the operators about how the damage occurred, he was able to advise on better production and usage methods. They were thus getting free production engineering advice or consultancy. Thirdly, the representative wrote his own orders, relieving the buyer of the task. A blanket open order was placed on the 1st January for the year and then monthly the supplier reported what was supplied – much simpler and less expensive for the buying company. Collectively, these benefits were highly valued by the buying company and reduced the overall cost of tool purchases.

However, we are not advocating single sourcing as the universal supply solution. Indeed single-sourcing is definitely not the answer in many cases. Dual-sourcing is a halfway house and could be beneficial and prove cost-effective over multi-sourcing. You and your organization must decide. The object of this chapter is not to take you through that decision-making process because that could be a book in its own right. We are simply raising the issue as a key operational decision. To help you in some of the considerations, however, Figure 5.3 summarizes some of the advantages and disadvantages of single- versus multi-sourcing. This table has been condensed from views and experiences expressed by managers of organizations working in this area. You will see that some of these aspects result from managers' 'historical' views on this area of operations. These are not always easy to change but we must be prepared to consider these new approaches for the benefits that may accrue.

	Multi-sourcing	Single sourcing	Comments
Pros	Spreads the risk. Competition keeps prices down. Buyer may 'feel' more comfortable.	Fewer suppliers to manage. Chance to get close – leads to greater understanding. Communication easier. Relationships easier. Joint teams feasible. Total cost lower.	Joint working parties can be very effective on cost reduction.
Cons	Many orders. Large number of suppliers to control. Too many relationships needed. All leads to high admin costs.	Perceived higher risk. Could lead to higher than market prices. Will fail if top management not committed. Destroys trust.	Risk minimized by careful supplier selection. Need to audit the market regularly to stay 'tuned' and challenge suppliers if necessary.

Figure 5.3 Single versus multi-sourcing

Partnerships

A natural progression from multi-sourcing through dual- to single-sourcing is the ultimate supplier arrangement; what many organizations are calling 'partnerships'. We believe that there are major benefits to organizations to think of suppliers as partners rather than as subservient sub-contractors. 'Partners' leads us to think about them in a different way, probably a more concerned and caring way. By caring we mean we set out to treat them as well as we would want to be treated ourselves, or would treat other members of our own organization. This gets away from traditional customer/sub-contractor adversarial thinking and into a recognition of the interdependence that exists between customer and supplier.

When a partnership is 'grown' (they take time to develop because such an arrangement is based on trust) both parties are working towards the solution of problems that occur within the working arrangements. Neither should be gaining at the other's expense; rather, solutions to problems are aimed at ensuring that both parties benefit from the results. At least, they should ensure that one party does not lose even if both cannot positively benefit.

In the UK this aspect of supplier management has been so recognized as key to the success of many world-class operators that the DTI and the CBI have jointly set up a special educational and advisory group to promote the topic. It is known as Partnership Sourcing Ltd, based in London. A valuable outcome of their work has been the publication of a range of short, pragmatic documents on how to go about setting up partnerships with key suppliers, and we would strongly recommend them to anyone interested; they provide real guidance. One element of the 'how to do it' advice covers a sample 'Partnership Agreement'. This is the sort of agreement you would have jointly with a key supplier; it is two pages in length, and covers twenty or so aspects of the working relationship. Some advice is controversial, such as sharing cost information or accepting year-on-year cost reductions as the norm. These require real commitment from both parties but, when effected, produce real benefits.

When partnerships are effectively managed, they produce real benefits for both parties. You may not wish or be able to implement full partnerships with your suppliers, but the rationale of getting much closer to the key suppliers is something everyone should be following. The catch phrase is 'Close, not cosy'. What we are aiming at overall is improved mutual understanding.

Even if a partnership is set up and effective, it can never be 100 per cent in achieving the win/win aims outlined above. The reasons are simple. Each organization is first and foremost responsible for its own success and survival, hence it cannot always put the other party's needs on an equal footing. When the chips are down, decisions made in one organization may impact badly on the other and so discredit the trust we spoke of. Another problem is that the customer is still the customer and in most people's eyes holds the balance of power. This preconceived notion can affect the partnership. The supplier never truly believes that the customer intends to act as a partner but only expects them to! When managers have had their fingers burned with these problems, they conclude that partnerships don't work. We take the view that the partnering approach may not yield 100 per cent of the claimed benefits at all times, but we should not be dismayed by this. We should strive for it but not expect too much too soon. The odd failure is not a reason to abandon good practices, and we believe partnership thinking constitutes good supplier management when used in the right context.

The internal supplier

When we ask managers who are responsible for both internal and external suppliers to nominate the most difficult category to manage, almost universally they select 'the internals'. Total quality studies show the same result. You might think that, as internal suppliers are part of the family, you would get better service and response to problems from them. The reality can be quite different. Because the supplier/customer relationship is indeed within the company 'family' arrangement, we rarely set up professional arrangements to manage the relationship. External suppliers *always* have formal contracts with requirements, delivery details and quality standards defined. Internal suppliers rarely do. So we start off with a major handicap. No-one is really sure what performance is required or expected, and there is rarely a penalty on the supplier for failure. When things go wrong, both parties expect the other to understand and make allowances. When this happens, as it often does internally, we are rubber stamping the status quo and supplier performance does not improve.

Two things are needed to overcome this problem. The first is for managers to recognize it exists and the second is a determination to tackle it. They should formalize the requirements and approach the supplying department positively to encourage their commitment to improve. This is not a time for internal politics, to score points or to apportion blame, but an opportunity to work together to find benefits for the organization. What we are trying to do is be as careful and professional as we are when dealing externally. We would advocate written agreements between departments – to mirror external contracts – and regular reviews of supplier performance. The same principles should apply to managing internal suppliers as apply to externals, and particularly so if they come into the category of key suppliers.

In organizations that have tackled the issue of sloppiness in the internal supply situation, we find new systems such as service agreements being used. For example, in an IT department agreements could relate to response times from help desks, screen update times, and breakdown emergency response for user departments. Performance is then monitored against these standards and regular reviews held to sort out problems and to find ways to raise standards progressively.

It should be easy to break down any barriers with your internal suppliers. This is where the 'family' aspect of the company can help. We need not ask, nor be invited, to go and talk to an internal supplier; we *should* all be working to the same overall goal – the successful performance of the company. In our experience this will not start, however, until the 'user' operation recognizes that it needs to operate more effectively with its internal suppliers.

Relationships, trust, fairness and communication

We have concentrated in this chapter on some of the fundamental supplier approaches aimed at producing good supplier performance. No matter how good these arrangements are, there will inevitably be some problems. One of the most important ingredients in finding swift, effective solutions to these problems is the network of relationships which exists between the two organizations. Good relationships carry us through the problems. Poor relationships can compound them! When relationships are good, people will give 120 per cent to try to find solutions to difficulties. It follows that we cannot afford to wait until problems occur to try to form these relationships – that is too late. Set out to build relationships from the first day that contact is made. Go and meet the key people to your supply situation. Do this in person even if it means travel; it is ten times more effective than telephone or mail. It takes time, of course, but over the long haul pays handsome dividends.

You must plan to set up and maintain these relationships. They will not just happen. Make an action plan and involve other key players in your team. Your MD should meet the MD of your top three or four suppliers. It may be up to you to make it happen. We cannot over-emphasize the value of having positive relationships with key suppliers.

A key element of strengthening of any relationship is trust. Work to build up trust, one with another. It is hard to build and easy to destroy. Probably the biggest cause of a breakdown in supplier/customer trust is poor, ambiguous or inadequate communication. You must have excellent systems of regular communication. When those close links from single-source, or partnership, arrangements that we described earlier exist, this communication includes sharing long-term forecasts enabling the supplier to plan ahead with more certainty. This builds trust.

Where suppliers are taken seriously, organizations have regular supplier briefings and conferences at which suppliers are told about such things as the customer's strategic objectives or market forecasts. In large organizations this may involve up to 200 supplier managers, in a whole day's conference. In smaller organizations it could be a lunch with three or four key suppliers and a two-hour presentation. The range of these events and their frequency varies widely. Just make sure you are doing enough to let your supplier know what your plans are. It gives them the best chance to perform well for you.

Trust is easily destroyed and in our view that happens mostly from one cause – *customers don't pay suppliers!* This is unforgivable. It is alarming how many organizations, some of them mighty companies, think it is good business practice to pay late, even when there are neither business nor legal grounds for so doing. They stand behind good cash flow management arguments. It is *not* good business practice. If suppliers have 'bust a gut' for you and met their promises, how can you break your promise (as in the contract) to pay on time?

How many managers would accept not being paid at the end of the month as good cash flow management?

If this situation exists in your own organization you may be the one who has to fight to get your suppliers paid. Take on the accounts department who are administering payments; make them see that it is harming a vital link in your operations. Suppliers who are not paid will not give us 100 per cent commitment when we need it, and understandably so. You may need to be their champion inside your own company.

Summary

- Supplier management is a vital part of operations management because supplies are vital to and a high cost element of effective operations.
- The value chain thinking can help us in finding sources of improvement in our links to our suppliers.
- We need to be continuously monitoring our use of suppliers to supplement our in-house operations. When suppliers can do it better we should seriously consider out-sourcing. However, never out-source the key strategic operational competences on which the business is founded.
- Choose suppliers wisely where you have a choice. If it is not your responsibility to choose but your operation will be affected by supplier performance, you must exercise influence in the choice.
- We must monitor suppliers' performance as it impacts on our operation. Set up systems to do so and hold regular reviews with suppliers. Target improvements.
- The general move is towards the use of fewer suppliers, moving from multi-sourcing to dual- and where appropriate single-sourcing. All operations should be alert to the high cost of multi-sourcing.
- Relationships are key when problems arise in the supply chain. Managers should not wait until that fraught time arrives to start the process of building relationships. Start today!
- Trust is vital to good relationships. Behave ethically towards suppliers, especially paying them on time.
- Analyse internal suppliers in the same way as for an external supplier. Set up formal arrangements if possible.
- Treat communications seriously and make real efforts to share information with your supplier.

Management checklist

- Do you have any arrangements for working jointly with your suppliers to find improved ways of working?

- Are there any areas of your own operation where out-sourcing would provide benefits?
- Is there a formal approach to your selection of suppliers?
- Do you know who your key suppliers are? Do you have excellent relationships with them?
- Do you rate your suppliers' performance? Do you use OTIF measures? Do you discuss the results with them?
- Is there a case for a supplier reduction programme in your own area?
- If you have any single-sourcing, do you have excellent partnerships with those suppliers?
- If you have internal suppliers do you have sound, formal agreements with them?
- Are your suppliers treated fairly and do you demonstrate trust towards them?
- Does your organization pay your suppliers on time? Do you need to represent them?

6 Organization and systems

Introduction

Chapter 1 reflects on the fact that most managers are in the position of inheriting an organization which has evolved over a period of time and that there is a need to examine that organization against the current needs of the business. Nowhere is this more important than in the organizational structure and the systems which derive from it.

The organization structure, because it is composed of people and reflects directly on their self-esteem, is a particularly difficult area in which to effect change, however much that change is needed. It is the area which canny managers leave alone as much as is possible. It is, therefore, the area in which there is likely to be a good deal of mismatch with the task in hand.

In the 1990s it is probably more difficult than it has ever been for managers to know what is the right thing to do to create an effective organizational structure. There are so many influences at work which both contradict and confuse that managers face an extremely difficult task in steering a best course. We have grouped these influences broadly under the headings of:

- functional/internal;
- economic/external; and
- cultural.

In the first part of this chapter we shall examine what we mean by these. As with most of this book we will not be attempting to give definitive solutions to problems, only trying to help you to find ways through a maze of economic and political pressures, social change and fads and fashions of thought to create what is the right organization for you.

One of the difficulties that we face is that while a number of different influences are at work at any one time, many of them seem to be in contradiction of one another. As business becomes more and more competitive and profit margins are narrowed, managements are continually searching for greater efficiency and productivity. At the same time legislation imposes increased duties, many of which add costs related to employment and environmental matters.

In addition, while costs have to come down, product and service quality has to improve by significant amounts. It is frequently by overhauling the organization and the systems which support it that improvements in cost and in operating effectiveness can be found.

When we explore the principles which affect systems design we shall be looking at the purpose for which systems are needed and the key items requiring control. We shall discuss the issues of computerized and manual systems and the use of ready-made computer packages and bespoke systems. We shall conclude with some thoughts on systems overhaul.

The chapter relates to the following management standards:

- M1/1.1: Maintain operations to meet quality standards.
- M1/2.1: Contribute to the evaluation of proposed changes to services, products and systems.
- M2/1.1: Identify opportunities for improvements in services, products and systems.
- M2/1.2: Evaluate proposed changes for benefits and disadvantages.
- M2/1.4: Implement and evaluate changes to services products and systems.
- M2/1.5: Introduce, develop and evaluate quality assurance systems.
- M2/2.3: Maintain and improve operations against quality and functional specifications.

The organization – functional/internal influences

Type of organization

What we mean by functional influences on the structure of organizations are those things which spring mainly from the nature of the enterprise itself. The first of these is the nature of the organization's business. If you manufacture a product are you engaged in a jobbing or batch or a continuous process? If you provide service is it highly skilled, as in a legal practice, or low-skilled, as in an office-cleaning company? Are the majority of workers of similar skill levels, as in a branch of a building society, or is there a complex mix of skill levels as in a hospital? Are employees in large groups, as in a factory, or small groups, as in a fast food chain outlet? Such factors are the primary features which will influence the shape of your organization.

When thinking of the way in which enterprises are organized, most of us think readily of hierarchical structures with a chain of command. That chain of command will be functional with senior executives in charge of each function and reporting to a chief executive. The terms are common to all types of organization whether they are in the private or the public sector of the company. Such structures tend to be seen as authoritarian and work, particularly at operative level, is reduced to simple, easily controlled repetitive tasks for ease of control and (assumed) greatest efficiency.

Some years ago the perception developed that some organizations appeared to be capable of reacting to fast-changing situations better than others. Those which remained very fixed in their hierarchies were termed 'mechanistic'. Those which were able to cope with rapid change were termed 'dynamic'.

Charles Handy identified four styles of organization in his book *Gods of Management*. Handy humorously names the styles after Greek gods, but because we feel that this might be confusing without his full text we will stick with his more formal titles.

Handy's organizational cultures each have their own characteristics, as follow.

The 'club culture'

Probably has a traditional functional organization but it is totally influenced by an all-powerful, autocratic boss. The power and influences of individual managers depends not on their formal position in the hierarchy, but on their relation and influence with the boss. In this situation the long-serving accounts clerk who joined the company when he was a member of the boss's football team, can have an influence in some matters which is as great as that of the newly joined finance director. What is more, the finance director will have far less job security.

The 'role culture'

A traditional hierarchical functional organization. This is probably the sort of organization that most people think of as the basic model. The whole approach is based on the rational idea of analysing work into manageable portions and defining roles or jobs to accomplish the work. Obviously personality plays a part in any organization but in this culture the role is more important than the personality. Role cultures are good for stable situations.

The 'task culture'

This is a less recognizable model but one which has been developing in the 1990s. It is concerned with solving problems or achieving one-off tasks and requires the effort of teams which form and reform in different ways, depending upon the skill and knowledge requirements of the particular job. Task cultures can be found in laboratories, consultancies and advertising agencies. In industrial situations they are to be found on construction sites and in aerospace where the matrix management approach is the one most often used.

Task cultures have small regard for hierarchy and it is the true ability of individuals which determines their prestige.

The 'existential culture'

In the other styles of management, in different ways, the individual is subordinate to the organization. In the existential culture, the organization serves to help the individual. It is more like a federation or a partnership and is often found with professionals. Examples are in small consultancies where individuals have their own clients but 'network' with colleagues and perhaps share office accommodation and administrative services. Another example is that of the Oxbridge college where there may be forty or fifty Fellows, all of whom have equal voting rights in the running of the College and who probably also elect the Principal.

In reality, these styles, which most of us recognize, get slightly mixed up. Within any one prevailing culture there will be sub-cultures operating in different ways and for different reasons. Sometimes those cultures will clash and cause difficulties. In a manufacturing organization with a typical role culture there can be difficulties in managing research or design teams who need to work creatively and who tend to despise hierarchy. In a hospital, consultants and senior medical staff will have an existentialist approach, junior doctors and nurses may well be working with task roles and yet there is also a huge volume of routine work of cleaning, laundry, feeding, patient administration, transport, and building maintenance which clearly requires a role culture.

Organizations do not only develop in response to the work that needs to be done, they are also shaped by the personalities in the management. This is particularly true of 'club' type organizations which are often run by the founder. Even when the founder has died or retired it is usually the case that his or her way of doing things remains the culture for many years afterwards.

Different people are comfortable in different organizations and so the people in them tend to reflect the values of the organization. There are consequently problems when organizations are forced to change their style. Public service tended to attract people who enjoyed the idea of serving the public, were more interested in doing a good job and enjoying security than in becoming rich.

When public services, such as the gas boards, electricity suppliers and the water boards became privatized, the people within them found it necessary to start adjusting to a culture which, if not entirely new, had some fundamental differences. Capital investment is something which has to be paid for out of earnings or raised from the investing public. Quality, as we have said earlier, is 'conforming to requirements' and not doing the best possible job, regardless of cost. There is a greater need to consider the customers and this means keeping them informed at times of crises. This requirement can seem very hard to an engineer in a water board battling to repair a burst water-main. As far as he or she is concerned it seems more important to focus all the attention on the burst main. Spending time to give progress reports for the customers' benefit is only slowing the job.

Re-orienting the organization in these circumstances becomes a major undertaking. People are, fortunately, reasonably adaptable and probably can work in more than one culture but as a corollary to this it must be said that you do have to recognize the culture for what it is. If you have been working in one type of organization and move to another, you may find that your behaviour intuitively reflects the former culture. The transfer is probably most difficult to make between 'club' and 'role' cultures. In each of these the formal organization looks similar on paper; the difference is that they do not work the same way and it may take some time to work it out.

Box 6.1
One of us once moved from a role to a club culture and took a very long time to spot the differences. The Chairman was the founder of the enterprise and had built it into a very successful public company. He pretended not to take part in its day-to-day running. From time to time he would make apologetic requests for help in semi-personal matters insisting that they should only be met if they were consistent with what the company was doing. It was some time before we realized that such statements were not intended to be taken at face value and that the Chairman actually did want special treatment.

Another factor which shapes the culture of the organization, particularly if it is a large one, is whether it is run centrally from a head office or whether local managers have a great deal of discretion. Some organizations lend themselves naturally to one or the other. Large national retail chains can be run centrally more easily than can a scaffolding company which does its business with local customers through a network of local depots. The need to obtain higher level authority necessitates procedures and records and certain types of staff which may not be necessary if operational decision-making is vested in local management.

The use of information technology, the extent to which work is sub-contracted, the use of techniques such as Just-In-Time are all influences which will reflect the way an enterprise organizes itself for optimum effectiveness.

These factors, then, are those which influence the way the organization is shaped as a function of internal aspects which derive from the business itself and the people in it. We would now like to examine some of the external factors, mainly economic, which also influence the way an organization operates.

External/economic influences

To some extent the influences on an organization which we have just been discussing have been within the control of the organization. However, by far the heaviest pressures which organizations have to cope with are those from outside and over which there is no control. The main pressures are economic, but there are also political pressures which are extremely important. Economic pressure is about competition. Political pressures are concerned with legislation and in Europe this means not only the legislation produced by each country's government but also that which is produced by the European Union. More and more these seem to be reaching into the 'nooks and crannies' of the way we run our operations.

By far the most important influence on the shape of business organizations is that of competition. Indirectly this influence has also affected government and local government institutions and public services of all kinds. In international terms competition is concerned with companies from other countries competing with us both in our own country and abroad. In specific terms it means many different things for different organizations.

In the private sector in the UK we have seen much of our manufacturing capacity put out of business by competition from other countries, particularly from Japan and the Far East. In the public sector the UK has seen the privatization of many companies and the employment of various devices designed to bring elements of competition into those public services which do not readily lend themselves to being run as businesses.

The effect of competition, in all its forms, for public sector organizations as well as for businesses, has been to make us focus on the fact that the most important influence on our organization is that of the customer. Some organizations have long been aware of this; we cannot remember when it started, but it seems as though it has been forever that Marks & Spencer have been willing to exchange articles of clothing, without question, regardless of the store in which the article was bought. While some have been long aware of the customer, many have not, and this is the case both in the private and the public sector.

In the manufacturing sector, particularly in engineering, British tradition has been driven by the product and in the past there have been many fine products – even now, after all its tribulations, Rolls-Royce is still a synonym for quality. Then we began to think in terms of being 'market-driven' and to develop 'customer-focus'. We had 'smile' campaigns in banks and hotels which often lost credibility because they were really only cosmetic applications with little concern for the customer. It is only with the arrival of total quality management that Britain is beginning to recognize the extent to which we have to go if we are really serious about reshaping our organization in order to achieve real service as a competitive advantage. Usually the older and better established the organization, the harder this is; practices are more deep-seated and it is traumatic to realize that principles which have served well in the past will not do so in the present and future. Younger companies, having developed in harder times, have a particular advantage if they are attacking markets in which other competitors have long histories.

Box 6.2
In 1994 the Unisys/Sunday Times Customer Champions Award overall winner was the National Breakdown Recovery Club, which also won the Consumer Service of the Year category. The company was founded in 1971, very much younger than the AA and RAC, and with a significantly smaller membership.

What applies to organizations as a whole applies to people as individuals. It is salutary to hear that when Nissan were recruiting for a new car factory in the UK they refused to recruit operatives who had previously worked in other parts of the UK car industry. They wanted to avoid people with 'old' habits and beliefs.

Customer focus finds an expression in organization terms in Porter's Value Chain which was described earlier. Barbara Spencer, an American business academic, gives a good summary of the effect.

> The organization is reconfigured as a set of horizontal processes that begin with the supplier and end with the customer. Teams are organized around the process to facilitate task accomplishment.
>
> (Spencer, 1994)

The implication for organizations is that the customer-focus emphasis may be pointing us to more of a task culture in our organizations than the traditional role culture. The effect would be to achieve better, faster responsiveness to the customer.

The other external influences which affect the way our organizations work are political and legal. Many British industries and organizations are being affected continually by the legislation being enacted by the European Union and the measures taken by our own government. Some of that law is concerned with employment practices – employees' rights and employers' obligations. Some is concerned with regulating competition; some is concerned with protecting the environment. Much of it affects businesses and employing organizations and will have its effect on the way they organize themselves. There have always been people in organizations accountable for the issues of pollution or employment but if laws become more stringent, those responsible have to become more forceful. This may mean different roles for personnel managers and more resources devoted to such issues as the control of discharged effluents. The legislation which affects employment is strongly connected to the social issues and it is here that we will deal with those influences on organization which we can describe as 'cultural'.

Cultural influences

How organizations are structured and operate reflect the way in which society operates. As attitudes change in society at large, so these changes are reflected in the way organizations conduct themselves.

In addition to social change we also find the influence of academic studies of management and of people at work. Their findings may also become absorbed into the culture of organizations and influence the way people manage or organize themselves to manage. Typical is the work being done on team-working.

As much as anything Britain also imports organizational ideas from abroad. At one time most of these came from the USA, but in recent years we have been especially influenced by Japan, from whom we are constantly seeking the secrets of economic success.

One organizational 'buzz-word' in the 1990s is 'empowerment'. This may mean different things to different people, but we see it as a further step in a series of developments which have been steadily taking place over thirty or so years.

This development includes McGregor's theory X and theory Y (see Appendix to Chapter 10); it includes the moves to 'job enrichment' and away from the soulless repetitive tasks of operations such as the continuous assembly-line; it includes the ideas of 'involvement', and of quality circles. All these concepts have been in vogue at various times and all have been moving towards a more 'open' style of management in which the individual worker is given greater responsibility for managing the task, including being responsible for his or her own quality control. Currently, too, there is a great deal of interest in the idea of organizing work in teams which either have a leader or which can be self managed. The psychological basis for this lies partly in the concept that better solutions to problems are achieved by groups, partly in the motivational aspect of encouraging people to manage themselves and partly in the notion that the people doing the job will actually be more expert than anyone else.

In addition to the psychological concepts there are also socio-political influences at work. British society is becoming more egalitarian and there are some who argue that concepts of 'superior' and 'subordinate' do not have a place in modern management. In the review of the MCI management standards some people are suggesting that all references to hierarchy should be removed. We do not, incidentally, find this particular argument credible in a real management context but will return to this later in the chapter.

One external influence which has had significant effect on the way business and the public services can organize themselves for work is in the changing attitudes and influence of the trade unions. Relations between managements and trade unions are becoming less confrontational and more co-operative. Where team-working is envisaged it may mean that people have to become multi-skilled. At one time trade unions would have fought tooth and nail to preserve single-skill demarcations. In many cases management would not even have contemplated a proposal for breaking down job demarcations because they knew how bitterly the unions would fight to preserve them.

Nowadays unions as well as managements know that they have to be prepared to think the unthinkable and abandon ancient sacred cows in order to survive in a competitive world.

Sometimes the socio-political influences can become a distraction to organization and managers must be alert to the need to maintain the organization's focus on the customer. Thus hierarchical role cultures are held to be associated with authoritarian attitudes and are 'bad' and task cultures, open management styles, team-working and 'empowerment' are 'good'.

Management theory has always been prone to fashions of thought and managements have always been on the look-out for the philosophers' stone which will transform today's average performance into tomorrow's pot of gold. The reality is, that very many of the fashionable ideas contain valuable concepts which when properly applied can improve performance. Their application, however, needs to be worked out and has to be made in the right context. Not all ideas are universally applicable and what may be right in one organization at a particular time may not be right for another – at a different time. The ability to make judgements about such issues is one of the manager's most important competences.

What we now propose to do is to look at some simple principles which managers can apply in practical situations.

The manager and the organization

The first essential is to understand the organization you are working in. Is it suitable for the type of business? Has it been moving with the needs of the modern world, or is it stuck in a time-warp? What are the external and internal pressures to which it is subjected and is it capable of dealing with them? Is it the right organization for you personally? Is the culture one which suits the way you think and the way you naturally behave? If not, you may have to modify your behaviour or at least be aware that you are not typical of the majority of people within it. This could be a disadvantage in terms of career prospects; it could also be an advantage in that you may be seen as bringing a refreshingly original view to bear on issues and situations.

Whatever managers do within their own operation has to reflect the culture and the practices of the greater organization – and only depart from them if they think that it will be successful. But where do you start when thinking about how your own operation is organized? You may expect us to say, having read so far in the book, that the first consideration must be the customer. In the past, in many cases the dominant factor in deciding the shape and culture of an organization has been the type of operating process in use. In addition to all this, as the manager of an operation within a management structure, you will have a boss who may well have had a hand in developing what you have already and certainly is the representative of the total organization. In practical terms, therefore, we believe that you may well end up considering all three of these issues at the same time.

The customer, the process and the boss

As far as the customer is concerned, whether external or internal, you need clear lines of communication for all eventualities. In different circumstances, the lines of communication may be different. When the customer places an order or a demand on your services it must be clear where the order is placed and what happens to it. If a customer wants to discuss the work-in-progress it must be equally clear to whom he or she speaks. Such clarity is also essential for any other external contact such as a supplier. It is no less vital for people within the operation.

Where as an operation you are dealing with the organization's external customers, the responsibility is probably clear-cut. If you are dealing with 'internal' customers you may need to think more carefully about the customer aspect. Within departments, or units of larger operations, people's main accountabilities are usually for the process being operated. It may be the job of these people to deal with the customer and the external world – or it may be the job of the manager. The choice should be on whoever can give the customer the best service. If this happens to be a member of the operating staff it is important that he or she is properly trained in dealing with this part of the job. It is no use putting the customer with the technical expert if that expert is inarticulate and incapable of presenting the organization's position.

The next consideration, as far as both the customer and the process is concerned, is to ensure that responsibilities are allocated for the things that you need to do to satisfy the customer. In some form or another, this will be concerned with both the quality of what you do and the timeliness of the delivery. If your business is servicing washing machines in people's homes, you will need a structure which ensures that technicians are trained and work to a standard; you will also need someone accountable for ensuring that they arrive on time and with the correct spare parts to carry out repairs.

If you are the invoicing department in a large organization you need to ensure that someone is responsible for ensuring that the invoices sent out correspond to the work which was done (how often does this not happen!); that when invoices are questioned, answers are given; that customer queries are not switched from one person to another;

that telephone enquiries are not lost as calls are transferred from one phone to another; that enquirers are given promises of a response if immediate answers are not available. The organizational structure will have an effect on all these activities.

Customer issues are frequently neglected because it is usually the technicalities of the process which dominate people's attention and which are the main influences which shape the organization. If you are making steel, you have a continuous process which needs to work round the clock, seven days a week. For this you need continuous shifts, and enough shift teams to cover a whole week; this involves a shift management structure as well as a day-working structure. Hospitals work around the clock but not in all departments. Retail stores are now increasingly working at weekends and structures will need to change to accommodate different working hours.

Some organizations are concentrated in one place – others are dispersed, and the type of staff and nature of the work make a difference. A school is a very 'flat' organization with few, if any, layers of management between the headteacher and the teaching staff. The supervision of a classroom teacher's work is slight, or non-existent. A national office-cleaning company needs a vastly different structure. Perhaps a head office in a major city; thirty or forty regional offices; cleaners working in teams of between one and ten in office buildings scattered all over a town and working between 6p.m. and 8p.m. Workers are part-time and staff turnover high; there may be a high proportion of staff who may not speak English; the opportunities for theft or making personal telephone calls in empty offices are high; a contract with the customer specifies the standard of cleaning to be accomplished.

Such a situation has a different management, supervisory and administrative structure than that of a school and the organization will need to match these requirements.

Sometimes, however, there is a tendency for operations to reflect the requirements of the boss as much as anything else. As we have said before, ultimately the boss is responsible for what we do (unless we work in the 'existentialist' culture). Normally, we would think that the boss's view of how the operation should be organized would coincide with ours. However, if people are more concerned with how the boss sees the organization than how they think it best serves the customer or relates to the process, there is the danger of failing to achieve the true objectives. This sort of effect is most likely in a 'club' type organization.

Cultural influences

Organizations are essentially communities and as such will reflect the attitudes of the community at large. Cultural change takes place unevenly; some individuals set the pace and eventually others catch up. Some communities change faster than others. Organizations can be ahead of change or lag behind, but never too far in either direction. If organizations want to break new ground, they may do so, provided they are not too far ahead of the community at large and provided they do so carefully. What they try to do must also be appropriate for the organization and people in it.

If a school became self-governing and parents and staff formed the governing body, it would not be seen as unacceptable. If the post of headteacher were abolished and the day-to-day management of the school carried out by all the teachers in committee, it might be seen as unusual and experimental, but not impossible. If the day-to-day running of the cleaning company were left to a committee of part-time cleaners it might well be perceived to be impossible.

When it is a question of empowering workers – turning over to them tasks and decision-making normally carried out by managers and supervisors – it has to be done in areas that make sense to the business and people have to be competent to carry out the roles. The area in which much of it makes sense is in the execution of the work. Deciding how to do a particular job, setting standards and deciding on the achievement of quality and also who does what, are all areas in which the operative can play a substantial part. Team-working without a supervisor or manager when you have a block of offices to clean is a possibility; team-working without someone specifically in charge in a heart transplant operation is more difficult to envisage.

At the core of the manager's job is the need to organize resources, bring them together and allocate work in the most effective manner. If you are selling highly standardized beefburgers much of the work can be carried out by technology and the rest by good team-work. If you are constructing a building with several hundred people working with a variety of trades and with different requirements for materials and equipment, you will need someone to control and direct. This is not because building workers are less capable and responsible than beefburger operatives – it is because there is a need both for a wide, specialized knowledge, which it would be impossible for everyone to have and for speed of action which you won't get if there has to be a committee meeting everytime there is a problem.

During a strike of hospital workers in the UK the porters took it upon themselves to decide which patients should be allowed urgent treatment. Most people in the country were probably very worried at the possibility of falling ill at that time.

Systems

Systems form an important part of any operation. They fulfil several functions but a convenient breakdown of these splits them into four types:

Enabling

The system provides triggerpoints, milestones or links between steps in an operation, such as sign-off points or hand-over points.

Monitoring

Progress will be tracked and reported using a systematic approach. The system provides the information required to kick-start any corrective action that might be required. It is often closely linked to control.

Control

A system may be used to control the operation by dictating ways of doing things or sequencing operations.

Informing

Systems are used to disseminate information and have become an important part of most organizations, particularly as the need for speed or responsiveness increases.

Most managers thinking about their own operation for a moment can fit their own systems into these categories. Sometimes one system will satisfy two or three categories. This is quite in order so long as the main function of the system is not compromised to satisfy less important needs. No-one should delay issuing enabling or controlling data because they are wanting to include some 'nice to know' general information on the same form or screen. In a similar vein, we need to ensure that vital controlling data is not lost among a welter of trivia. This is a danger with the growth of the electronic mail systems – 'E-mail' – that we all see so widely used. Among maybe thirty messages sent each day will be fifteen general information items, three instructions, one of them vital to several individuals, and eight advertisements of cars and TVs for sale. Have the busy recipients seen that one vital entry?

The systems used must serve the needs of the operation and its organization. While this seems a very obvious statement our experience is that this does not always happen. In fact we would go further and say that it rarely does. Systems are designed by organizations for a variety of reasons, as we have said, and very often by people who will not be required to use them. Little wonder they rarely match the needs of individual parts of the operation, let alone individuals within the operation. Managers must guard against this and fight for systems their teams can use – the phrase 'user-friendly' comes to mind!

System design and capability has been developing with ever-increasing pace. It is most likely then that for any system that is more than a few years old, say three, there is a more effective way of doing the same thing available today. This is an area where computers have made and are making massive improvements. These improvement are available to us all and no-one can afford to be ignoring this field of development for a any length of time. It is an area which every manager must stay abreast of, otherwise opportunities are missed. The first effect in those circumstances may be when the competition does something in the market place that we cannot do. Systems design offers this opportunity . . . and threat!

So, new systems offer great opportunities to those operations adopting them and getting it right. They threaten greatly those not doing so. When Federal Express offered their 24-hour guaranteed delivery service in the USA, they could only do so because new technology made it possible. Couriers and drivers carried hand-held digital units on which they entered the customers' information. The data could be instantly transferred into the company's main computer controlled systems, enabling much faster routing, customs clearance and billing.

This is an example of a total business leap-frogging the capability of its rivals and posing a threat to their businesses. On a smaller scale, within departments and sub-units, similar advances can be made.

Know what is key

If a manager wants to run an effective operation, he or she needs to keep control of a few key measures. We have spoken at great length about the need for clarity of focus and control. It plays a major role in helping to decide what systems are needed within the operation. Box 6.3 makes a comparison between managing an operation in a business or service organization and flying an aeroplane.

There are a few keys to success and systems are needed to enable, monitor and control all of them. In business they will be revenue, defect levels, order intake, customer service levels, costs, and cash management. Key ratios on which the business will be managed, such as return on capital, are derived from these. Chart these ratios so that trends can be seen clearly.

In the same way, every operation has key elements around which the systems must be designed. Every manager needs to know what the 'aids to flight' are and we refer to this in Chapter 8.

A manufacturing operation will need, for example, systems for scheduling, raw material supply, work-in-progress and cost control and the quality systems we have covered earlier. High volume businesses need different systems from low volume or bespoke operations (see Box 6.4).

Box 6.3
Even a simple plane has a wealth of information provided to the pilot. However, there are five of six key measures needed to control the operation of flying the plane. These are the things the pilot must be aware of at all times.

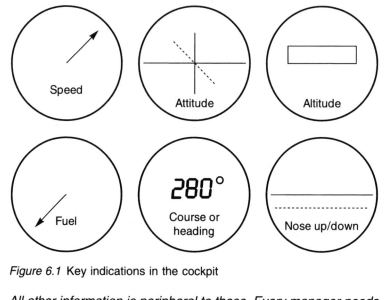

Figure 6.1 Key indications in the cockpit

All other information is peripheral to these. Every manager needs the equivalent key indicators for their operation.

Box 6.4
New systems are being developed in all these areas, whether they be the latest versions of these scheduling systems known as MRPI+II (Materials Requirements Planning) or the system of working known as Kanban. This is a philosophy of operating where the work is 'pulled' through the system by the customers' needs, rather than 'pushed' through by the company's schedule. Operating managers within a manufacturing environment need to be aware of these latest developments and employing them where appropriate.

In the service area systems are having great impact on the service delivery system. They enable faster more bespoke offerings to be made and provide customers with added value as Box 6.5 shows!

Box 6.5
On our first one-night visit to a hotel in Malaysia, we were greeted at reception and asked to fill in the usual form with our details – home address, passport number and the like. In our room later, we noticed a nice touch, a little card signed by the general manager saying 'Welcome to the Ming Court Hotel. We hope you enjoy your stay.' Over the next few months regular visits were made to the hotel. On checking-in each time, we were presented with a ready completed details card from their system and simply asked to check it for corrections and sign it. Very helpful at the end of a long tiring journey. In the room we noticed the card now read 'Welcome back to the Ming Court Hotel.' This promoted that individual feeling 'they know and care about me.'

During the same period we were also making regular visits to a hotel in the UK. Each time we had to fill in our personal details afresh – and there was no welcoming card. We might not have thought anything about it but for the contrast with the Malaysian hotel using their computer to help them set another standard.

Incidentally, the UK hotel had computers; guests could see them in the office behind reception. The management had just not made the mental leap to consider how to get the best from them. They had the cost without the benefits.

Finally, here is a tip when updating your own key information. Physically mark up the charts yourself, rather than 'hitting the keys' to obtain a plot. Taking a plot from the computer does not have the same 'gut-wrenching' effect as plotting the results and finding, say, output is down by 10 per cent. Plotting the point on the chart in person does bring home what is happening and instil in the manager the need to do something. We know this may sound old fashioned when high speed systems do this so well, but we strongly recommend it as a practice.

Manual systems or computer systems

Should systems always be computerized? The decision whether to computerize can be very difficult. In our experience trouble often results from trying to computerize a poor manual system. That rarely works. Before any system can be successfully computerized it should be validated as a system. With new systems, what we are talking about is at least designing the system on paper and testing the idea out on the users before committing to a software development programme. There should always exist what everyone believes is a working paper system design, before computerizing.

A watchword at this stage is simplicity. If the system design is not simple, it is less likely to be successful. Your aim should be to ensure simplicity by removing unnecessary complexity.

Generally, people computerizing systems are looking for improvements. In most operating systems the advantages of computers are in their ability to process large amounts of data, such as long client lists, to work at high speed, and to take the drudgery out of repetitive work.

Another ability is to interface with other systems either within the organization or outside it, such as with suppliers being linked to their customers' scheduling systems. This interlinking capability can offer significant advantages where high speed transfer of data is of value to the operation.

Computer miniaturization has moved from the personal desk computer through the laptop and onto the handheld unit. This opens up many new applications from which our systems may be able to benefit.

There is still a place for paper-based systems, particularly where teams sit close to one another so that information transfer is easy. There is a real advantage in using simple forms where the operations staff are not using keyboards regularly and so do not have the opportunity to develop the necessary computer skills.

If a decision has been made to computerize, there is much to be gained from visiting an operation similar to your own which is computerized, before you finally take the plunge. You can learn things from them about the hardware and the software, implementation and training phases, and problem areas.

If you are not sure who to visit, ask around. Ask the hardware suppliers and the software suppliers; ask your boss; ask the IT department; ask your customers or suppliers. Eventually you will find someone. If you are the first using a particular application you may not be able to find a comparison in which case you need to be cautious as you proceed. There are great gains to be made by being first, but trailblazing is risky.

Standard or tailored systems

Standard systems are usually instantly available, low cost, proven, easy to learn. Tailored systems are closely aligned to your needs, more effective and designed to maximize the particular operation. However, both have drawbacks. Standard systems may not 'fit' the operation well, meaning that you compromise the optimum operating results. Additionally, staff may never see the systems as their own, because it is a standard package. The drawbacks of tailored systems are their high cost and the long timescale which they need for development. Additionally, they may never deliver the benefits promised and may need a great deal of de-bugging.

So when a choice has to be made, the answer may lie in the issues we have raised. How important is system performance to the success of the operation? How much compromise would be needed to use a standard system? Can the compromise be tolerated? How much money and time is available? Only by debating the issues will the answer be found. Sometimes it will still not be clear, in which case managers should follow their own preference. This produces owner-ship which is more likely to produce success.

Whatever approach you select, visiting others using similar systems is one of the most useful things you can do. The system 'design' is vital so explore it through these visits. In the case of a standard package you need to gather as much information about the actual design as possible. In the case of a tailored solution you need to gather information about the capability of the designers. If your own internal systems department is tailoring a system for you, go and talk to another department which has done something similar. It will be helpful to give you insights into how they work, their effectiveness, which aspects can they be trusted with and which not. This is invaluable information to you and enables you to plan ahead. It may influence the overall 'standard or tailored' decision.

Maintenance of systems

Systems are like any other equipment you are using in the operation. They will need maintenance and perhaps overhauling, which needs a regular process and a rigorous routine.

Too often systems are designed once and never reconsidered. The poor users struggle with their inadequacies or overweight design. There can be major advantages from regularly looking at shortcomings through the eyes of the user and amending them to overcome the failings.

There are a few questions to be asked when overhauling. The first is how much of the system is actually used, and how often. This will tell the owner of the operation how useful that system is to the staff. They will use systems that help them do the job and neglect others. If you conclude that whole systems, or parts of systems, are not being used then their design or very existence should be questioned.

The second area of questioning is a matter of detailed usage. When using forms or screens, how much of the information is used/needed/ entered? What we find is that some 60 per cent of the content of forms or screens is not used. Things which were included as a 'good idea' at the design stage but have never been used should be deleted. They confuse, distract, waste paper, waste time and use valuable computer memory.

The people using the systems should be deeply involved in these moves. They are the ones who know why they do what they do and what they need to get the job done. Any 'cleaning up' activities on the systems should involve them.

... And finally, understand them

Every manager should fully understand the systems that are used in or impact on his or her operation. This is rarely the situation, and the larger the organization the more rare it is. It seems that there isn't time for managers to research the systems that exist. Yet often we have come across cases where busy managers spend valuable time designing a new system to do something, only to learn that such a system already exists – it just isn't being used. Or they learn that what they want is within the capability of an existing system but no-one knew, therefore it has not been employed in that way. Time should be allocated to learning how all systems work and researching their inputs and outputs if they extend outside the operation. This is particularly true if either the operation or the manager is new. The knowledge gained will be most valuable in managing the operation in the future; additionally the staff will be impressed that their manager is taking time to find out about their day-to-day work.

Box 6.6
One of us once worked for a defence supplier contracted to the Ministry of Defence. MoD appointed a new head of contracts from outside that division and we all were interested to see the effect of this new man. For six months nothing appeared to happen and we wondered what he was doing. Rumours started of an ineffectual manager in the seat.

What he was actually doing was researching all the systems in use in his department and in particular how they interfaced with other decision-making departments. In the bureaucratic civil service of the day, systems of working were everything. By learning and applying the systems he was able to get much more done than if he had fought those systems, as some of his predecessors had done. After a year or so, we all agreed he had become one of the most effective mangers we had seen in that post.

The manager's role is also to see that all relevant staff know the systems they have available to them and understand how to get the best from them. This means they must be given time to learn these systems, particularly if they are new to the operation. Do not rely on the hit and miss approach – 'you'll pick it up as you go along'. They will only pick up 50 per cent – it might be the other 50 per cent that holds the key to more effective operations.

Summary

Organization structure is based on the type of business and the type of process in which the organization is engaged. Some organizations react better to rapid change than others. Organizations also have their own culture and Charles Handy has categorized these as:

- club culture;
- role culture;
- task culture; and
- existential culture.

Culture is a result both of the type of work being done and the influence of the management.

The principal external pressure which can affect an organization's structure is that of competition. Structures and cultures need to be adapted to customer and market needs. Social pressures are also shaping the way organizations are structured. Management is becoming more 'open' and people are having more influence on the way that their own work is being structured. The power of team-working is becoming more understood and developed.

Managers need to understand the type of organization they are in and seek to adapt their operation to this and to changing cultural and competitive circumstances. There is a dominant need for clarity in the organization when dealing with customers.

We described the different functions that systems normally fulfil, and offered some advice on the value of ensuring that the systems in use do actually serve the operation.

Modern systems are highly capable of providing the operation with 'competitive-edge' performance. By using this available capability managers can provide their organizations with new business opportunities. Conversely, managers who are not exploiting this facet of systems performance, may be handing market share to their competitors.

We explored some of the difficulties of deciding whether or not to computerize systems and offered some advice on this issue. The decision of whether to use standard or tailored systems has been covered and, again, we outlined the advantages and disadvantages of each.

Many systems will have been in use for a long time and would benefit from overhaul or maintenance. Some guidelines are offered, which centre on the value of removing unnecessary elements or features, and simplifying where possible. Remember to involve the staff in this.

Finally, we emphasized the need for managers and their staff to fully understand the systems employed within their operation. This will help when looking to exploit the system's capabilities in the future.

Management checklist

- What sort of management culture exists in your organization? Is it suitable for the type of work you do? Does your operation reflect the organization culture? (Handy's definitions are useful and we find them valid but organizations do not fall neatly into categories.)
- Has the organization needed to change in recent times? Should this affect the way it, and your operation, is structured?
- Is your operation structured so that everyone (internal and external) knows how to get things done? Have you checked this with members of your staff?
- Does the structure of your operation make it easy for the customer to deal with you?
- Are your systems user friendly? Do they match the operation? If 'no' what do you need to do about it?
- Would improved systems provide any new opportunities for your operation? If 'yes' where and what?
- Are you clear what your key measures are? Do you have systems in place for all of them?

  My three key measures are: ....

  ....

  ....

- Is there a case for computerizing any of your systems?
- Are your systems standard or tailored? Record an example of each if you can:

  Standard ....

  Tailored ....

- Have you ever visited an organization to check out something before adopting it? Is there a need now? Who might you visit?
- Do your systems need a clean-up? When was that last done? Which could you start with?
- Are you clear about all the systems used in your operation? If 'no' what will you do? Do you need to take any action to ensure staff understand their systems?

7 The right working environment

Introduction

Whatever the circumstances of any particular situation, managers must always regard themselves as responsible for the environment in which they are working. There may be distinct limitations on the extent to which physical working conditions can be altered, but staff will always see the managers as responsible – as, indeed, they are. As a result, staff will draw conclusions about managers' concern for them, from the way they deal with questions affecting their security, comfort and convenience. If air-conditioned, clean rooms are provided for computers, and staff work in poor light or shabby offices, they may be forgiven for concluding that the management think more of machines than of them. Staff usually have an understanding of what is in their manager's capability to fix and what is not. Additionally, managers have a powerful influence on the psychological environment; their behaviour sets the standard for the particular workplace, and the way work is done will derive from those standards.

Before going into greater detail it is relevant to look at some investigative work carried out by three psychologists; Frederick Herzberg, Bernard Mausner and Barbara Boch Snyderman (the work is often referred to as Herzberg's). The work was concerned with identifying what it is that motivates people to work, and they concluded that there were two classes of motivators which they called 'satisfiers' and 'dissatisfiers'. The 'satisfiers', as the word implies, are the factors which they found give greatest satisfaction in the job and which can motivate people to greater efforts; the 'dissatisfiers' are the things which make people unhappy at work. Figure 7.1 shows the results of Herzberg's work and how the various factors in the study fall into the category of either 'satisfiers' or 'dissatisfiers'.

Herzberg concluded that what people want from their jobs revolves around feelings of success in their work and the possibility of professional growth. The factors which make people unhappy at work are the things which are not associated with the job itself but with the conditions which are associated with the work and which constitute 'an unhealthy psychological work environment'. They called these factors 'hygiene factors' by analogy to principles of medical hygiene and on the basis that good hygiene results in removing health hazards but does not cure disease – it prevents but it does not cure. Getting these things right will not supply a strong motivation for people to work, but getting them wrong will demotivate them.

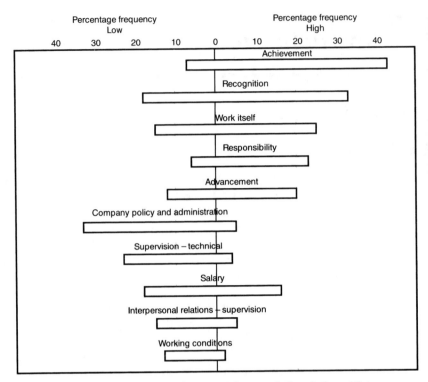

Figure 7.1 Herzberg's comparison of satisfiers and dissatisfiers. High percentage frequency of responses indicate 'satisfiers' or factors capable of motivating people positively. Low percentage frequency indicates 'dissatisfiers' or 'hygiene' factors

The things that we are concerned with in this chapter are among Herzberg's 'hygiene factors'. Working conditions, technical supervision and interpersonal relations with superiors are all things that we shall be concerned with and all of these fall clearly into the group of 'dissatisfiers'. (It is interesting to note, too, that not only is pay seen as a 'dissatisfier', it is also seen as less important than working conditions.) As a manager, therefore, getting these working conditions right is seen as essential in removing poor attitudes to work but, of themselves, are not likely to create significant gains in job satisfaction. The issues with which we shall deal will be:

- the physical environment;
- health and safety;
- the best possible working conditions;
- doing something worthwhile;
- communicating;
- building improvement into the working environment; and
- the customer in the workplace.

This chapter relates to MCI Management Standards:

- M1/1.2 and M2/2.4: Create and maintain the necessary conditions for productive work.

The physical environment

Most of us have to work in a particular building, office or workshop with little control over its location, age or general condition; as managers, however, it is up to us to ensure that they are as good as can be for the work we are doing.

In larger organizations there are usually managers with specialist responsibility for 'facilities' or maintenance or health and safety and these can make life significantly easier for operating managers. It does not mean, however, that operating managers can abdicate responsibility. Answering three questions can help to determine whether you have the optimum working conditions within your area of responsibility.

- What needs to be done to ensure a safe and healthy environment?
- What needs to be done to ensure that you have the best possible working conditions?
- Can anything else be done to help achieve effective working?

You can also ask whether you would want to do the work yourself. If the honest answer is 'no', then you know that action is needed.

Box 7.1

One of us worked in a large, design-based organization, staffed mainly by professionally qualified people. The company had very close links with a number of key nationally-known clients whose representatives were regularly on the design premises. At one point there was a strike of the support staff who cleaned the lavatories. Because of the significant number of client visitors and, in the circumstances, the inability to hire contract substitutes, managers took on the task of lavatory-cleaning. This was done quite willingly except that additional equipment was demanded by the managers in order to do the job as hygienically as possible. When things returned to normal the additional equipment was retained precisely on the basis that we should not expect others to do work in a way which we did not find acceptable ourselves.

Health and safety

Managers' responsibility for health and safety matters varies to such a large extent that we can only deal with this area in terms of principle. The manager of building society branch has a different set of problems from the manager of a construction site. Where there are hazardous conditions such as on building sites, in factories, in chemical plants or mines, managers have a very heavy responsibility for safety; regulations are usually comprehensive and the big problem is to ensure that they are adhered to – not only by staff but also by sub-contractors and visitors. However, in every case line managers must be aware that, in the eyes of the law, they are responsible, as agents of their organization, for the safety of staff and visitors at all working times. This applies even if they are careless or negligent.

Obviously, managers' first task is to ensure that they themselves are fully conversant with regulations and health and safety legislation. It is unlikely that operating managers are starting from scratch in this respect, and organizations will have systems and training procedures for ensuring that managers and other personnel are properly trained. If, by any chance, this is not the case, the Health and Safety Executive is the obvious place to start seeking help.

The next task is to ensure that staff are fully trained and that they work safely. Just as with measures to maintain and improve quality, the total involvement of staff in the safety process is crucial; only if everyone continuously 'thinks' safety can the manager be satisfied that everything possible is being done to ensure safe working conditions. For this, procedures must be laid down clearly and simply and staff trained in their practise. Above all, managers have to set the standards by their own behaviour. This includes encouraging the reporting of any incident which might have led to an accident, taking action and being seen to be taking action.

Safety committees are a standard means of involving all staff in safety matters and as a means of focusing attention on the subject in a regular way. As with all regular committees, there is always the danger that they can become stale and routine. Above all, the safety committee must never be used to avoid responsibility. In safety matters, the management always takes responsibility and the safety committee can only operate as an adviser to the manager.

In workplaces where there are no obvious hazards – particularly in offices – health and safety does not have to be such a critical feature of the manager's job. For this reason there may be a temptation to ignore the matter altogether. Our advice is to resist temptation and remember that, although you may not be in a hazardous environment, you are still responsible if anything goes wrong. Fire drills can be a good way of reminding staff, as well as oneself, of the importance of safety measures, even in safe areas. Most fire drills tend to be half-hearted affairs with people responding in a very sheepish and self-conscious way. Managers, here, can set a serious tone and remind people of the need to ensure good practice. The clearance of a floor or a building can be timed and an estimate given of the degree of hazard involved in such a timing. Fire wardens need support for doing a thankless task and this can be the opportunity to make them feel that they are doing something worthwhile.

The Health and Safety Executive has a useful booklet published by the Industrial Society, called Health and Safety Management. This contains a useful checklist for managers, which is reproduced in Box 7.2.

Box 7.2 (Health and Safety Executive, 1988)
The following questions are intended as an aid to managers. They are not exhaustive but are intended to cover the main issues addressed in the text.

Where to start

- Do we have a safety policy statement? When was it last revised?
- Is is comprehensive? Does it specify the organization (i.e. people and their responsibilities) and arrangements (i.e. systems and procedures)?
- How is the policy commitment to health and safety promoted throughout the organization?
- How do individual managers demonstrate their own commitment?
- How is a 'safety culture' promoted?

Organization for health and safety

- Is the delegation of duties logical and successive throughout the organization?
- How are people made aware of their responsibilities?
- Is final responsibility accepted by the relevant director?
- Are the health and safety responsibilities of senior managers specified in job descriptions?
- How is the safety performance of managers measured? Is it an ingredient of their annual review?
- Are the roles of key functional managers clearly defined?
- How are managers made aware of the requirements of health and safety legislation relative to their own departments?
- How is compliance with legal requirements assessed?
- Has a competent assessment been made of all hazards associated with the company's activities?
- Has an assessment been made of occupational health needs?

Monitoring for effect

- Is there a comprehensive established system for monitoring compliance with standards and procedures?
- Are there sufficient staff with adequate knowledge and facilities to carry out the monitoring?

- How well do we comply with the law on health and safety?
- How far have we met our own policy objectives?
- What is our own accidents and ill health record? Is it acceptable?
- What deficiencies have we identified? How are they to be remedied? What more needs to be done? Now? Within the next year?
- Are the results of monitoring made available both to the managers concerned and to senior managers?

Accident/incident investigation

- Are there clear criteria for reporting and investigating accidents and incidents?
- How well are they understood?
- How are near-miss incidents identified?
- How far does the accident-investigation system seek to identify fundamental causes and failure in management control?
- Is information obtained from accident investigation analysed to establish trends? Do we make good use of it?

Training for health and safety

- What is the system for identifying training needs?
- Does health and safety training cover all levels from senior management to new entrant?
- What 'special risk' situations requiring training exist?
- Are sufficient people trained to cope?

The best possible working conditions

First, make sure that people have the best tools to do the job. Whether we are talking about expensive machine tools, or simply a pair of scissors, a word-processor or a pencil-sharpener, it pays to make sure that people have the most appropriate tools and equipment for carrying out the job. This does not necessarily mean the most expensive, newest or most fashionable, but it does mean careful appraisal of what is available (see Chapter 5). Ensuring the best tools and equipment will not only help to obtain the most efficient working, it will also signal to employees that you are seriously committed to the quality of the work and that you are seriously committed to supporting them in producing high standards.

We cannot be quite so clear-cut when it comes to advice on how to achieve the best physical working conditions to suit the needs of your particular operation. We believe it is important, however, to understand what Herzberg says about working conditions being 'dissatisfiers' rather than motivators. The reality of this means that if you don't get conditions right you may find that it can disrupt you and your team's work performance. Conversely, if you put a great deal of effort into improving conditions, the effect that it has on output and even on people's attitudes may be hardly noticeable. People soon get used to improved conditions and then take them for granted.

Getting it 'right' is not absolute; people's expectations change with changing social expectations, and what was acceptable twenty-five years ago is not acceptable now. (You only have to look at the change that has taken place in public houses to realize how much social expectations have shifted in a relatively short time.) This means that you must never expect to have got it right permanently – there will always be changes to be made.

The other idea that we think applies is less scientific than Herzberg, but is embodied in the Yorkshire saying 'There's nowt so queer as folk'. Even if you are very experienced in dealing with people you will continue to be surprised by the things that they find unacceptable and those that they can ignore. So one of the rules must be to listen to what people say and try to make sense of it. What seems to the management to be an improvement may not appear so to the staff. When listening, be careful of the talkative one who has plenty of views about what needs to be changed. The silent majority might prefer things left as they are and you will not be told this until after you have rearranged things.

The best way to maintain a proper understanding of what features of the working conditions are likely to impair people's effectiveness is to keep in touch; to 'walk the floor'; to observe with your own eyes how people are working, and to keep listening. This is sometimes known as MBWA, or 'management by walking about' – more of which later.

Making minor improvements is something that managers should be able to do fairly quickly, if not instantly. Fast action from the manager sends messages about commitment – a 'can do' approach which sets an example for others to follow. Great improvements in environment and attitudes can often be made through relatively small changes and minor expenditure. Managers should always be on the look-out for opportunities of this sort.

Anything requiring significant expenditure may need consideration against the budget. There will probably be budgetary limits on what may be spent on improving overall working conditions and it is therefore necessary to give consideration to these, preferably in advance of the time when budgets are fixed. If planned in advance, this is a time when, if there are priorities to be set or choices made, you can give the staff the opportunity to express where they would prefer to see the money spent and also get them to understand that, probably, you cannot do everything that they may wish for in ideal circumstances.

The working environment is, of course, more than just the physical working conditions; it also includes the whole social and psychological atmosphere of the workplace. This will be significantly affected by the sort of culture which is engendered by the organization as a whole.

Herzberg rated this – 'Company Policy and Administration' – as the most significant of the 'hygiene' factors, i.e. the factor with the greatest potential for causing dissatisfaction. This might include personnel policies – perhaps a sloppy sickness absence policy which allow individuals to get away with malingering – or credit control policies which dictate withholding payment for ninety days to small local suppliers who are hard-pressed to survive.

While these things are not in the control of many managers, they are not totally powerless to do anything about them. Indeed it is the responsibility of managers to raise these issues with their boss or the appropriate person and make every effort to achieve improvement. If managers do not highlight these matters of company policy which are having an adverse effect on employees' efforts, a trade union representative probably will, leaving managers open to the charge that they are not concerned about their people. If there are no trade unions it is even more important that managers fight the issues; in this situation, people must genuinely believe that the boss is keen on looking after their interests.

Much more within the control of the manager are those other of Herzberg's dissatisfiers which are, perhaps, the most influential factors affecting the psychological atmosphere of the workplace. These are 'supervision' (by which Herzberg means technical supervision) and the relationship with the supervisor that managers can affect directly. The way you treat the supervisors who work directly for you will greatly affect their morale and the way they carry out their tasks – it will also have a knock-on effect on the way in which the supervisors treat their subordinates. Thus, within a framework of organizational culture and organizational policies, the manager sets the tone, creates the atmosphere in the workplace – or should do. This is the element of the manager's role which can best be described as leadership.

There has also been, and probably will continue to be, a great deal of discussion about what constitutes leadership, and it is not our intention to become involved in definitions. Sometimes, however, there are definitions which attempt to separate management from leadership as though they are two distinct functions and this, we believe, can lead to misunderstanding of the role of manager. Whatever the definitions, it is our belief that within the role of manager there is a strong element of leadership, and that it is this element which, in the final analysis, distinguishes the good manager from the ordinary manager. It is this element which helps the manager to create a positive atmosphere in the workplace – the thing which produces the buzz which tells the visitor that people are going about their work in an energetic and purposeful way.

Along with most people we feel that we can recognize good leadership when we experience it, but find it difficult to describe. What we will do however, is refer in the rest of this chapter to some of the things a manager can do to help create a good and positive attitude to work.

Box 7.3
Most of us have been in hospital wards at some time or another, either as patients or as visitors, and will have noticed the dramatic difference there can be in the atmosphere when different ward sisters are on duty. There are those that seem to make the whole ward come to life when they walk in; nurses and auxiliaries move more briskly and patients show a livelier interest. Conversely, there are others who seem to generate a general gloom which envelops staff and patients alike.

Creating a positive attitude to work

In Herzberg's list of motivating factors, the three most important are:

- a sense of achievement;
- recognition; and
- the work itself.

In rather more everyday terms, this could be summed up by saying that the most important thing in getting people to work well is for them to feel that they are doing something worthwhile. It is highly enlightening that Herzberg found that pay is not among the factors which motivate people to work. Pay is necessary – fair pay is vital to avoid demotivating discontents – but pay does not make people look forward to coming into work in the morning; it does not make them 'go the extra mile' to satisfy the customer; it does not make them spend their lunch-hour working out ways to do things a little bit better.

A sense of *achievement* is both a personal and a social thing. People want the self-satisfaction of doing something that is valued and that they do well – some people are not content unless they can feel that they are the best. The other part of achievement is the *recognition* which can come with it. To do a good job in a successful company means that you have not only self-respect, but the respect of those around you, at work, your neighbours at home and your friends in the pub. People do not achieve those satisfactions in isolation. Management have to set standards of quality and ensure that people work to them. That is, managers have to tell people what constitutes a good job, tell them how it is measured and tell them how well they are doing. Obviously, how that is done will vary immensely from one organization to another, and from one type of job to another, but it is essential in all operations. If we want to see effective and continual improvement in our operation we have to work hard at setting standards, measuring and communicating results. Part of the manager's job is to work out how best this can be done for the people working for them, but it will need both the skills of communicating and of listening. Many people are not good at expressing their own preferences and managers have to be alert to the need to interpret what they say and to ensure, either by coaching or by other forms of training, that their supervisors are also sensitive to this particular problem.

The importance of recognition, making people feel appreciated for what they do, is universal, and methods can come in many forms. We are not thinking here of the razzamatazz of the annual sales conference, where awards are made and the 'Sales Rep of the Year' is declared – this is a form of recognition designed for a specific purpose. We are more concerned with what needs to be done day-by-day, week in and week out. At one time it used to be commonly felt that the only times one's work was remarked upon was when something had gone wrong. People were paid to do a job, and managers did not expect to have to praise them for doing what they were paid to do. Now the value of management's recognition and appreciation of a job well done is seen as a positive motivator. The carrot is seen to be a better long-term motivator than the stick. Although appreciation of effort does encourage people to maintain that effort, praise for its own sake can debase the currency and becomes valueless in the eyes of the worker. Managers need to strike the right balance and the first rule is to understand what constitutes good performance as opposed to the norm. Employees understand this and if managers do not they will lose respect.

There are dangers, too, and one of the worst occurs when trying to be encouraging to the poor performer. In trying not to damage someone's self-esteem, managers tend to sugar the pill by mixing criticism with some sort of praise – the effect can be that the criticism is either forgotten or not heard, and only the praise remains.

Box 7.4

Bill was a good engineer with a total inability to work with other people. Business was good and good engineers were very hard to come by. Over a period of ten years, Bill was moved into different jobs, under the guise of promotion, gradually losing responsibility for people and ending with the title of consultant engineer and working on his own. When recession came and staff cuts were necessary, Bill was made redundant at the age of forty-seven and three years later was still out of work. Bill was devastated. He had been told that he was being promoted (they had given him salary increases) and never understood how difficult he was to work with. In his thirties some sensitive handling might have helped him to improve – the effect of not providing this was to put him on the scrap-heap at the age of fifty.

But what can the manager do in relation to Herzberg's third principal motivator, *the work itself?* Getting satisfaction out of work itself is very personal and, thankfully, what different people find interesting or stimulating or generally congenial varies to a great degree. We say 'thankfully' because otherwise we would not be able to get done all the different things which need doing.

Having said that, people are very adaptable and, with the right handling, can accommodate themselves to doing things which, at first sight, might have seemed unlikely. Managers need to work in three areas in order to help people to get the most out of their jobs and at the same time to work most effectively. These areas are:

- initial selection;
- team building; and
- job significance.

Where the skills of a job are well-defined, the selection process concentrates on finding people with those skills which in itself is some sort of indication that an individual will be suitable. If no skills are required you may be looking to aptitude. This is much more difficult to detect and managers must spend time establishing what sort of aptitudes are required by different sorts of work and how, in a total selection process, you can identify them in individuals. Job satisfaction also depends on how much people are temperamentally suited to the work, the workplace and the other people in it. Again, temperamental suitability is difficult to identify and will usually depend on the skill and the experience of the manager in making judgements about people.

Those judgements are, of course, much easier made when people are known to you and it is then that team-building opportunities can occur. No matter how sophisticated the initial selection process may be, it can never substitute for real knowledge about people in a working situation. Once managers have that knowledge of people they can make better-informed judgements about the combinations of people's skills, aptitudes and temperament. Furthermore, if things are handled properly, experiments can be made by moving people around to see how they perform in different jobs or in different combinations of working groups.

We say 'if handled properly' as a very important warning. Some people like change, most don't. Most people feel insecure about their talents and abilities and are quick to assume that any change implies a criticism of their work. So they are defensive and can react badly if you are not careful. Experiments with people's jobs, even with the best of motives, have to be conducted with careful preparation and patient explanation. It can be done if people trust you – something which is built up over a long period. If, however, you are going to get people into the jobs that most suit them – square pegs in square holes – you must aim to achieve the sort of flexibility which allows you to experiment with your teams. Creating a good team is not only about getting the right mix of skills and aptitudes but also about getting the social mix right. We all obtain a great deal of social satisfaction from being at work and if we are working in a group in which we feel wanted and respected we will have a much more positive attitude to work than if we feel outsiders. So, if in addition to getting the right mix of competence and experience we can also achieve a high degree of compatibility, we will be well on the way to achieving high effectiveness.

Finally, when it comes to making people feel that they are doing a worthwhile job we come to what we have called 'job significance'. This is about getting people to understand how their department and their job fit in to the overall scheme of the organization and also about the importance or the significance of the job in the overall scheme of things.

It is said that a mediaeval bishop, visiting a construction site, asked three stonemasons what they were doing. One answered that he was cutting stone into building blocks; the second said that he was making building blocks for a doorway; the third said that he was helping to build a cathedral.

If people can understand the sort of cathedral that they are helping to build, it can give them a greater satisfaction with the work they are doing. Even this, though, needs working at by the manager; not everybody professes to want to understand the big picture and how they fit in to it, and some make a point of taking the opposite view. We believe, however, that most people do want to see their work valued in the enterprise as a whole. Those who take a very negative and sometimes cynical attitude are in a minority but need to be taken seriously. Negative attitudes towards one aspect of work may be reflected in others.

It is the presence itself of the manager which acts as the catalyst to make things happen. Managers must always be available to their immediate subordinates and must be visible to their staff. Managers are only people and they come in all the usual shapes and sizes. Each of us has our own style of operating and it is important not to try to acquire a style which is alien to us as it will soon be seen as false. Within that particular style, however, we have to seek to do and say things which, when we are in our own workplace, will inject a little extra electricity into the atmosphere.

Communicating

The basis of much that has just been said depends on good two-way dialogue between managers and their team. Much has been, and continues to be, written about the need for good 'communications' in the workplace, with the implication that it is all so simple if people only took a little trouble. If it were that simple, problems would have been solved years ago and we would not still be hearing about them.

We don't like the term 'communications' because the word is used as a catch-all phrase to cover too many situations. Managers need to think clearly about the different communication issues which can damage the working environment and affect people's morale.

With the best will in the world it will always be extremely difficult to eliminate totally the idea of an adversarial relationship between management and other employees – the conflict of interest between 'them and us'. Thus employees can be very quick to become suspicious and doubt the intentions of management, however good the relationship might have been beforehand. Managers should always bear in mind this latent suspicion, however unjustified they feel it may be, and be prepared to compensate for it.

Many of the problems which are described as 'communications' problems within a workforce are concerned with general information about an organization's affairs – either about the corporate whole or about a department or workplace. If people do not receive information to which they feel they are entitled – or if they receive it in a way which they feel is inappropriate or insensitive – the general tendency will be to attribute the situation to management ill-will, or perhaps to management incompetence. In either case, employees can be very unforgiving. Organizations are much more aware of the need to provide general information to employees, particularly through the medium of company magazines and journals, and it is sometimes the case that more information is provided than employees want. Middle- and first-line managers who are in direct contact with the bulk of employees are in a better position to understand the concerns of people, and need to be aware of those things which they really want to be informed about. In simple terms, this means those things which are likely to affect them directly. It may sound rather cynical to add, too, that people do not want to hear bad news unless it is likely to affect them directly. Some years ago, when one of us was involved in a scheme to give employees monthly information about their department's production, including the state of the order book, one representative said that they did not want that sort of information because they did not want to know if the order book went down, because 'managers are paid to have ulcers, we aren't'. Employees, too, have lessons to learn and part of the manager's job is to find ways of getting across both bad and good news, clearly and regularly.

Managers are not mind-readers, but sometimes they seem expected to be. However, if they want to know what employees' concerns really are, the employees have to tell them. Good personal communication between manager and managed is a two-way street. There are two sets of problems which the manager has to recognize: the first are those which revolve around trust, the second around language.

Trust

Although both management and workers wish to see the success of the enterprise, each has a different agenda. All employees, whether managers or workers, are well aware that success means productivity, and productivity usually means fewer workers. Jobs for life and the security that entails is no longer a part of industrial and commercial philosophy. Therefore workers are going to be cautious about opening their hearts to their boss. If a worker complains about unsafe working practices, will he or she be seen as someone who could slow down production or is at best a trouble maker? If the boss suggests reorganizing the order intake system in order to improve service to the customer, does a worker tell the boss that it will probably create enough extra work to require an extra member of staff, or does the worker decide to keep quiet in case the boss thinks that the worker is negative on customer service? These are real dilemmas for workers and they need to feel safe if they are going to make valuable contributions to a workplace dialogue. They need to understand that the survival of a business needs them to make that contribution and that management will act on it wisely.

Language

People's powers of expression sometimes do not allow them to say what they want to say, and conversely prevents them from understanding what is being said.

In addition to the sheer inability of many people to understand what is being said, there is also an attitude which allows people to interpret what has been said or written in the way they feel it ought to be interpreted, regardless of the actual words used. The onus is on the manager to ensure that those sort of misunderstandings are resolved. The manager must also ensure that messages are conveyed in a way which is clear to staff.

Box 7.5
During a discussion on canteen meal prices, the trade unions representative and the manager were at loggerheads over canteen subsidies. The manager eventually realized that they were defining subsidies differently. The representative's definition was that the company canteen subsidy was the difference between what employees paid as the price of a meal and what the ingredients actually cost. Mistakenly, the manager tried to point out that subsidy involved such things as maintenance and renewal of equipment, staff wages, fuel and power. Genuinely, the representative could not understand this.

Building improvement into the working environment

Working with an 'open' management style which attempts to create trust between management and other employees is not easy for the manager. If you attempt to give information it is very easy to be criticized for not giving enough, for not giving the right sort, for withholding particular things. By creating dialogue between manager and worker you can raise expectations about the right to be involved; people can become disappointed if you don't agree with them; decision-making can be slowed because of an extra element of consultation. However, these are dangers which need to be overcome for the benefit of creating the genuine involvement needed for world-class operation.

We believe that a great danger is that managers and staff can mistake a 'consultative' style of management for a 'consensus' approach, and come to expect that every management issue has to be the subject of debate and that all decisions are arrived at by joint agreement. Although there are issues which must have consultation and discussion, the essence of the effective management of an operation is in prompt and decisive execution of day-to-day matters. This requires workers to understand clearly what they have to do and managers to deal with non-routine matters without too much debate.

This is particularly true when competitive pressures are ever increasing for commercial enterprises and demands for greater efficiency are pressing upon the public sector. As a result of these pressures there has to be a constant search for improvements to products and procedures which affect the working environment and lead to a climate of constant change. Change, for whoever is concerned, is uncomfortable, and can create a more stressful environment. In these circumstances the existence of an atmosphere of trust in the workplace can smooth the path of change. The feeling that the boss understands the concerns of the workforce and will consult about them can overcome the sort of suspicion which makes people want to question and discuss the reasons for changes every time a light fitting is re-sited. If people know that they can raise issues and that genuine concerns will be dealt with, they will not be looking for management conspiracies behind every change and will help to make them work. Back, again, to the issue of 'trust'.

The customer in the workplace

In the retail business and in building societies, hospitals and many offices, the customer is very much part of the workplace. It is, in fact, partly designed with him or her in mind. In many other organizations – particularly in industry and commerce – where there is a business-to-business operation, the customer is not usually involved in the actual workplace. Although it may not always be appropriate, we believe that, in these cases, it will be worth considering involving the customer more. Modern quality procedures demand access for the customer – much better to be ahead of the mandate and invite them in first.

Where a business involves major contracts lasting for long periods, there will of course be initial visits from customers who wish to assure themselves that the organization has the facilities to carry out the required work. In these cases, it is of value to ensure that those visits are continued just as it is to encourage customers who might not otherwise come.

A general objective will be to strengthen the ties between your organization and the customer by creating a better understanding of the way you work. More specifically, both you and the customer can think in terms of the value chain and the effect that your working procedures can have on the product. When customers see the way you do things they may see alternatives which could improve the product for them and make things easier for you.

You must, however, be sensible about such exposure to the customer. Before embarking on this course, try to view your operation as a customer would view it and ask yourself whether it comes up to what he or she would expect. If not, you first need a plan to improve anything which might undermine the customer's confidence in your ability to fulfil your commitments. Only when you have fulfilled that plan should you open up the operation to what would be a very critical scrutiny.

Finally, in operations where the employees do not generally come face-to-face with the customer, there is an added advantage of some customer contact. If you are trying to make all employees aware of the need to satisfy the market – to give service to the customer – it can be a difficult message to get across if the customer is never seen. Anything which helps to make customers more real is beneficial.

Summary

Managers are responsible for the working environment. The physical environment should be examined both in terms of health and safety and in terms of plant and equipment. Ensuring the right working conditions may not be a positive motivator but it will prevent dissatisfactions. People are more likely to be motivated positively by psychological factors and the manager is a powerful influence on this. The manager's role in selection, team-building, training and reward is vital in creating the right positive environment. The ultimate aim is to create a trusting relationship between manager and staff. In some circumstances the involvement of the customer in the workplace may benefit the working environment.

Management checklist

- Review the health and safety requirements of your operation with the aid of Box 7.2.
- Review working conditions under two headings:
  - buildings and accommodation;
  - plant, equipment and tools.

  List any items which act as 'dissatisfiers' to your staff and state what actions are needed. Examine implications for the budget.
- Are there any issues of company policy which create dissatisfaction? Are there procedures which ensure that you can get these examined at the right level? What action are *you* taking?
- Are any of your supervisors or junior managers the cause of dissatisfaction with the staff? Are there actions which can be taken to improve the situation?
- To what extent can you match the work to individuals? Are you sure that you and your supervisors understand individual preferences and aptitudes for work among the staff?
- To what extent is it productive to organize your staff into compatible teams? Can you measure the effect on performance?
- How do you communicate a sense of recognition and achievement to your staff – both collectively and individually?
- Are you able to 'measure' work output, quality and customer satisfaction? Are these capable of being communicated to staff?
- Is there a 'them and us' attitude among staff? If so, is there anything that you can do to improve it?
- Do you know what your staff think of the management in general and you in particular? Do you have their trust? How can you be sure?
- Do your staff have a clear association with your customers and what they need? If not, are there measures which could be taken that would improve the operation's effectiveness in this respect?

8 Keeping track of your operation

Introduction

This chapter proposes to focus in simple terms on one of the central issues of every manager's job – the need to keep track of how well he or she is doing in order to achieve the right levels of performance. We shall try to use simple terms because we believe that it is helpful to our readers to remind them of simple truths at a time when managers' jobs appear to be becoming more and more complex.

Managers are usually agreed that one of the greatest difficulties at work concerns the pressures on their time. Courses on time management have flourished for decades and continue to do so. All general management training programmes include a session on time management, and new books on the subject appear regularly. A survey into managerial stress conducted by the Institute of Management in 1993 concluded that 75 per cent of managers had seen their workload increase, and 86 per cent cited time pressure and deadlines as a source of stress. This chapter is not specifically about time management but it is about priorities: identifying the things which matter and which must be concentrated on.

There will be many different reasons, in different organizations, for managers working longer hours; overall there is an inexorable increase in competition in commercial organizations and the drive to reduce staffing and bring about change in all types of organization. Managers, too, have to contend with more and more constraints on their actions as employment legislation becomes more onerous and employees' expectations increase.

After the removal of whole layers of managers, those who remain have to rethink their jobs and responsibilities; business process re-engineering may be changing the face of the organization so that jobs have to be carried through quite differently; the move from product-driven to market-driven, from public utility to privatized company; the introduction of total quality management and customer care campaigns can create a change overload which can easily cause managers to take their eye off the main purpose of their particular operation. It is possible to argue that organizations try to make too many changes at once but sometimes they do not have much choice.

This chapter is about monitoring the performance of your operation and will be concerned with how managers can cope with achieving the results that are expected of them, while at the same time dealing with the pressures of change and constraint in their many forms.

The chapter will be concerned with:

- the need to measure;
- what to measure;
- performance measures;
- how to measure;
- internal and external measures;
- setting targets;
- motivating; and
- informal measures.

The chapter relates to the following MCI Management Standards:

- M1/1.1: Maintain operations to meet quality standards.
- M1/2.1: Implement and evaluate changes to services, products and systems.
- M2/1.4: Implement and evaluate changes to services, products and systems.
- M2/2.2: Establish and agree customer requirements.
- M2/2.3: Maintain and improve operations against quality and functional specifications.

The need to measure

Some managers say that if an activity cannot be measured it cannot be managed. It is, of course, much easier to measure some things than others and frequently one finds that those things which can be measured easily become more important than those which cannot.

It is easy to measure the volume of sales of a range of products and it is tempting to be seduced by simple and unassailable figures of this sort. But we all realize that volume is not enough and that it also requires quality and customer satisfaction and profitability; and as we find so often in management there is a need to achieve a balance across all of these. What we would say, therefore, is that if something is important in management it must be measured.

The word 'measure' can be difficult because it implies a degree of precision which it is not possible to achieve in many areas of an organization. It is possible to say how many children will be eligible to start at a neighbourhood school at the beginning of the next year, but it may be much more difficult to predict how many parents, given a choice, want their children to go there. Currently, it may not be important to know whether a school has a good or a mediocre reputation. However, if parents are in a position to choose where to send their children, schools will need to be able to measure their attractiveness to parents in order to make some sort of assessment about the future intake. If their popularity is low and they take steps to improve it, they will need to keep measuring in order to know whether their steps are succeeding. If a management training programme is started to improve an organization's performance, that performance needs to be measured to see if it is working.

But measuring things like a school's reputation, or the effects of a management training programme, or such things as investment in research or customer satisfaction, are not quite the same as measuring volume of sales or numbers of patients attending a hospital casualty department. We are accustomed to dealing with so called 'hard' items which we can put as precise figures in budgets and balance sheets. Measuring so called 'soft' items, such as morale or customer satisfaction which cannot be quantified with precise figures quite so easily, requires a different approach and one which is less familiar to us. This lack of precision, together with the lack of familiarity, tends to make us sceptical of the process and encourages the view that some things are too vague to be measured and consequently lose importance. More and more, however, modern management is recognising the significance of 'soft' issues in the success of their operations, and more and more they are seeking ways of identifying them and designing new ways of putting some sort of measurement on them. If an activity is important to the business, we need to keep track of how it is doing and how it is affecting the total operation. Somehow we have to turn 'soft' issues into measurable ones.

Box 8.1

If we want to see whether customer service is improving, we can identify and measure customer complaints; delivery of goods in full and on time, numbers of incomplete or incorrect articles delivered or sold; which customers are affected. From this information, we can set standards of performance which we need to achieve. We also need to ask customers what they themselves consider to be important. Different customers value different aspects and finding out what these are can give us a few surprises. Finding out what is important to the customer is relevant, whether the customer is external or internal to the organization.

It may already seem that we are complicating things rather than keeping them simple. By 'keeping it simple' we are concerned with identifying a minimum number of performance objectives – perhaps four or five broad items which are what your operation is about – and then understanding them thoroughly. In total organizations they will be such things as customer service, patient care, high quality product, lowest price, state of the art technology. In departments within organizations, they will reflect the organizational goals, but will be more specific to departmental operational needs. This could mean such things as numbers of properly skilled personnel, rapid order processing, production throughput, transport scheduling, machine availability, absenteeism.

In any operation there will be a small number of activities which will be critical to the whole enterprise, and these are the ones which the manager needs to focus on. Some of these things, like the weather, are things which are not in your control. But if you are a brewer, an ice-cream vendor or a water company, you really need to have as much meteorological information as possible, so that you are not taken completely by surprise by a long, hot summer. Even though you can't control everything, you need to be informed about critical events in order to avoid nasty surprises. Other things, such as a shortage of skilled personnel, if not completely within your control, are capable of being strongly affected by your actions.

You need to know in broad terms the handful of activities – the key performance factors which are vital to the success of your operation – and you need to carry around in your head some very simple rules of thumb which can alert you speedily to the possibility that something may be wrong. Such performance factors are, however, too important to be solely left to rule of thumb, and once they have helped to alert you to a problem, you must then enter into the rigorous investigation which requires detail.

Performance factors for every operation will be different and infinitely varied. Only the managers concerned can define what they should be for their own responsibility. We believe, however, that there is a simple principle which can help to determine what they are.

What do you need to measure?

Within any organization there are broad groups of individuals who have a strong involvement in the enterprise and in its success. These groups are usefully known as the stakeholders and we believe that managers can usually define their performance factors by reference to their stakeholders. These will be concerned both within the organization as a whole and with a particular manager's area of responsibility.

In a public limited company, the main stakeholders are:

- the shareholders;
- the employees;
- the customers; and
- the suppliers.

In 'not-for-profit' organizations there may be no shareholders, but there will be an equivalent. In government, local government and public services, it is the tax payer and the council tax payer who are the shareholders and there are some similarities in the roles. The vital principle for managers at all levels is to maintain a correct balance between the interests of these various groups, and as is usual in management this is more an art than a science.

We have, too, included suppliers in the group of stakeholders when many people would not. Certainly, in most cases, suppliers are the least influential of the stakeholders, but gradually organizations are coming to recognize the value of supplier involvement as an essential part of business strategy; something which companies like Marks & Spencer have recognized for many years. In her book *Managing Today and Tomorrow* Rosemary Stewart gives some extended views of organizational stakeholders which are reproduced here in Appendix I to this chapter.

Partly due to circumstances, partly due to fashions of thought, at any one time there is often an emphasis on one or another group of stakeholders, at the expense of the others. But this cannot last for long and the balance has to be redressed.

Following the Second World War there was a great shortage of most things, and the UK had a 'rationing' mentality. Industry was production driven, customers scrambled to get whatever was available and customer service was not an issue. Customers often came a poor third to shareholders and employees.

There are a great many people who genuinely believe the slogans which convey the idea that the only reason for running a business is to satisfy the shareholders. Then too, in the hey-day of trade union power, many people acted in the belief that employees were entitled to earnings and a certain standard of living, whether or not they made a contribution, and whether or not they were employed by a viable business.

Now the slogans are focused on customers, because competition, particularly from abroad, offers them choices which did not exist in the days of post-war shortages. The slogans serve to focus our minds on the priorities but wise management understands that you can't run a business without shareholders and employees, and their interests still have to be served, even when the customer is at the top of the tree.

In the book *In Search of Excellence* by Peters and Waterman, one industrialist is quoted as saying that customers come first, employees next and shareholders are last. What it is really saying is that, if you look after your customer as a first priority and your employees as the next, the shareholders' interests will be automatically taken care of.

As managers, then, we need to recognize at *all* times the claims of *all* stakeholders in our business, even though we may give them different priorities. These claims give us a foundation for determining our performance factors. If, as will be the case for many of our readers, your own operation is a department or division of a larger organization, you will need to decide who are the stakeholders in your own department. Are your customers different from those of the rest of the organization? Are you part of an internal value chain which does not deal directly with the external customer? Your suppliers may well be

Box 8.2

David is the manager of the transport department in an engineering company which manufactures capital goods. His responsibilities include running a car pool for general use; assisting in buying company cars and supervising the fleet; providing a pool of light vehicles for goods transportation; transporting heavy loads to customers in hired transport; operating a small maintenance unit.

David's customers are:

- the company's customers to whom he delivers finished goods;
- the sales manager who takes overall responsibility for the delivery of finished goods;
- company executives, senior managers and sales staff who run company cars; and
- the purchasing manager and various members of the production management for whom he supplies collection and delivery services.

David's suppliers are:

- local haulage companies from whom he sub-contracts heavy vehicles on a regular basis;
- a national car distribution company from whom company cars are purchased;
- a leasing company which leases some company vehicles;
- a national oil company which supplies petrol and diesel fuel for the company pumps; and
- the insurance broker who deals with vehicle insurance.

David's shareholders are, of course the company shareholders, but represented by the senior management of the company to whom he reports.

Employees are those people who report directly to him, but also those who work for him indirectly:

- staff in the invoicing and bought ledger sections;
- purchasing staff;
- members of the personnel department;
- staff in production and production control; and
- members of the sales department.

another department within the organization, in which case their involvement within the organization is one of total commitment. In such circumstances, where customers and suppliers are internal and shareholders are dealt with at a more remote level, higher up the chain of command, it is easy for the employees to appear to be the most important stakeholder – an imbalance you must very seriously strive to avoid. When you have decided who are the stakeholders in your operation, you can then begin to decide what are the critical requirements which they need from you, and from this you can begin to work out your own performance factors.

Performance factors

Having decided who are the stakeholders in your particular operation, it becomes easier to identify those factors which will be important to each individual group. At the same time we can consider how frequently each factor needs to be reviewed. Frequency of review does not necessarily indicate importance, but it does indicate urgency. Some activities need to be reviewed over a long period, others require immediate review. In the case of our transport manager from Box 8.2 we might end up with a list which looks as Box 8.3 shows.

How to measure

Managers will be working to a budget and it is normal for actual departmental costs and expenses to be the subject of a monthly report comparing them with budgeted figures. It may be a valuable document but it cannot do everything a manager needs. The first weakness that must be recognized is the fact that it may not be available until two or three weeks after the end of a month. Thus, information could be over five or six weeks old. In the case of our transport manager (Box 8.2), a sudden change in petrol prices could have a serious effect on costs in such a length of time. Similarly, the effect of an exchange rate fluctuation to an exporter cannot be allowed to wait for the appearance of a monthly report, before the implications are considered.

Another problem with budgets is that they have not always been designed with the departmental manager in mind and thus do not give the information in the most suitable way. Managers must therefore have clearly in their mind that information which they need in order to be on top of events on a daily or weekly basis. They must also be prepared to negotiate with management accountants in order to get the information they need.

Not everything the manager needs to know will appear on the budget report, and if we look at the transport manager's perform-

Box 8.3

Customer	Performance factor	Review
Company customer	On-time delivery	Daily
Sales manager	Satisfy company customers	Weekly
	Reliable and cost-effective sales force cars	3 monthly
Company executives	Reliable and cost effective management cars	3 monthly
Other managers	Vehicle availability	Weekly
Suppliers		
Vehicle sub-contractors	Availability	Monthly
	Reliability	Monthly
	Cost	3 monthly
Car distributor	Discount levels	3 monthly
	Service	3 monthly
Car leasing company	Cost	6 monthly
	Service	6 monthly
Oil company	Cost	As delivery
	Service	As delivery
Insurance broker	Cost	Yearly
	Effectiveness of claim/process	As necessary
Employees		
Drivers	On time delivery	Daily
	Customer relations	Weekly
	Accident record	Weekly
	Care of vehicle	Weekly
Admin. staff	Timely, accurate and reliable documentation	Weekly
	Customer relations	Weekly
	Team working	
Other company staff	Positive support for department	As contact
	Professional competence	As contact
	Timeliness	
Shareholders		
	Cost effectiveness	With budget

ance factors, we find some which lend themselves readily to numbers and others which do not. On time delivery, vehicle availability, vehicle reliability, accident record are all things which can readily be measured in figures. Delivery can be recorded to show precise levels of lateness; vehicle availability can be recorded in terms of demand and waiting time; reliability in terms of times unavailable, and accident records in terms of incidents and time unavailable.

Measuring some of the other factors, such as the effect of drivers or administrative staff contact with customers, is more difficult. Such information is probably best acquired by direct personal contact with the customer and the customer's staff on an informal basis. The ability to achieve reliable information of this sort depends on establishing a good relationship with the customer, and if this is achieved, the manager has that vital early warning system which can warn of, and deflect, disasters.

In these unquantifiable situations this will not be enough. In normal circumstances we only expect about 10 per cent of dissatisfied customers to complain. If you have a good system of contacts you may expect a much higher percentage, but there will still be a number of dissatisfactions which you may not know about until a major crisis appears. One way of tackling this is to assume from time to time that a registered dissatisfaction is not an isolated incident, but could have been repeated many times with different customers. Thus, speculative investigations could be made to check that there are not more instances of a problem than appeared on the surface. Random events in the field of customer satisfaction are more the exception than the rule and, in our experience, it is usually safe to assume that there is 'no smoke without fire'.

Audits and surveys also have a place in flushing out information, especially from customers and employees, and can be used to good effect. There are, however, certain pitfalls which managers should be careful to avoid with employee surveys:

- Don't use them as a means of delaying taking unpopular actions which are inevitable.
- Be prepared to act upon unpalatable information.

With customer surveys, don't give the impression that you do not understand what the market is requiring.

Internal and external measures

When setting measures of performance for your department or your organization it is useful to consider the balance of measures between those that are internal or inward-looking and those that are external or outward-looking.

Internal measures would be concerned with:

- production volume;
- scrap;
- work in progress;
- stock levels;
- headcount;
- productivity;
- absenteeism; and
- staff turnover.

External measures would be concerned with:

- customer complaints;
- delivery performance;
- competitor benchmarks;
- market share;
- product development; and
- community investment.

Traditionally, most of our organizational measures of performance have been inward-looking and usually financially based, much of it based on budget reporting. We recently worked with one division of a major UK international company which set out to establish a programme leading to world-class performance. When its established performance measures were reviewed, it was recognized that all measures were internal measures, and none was directed towards the division's performance in its marketplace – the arena which determined its existence. The list of measures which were subsequently generated was significantly changed to reflect performance in the marketplace.

As a rule of thumb we recommend that, when devising performance measures, an organization should start with at least half of them externally based. As the organization grows in confidence and looks towards world-class standards, it may well find that the proportion of externally-based measures increases.

In the USA for some years there has been a scheme to promote quality on a national scale – the Malcolm Baldrige National Quality Awards. Companies entering the competition are judged on their organization for quality achievement under a series of categories which are allocated a points weighting. Although these are not aimed at the total performance of a company, these categories, together with the points weighting, offer a valuable example of how different aspects of performance can be identified. We have reproduced their scheme of judgement in Appendix II to this chapter. It is significant that in allocating 1,000 points to seven different factors, 300 points are allocated to customer satisfaction.

Setting targets

Identifying those things which you want to measure is a first step; the next step is to decide what level of performance you need to achieve, that is, what your targets are for satisfactory performance.

Unless you are in a situation in which an activity is obviously performing well below the norm or there are catastrophic circumstances, targets should not be over-ambitious to start with. You may, as a manager, see the need for very significant improvements, but unless you are making radical and dramatic changes to the process it is as well to keep those to yourself. Psychologically, people will try hard to achieve improvements which they see as attainable but will become demotivated if they feel that the impossible is being asked.

Targets should, therefore, be stretching but realistic; they should be seen as a challenge but not as unachievable. As managers we should have a highly-informed understanding of what is possible through knowledge, experience and research in our own particular field. We should know how our processes and resources compare with our competitors', and thus be able to make judgements about what should be possible. If we are already ahead of the field we should understand that if we are complacent we will not stay that way for long, because our competitors will see us as the target to beat. Thus if we are the leaders in our particular field we should set arbitrary targets of, say, 5 to 10 per cent improvement, and then be innovative about how we achieve them. If we are not the leader, we may be able to learn from others.

Lately, the idea of learning from others has been recognized as a valuable item of management practice, and many of you will have come across it under the term 'benchmarking'.

Benchmarking is simply the idea of making continuous comparisons of key processes with the best practices from the industry or even outside it, if appropriate.

It has particular relevance to private sector activities where companies are in competition, and in these circumstances it may be more difficult to discover how the opposition goes about its business. In non-competitive organizations the exchange of such information is much more readily accomplished, through formal and informal relations with organizations in the same field. Professional associations are a useful meeting place for the exchange of ideas as these can represent neutral ground for people in the same field.

Setting targets, then, is not an arbitrary decision, nor is it concerned with guesswork. The minimum level of target for key performance areas needs to be decided rationally. If comparisons tell you that your performance is 40 per cent worse than others in the field, that may have to be the target. But an improvement of that magnitude – particularly if it needs to be accomplished quickly – indicates radical action. It may require completely redesigning the process and some capital investment. If you are in business you may have to consider seriously whether you will ever be able to catch up to such an extent.

Given, however, that performance targets are not dramatically different from your current achievements, you need to consider your reasons for setting particular levels. Target levels can be identified either because external pressures require them, or because you or someone within the organization decide that they are appropriate.

In the first case, external pressures can come in various ways:

- Costs are increasing but you cannot increase prices.
- You need to increase output without extra facilities or people.
- In a hospital you need to reduce the waiting time for operations.
- In a bank you need to meet a range of customer service quality requirements laid down centrally.

Such external pressures often give you little choice of setting the targets because they are set for you.

In many cases, when we are working within a philosophy of continuous improvement, we have choices of where and at what level we set our targets – stretching but not unattainable. In the end, they will usually represent a judgement on the part of the manager, but a judgement based on fact, experience and the involvement of those concerned. Wherever possible, situations should be carefully analysed so that you can see the contribution to be made by different parts of the operation. However, experience and knowledge will tell you that a 5 per cent improvement over a year is reasonable in one area, but totally unattainable in another. A critical factor in setting targets, however, is the involvement of the employees concerned. Not only will they have a good understanding of what is possible and not possible but also their ownership of the targets is a vital ingredient in their achievement.

Motivating people to meet targets

A great deal of effort goes into developing ways of motivating people towards the achievement of organizational goals, much of it revolving around linking pay to performance. We certainly believe that in order to achieve targets it is highly valuable to focus people's minds through the reward system, but that this must not only be concerned with pay; we need to take a broader view.

It is a good principle to assume that the first step in motivation to meet targets is concerned with 'ownership', and the more involved people are in defining targets, the more committed they will be to meeting them. As with other aspects of management, the imposition of targets, whether reasonable or not, is unlikely to generate as much enthusiasm from people as when they develop and set them themselves. Sometimes in these circumstances people can be carried away by their own enthusiasms and set targets which are over-ambitious. Managers must be prepared to temper enthusiasm with good judgement.

On a general level, Chapter 7 referred to Herzberg's ideas on the factors which motivate people at work. Another useful general model of motivation is that of Maslow, who saw people's motivation to work driven by their needs, which range from the basic need for food and shelter to the highest need for self-fulfilment. A fuller explanation of Maslow's Hierarchy of Human Needs is shown in Appendix III of this chapter, while Appendix IV shows how Maslow's model compares with Herzberg. Motivating people to achieve specific targets in a much narrower way is rather different. Another psychologist, E. Lawler, has produced a different model which considers the direct relationship between effort, performance and reward. He sees people's motivation to perform requiring three sets of conditions:

- There needs to be a reasonable likelihood of achieving the required target. This condition is dependent on:
  - their ability to perform the job;
  - knowing what to do; and
  - availability of resources.

  All three of these sub-conditions sets a clear onus on managers to:
  - ensure adequate skill levels;
  - give clear instructions; and
  - make resources available.

- If rewards are dependent on achieving targets and those rewards are what people value, they will be motivated to perform. This condition is affected by:
  - the link between performance and rewards; and
  - the value of rewards.

  Managers should ensure, therefore, that there is:
  - a clear relationship between achieving the target and receiving the reward; and
  - the reward itself must be worthwhile.

- The reward must be fair in relation to the effort expended. This is influenced by prevailing notions of what is 'fair'.

When considering rewards we naturally think of pay and there is in the 1980s and 1990s a heavy emphasis on performance-related pay in all sectors of the economy, particularly in public service organizations where the concept is relatively new. There have always been difficulties with performance-related pay schemes (or payment by results, as they used to be known), because they often do not seem to work in practice. Even when results ought to be relatively easily measurable, such as in factories where outputs can be measured precisely in physical terms, there are manipulations and distortions which undermine the whole process. It has to be said that in manufacturing operations, where piece-work and bonus rates used to be the norm, most managements have been trying to get away from such systems because of the difficulty of administering them to give the desired motivation. Where targets are less precise it is necessary to be extremely careful in designing schemes, and we believe that Lawler's principles make valuable guidelines.

Having said that, we believe that if you can clearly identify key activities and set measures on them which can be obviously linked to a reward system, improvements in performance will result.

We said earlier, however, that rewards involve more than just the pay packet. Herzberg's top two motivators are 'achievement' and 'recognition', and setting and hitting targets can bring in both of these. It is self-evident that, when you have hit the target, you know that you have succeeded. Recognizing this means that other people need to know as well. What you do to generate this recognition will vary enormously according to circumstances. A very simple example is the posting of output figures in a factory; perhaps there is a daily progress chart with a weekly or monthly target to meet. At the other extreme there is the 'razzamatazz' sales conference with awards and elaborate prizes. In between there is a whole range of events, awards, prizes and publicity activities which give recognition to success and at the same time generate a buzz of excitement and a bit of fun. Not every activity lends itself obviously to the public event but there is usually something which can be done in simple ways to show people that their efforts are appreciated. At its basic level it is no more than a word of praise from the manager for something well done or a little extra effort. Any letter of appreciation or thanks from a customer or a senior member of management can be circulated. We know of one small office where the boss gives a bunch of flowers to someone who achieves something that is a little bit extra.

The best manure is on the farmer's boots

You can't run a farm by sitting in an office; farmers need to be covering the ground to see what is going on and getting their boots muddy in the process. The same principle applies to managing organizations and has inspired the phrase 'management by walking about'; or, as Tom Peters calls it, 'management by wandering around' – both known as MBWA. We want to link this, finally, to what might be called informal systems of measurement.

The good manager is one who understands what is going on in his or her area of responsibility in all aspects. Reports of all sorts are vital to know how effectively the operation is achieving its objectives but, as we said earlier, formal reports can sometimes take time to arrive.

On the sails of yachts are sewn small lengths of wool known as 'tell-tales'. When the tell-tales are horizontal and lying flat against the sail, the person at the helm knows that his or her course is correctly set to take advantage of the wind; if the tell-tales begin to drop he or she is losing the wind; if they hang vertically, the wind has been lost.

The manager needs tell-tales to give instant warnings of how the operation is doing. Many such indicators will be the result of acquired experience and will seem more like instinct than applied knowledge. Additionally, the experienced manager will look for and register the tell-tales almost unconsciously, when walking from one part of the operation to another or when holding a discussion in the workplace.

Tell-tales are often simple things, the number of cars in the car park may tell you something about volume of customers; the type of noise in a factory can indicate a level of activity; the number of empty desks in an office; the size of queues in a bank or building society; the busyness of the shelf-stockers in a retail store; the number of staff on coffee breaks – all tell the experienced manager something about the way the operation is running. They don't, of course, control the operation, but they give to managers the sort of sixth sense which enables them to anticipate problems almost before they actually happen.

Box 8.4

The chief executive of a major international company was in the habit of walking around the factory every Saturday morning. Saturdays are not a normal working day but there is usually a certain amount of overtime being worked.

The factory assembled very large pieces of sophisticated electronic equipment and on Saturday mornings, when the pressure was off his daily load, he was able to take a little time to see the progress being made on each job. Employees in the factory resented this, because as most of them were not present, they considered he was 'snooping'. Although he was an extremely able and conscientious chief executive, he lost a certain amount of leadership effectiveness because of this.

The experienced manager will have a number of tell-tales for his or her operation, but in order to make use of them the manager will need to be in close touch with the day-to-day activity – hence MBWA.

'Management by walking about' is not only about spotting the tell-tales. It is also about leadership. It is important for the manager to be seen; to talk to people, not only to know what is going on, but to be seen to know and be involved.

So, as with many aspects of management, doing the right thing is not always straightforward, and even with the simple business of walking about the workplace it is advisable to consider how you do it. When you are in a leadership position, at whatever level, people will interpret what you do and what you say, and very often infer intentions and motives that are totally incorrect. Often you will be unaware of these false interpretations of your actions and so you will never have the opportunity to put the record straight – certainly not a single opportunity, that is! However, you have to believe that if you are doing the right things with the right intent, your staff will understand over the longer term. And it does not alter the original premise that, to manage successfully, you need to keep closely in touch with the everyday activity, picking up the vibrations from your operation as it is taking place, and instantly being warned of any developments and problems as soon as possible. Like the person at the helm of a sailing boat, being able to make the small, immediate adjustments needed to take best advantage of the changes in the wind makes the difference between average performance and out-standing performance.

At the same time, just as the effect of the helmsman's skill will help to inspire the crew to greater efforts, so the presence of the manager in the workplace will help to motivate the staff and improve perform-ance. Which is where we return to agriculture and our heading that 'the best manure is on the farmer's boots'.

Summary

If an activity is important to the organization we have to find ways of measuring it – even if it canot be quantified. Measurement is the only means of identifying improvement. Activities to be measured should be kept to a minimum and can be identified in relation to the organization's stakeholders.

Departmental managers need to think through those activities which are most critical to their own activity. Care should be taken to identify external measures of performance. People should be involved in the development of targets and rewarded for achieving them. Reward is not just a question of pay. Managers need to keep in close touch with their operation and be visible to their teams in doing so.

Management checklist

- What activities in your operation are measured now?
- Are there others which should be measured?
- Who are your stakeholders?
- What measures exist in your operation to serve each group?
- What are your 'performance factors'? Do you have a review time-table for them?
- Do you have 'performance factors' which are difficult to measure? Do they get less attention because of this? Can you improve the measures?
- What is your balance of internal and external measures? Could it be improved?
- What sort of improvements could be achieved in your operation? What are the priorities? How will you target them?
- Do you know how your performance compares with other organizations?
- Are your staff satisfied with performance or are they keen to improve it?
- Are all staff competent at their tasks? If not, how can you improve their competence?
- Does the reward system relate to your targets? Does it reward effort, or results?
- Are there psychological rewards?
- Do you have any 'tell-tales'? Can you anticipate problems before they occur?
- Do you use MBWA?

Appendices to Chapter 8

Appendix 1 Different types of stakeholders

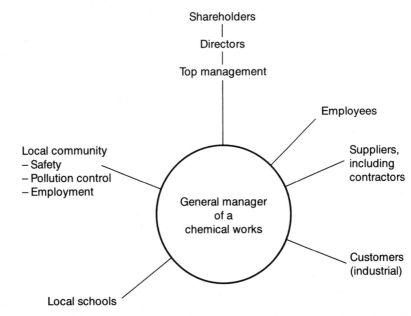

Figure 8I.1(a) General manager of a chemical works (Source: Stewart, 1991, by permission of Macmillan Press Ltd)

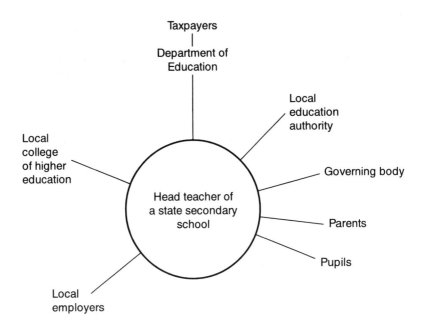

Figure 8I.1(b) Head teacher of a state secondary school in England (Source: Stewart, 1991, by permission of Macmillan Press Ltd)

Figure 8I.1(c) General manager of a teaching hospital in England (Source: Stewart, 1991, by permission of Macmillan Press Ltd)

Appendix II 1991 Examination categories and items – Malcolm Baldrige National Quality Awards

Examination Categories and Names

1.0 LEADERSHIP (100)

1.1 Senior Executive Leadership (40)
1.2 Quality Values (15)
1.3 Management for Quality (25)
1.4 Public Responsibility (20)

2.0 INFORMATION AND ANALYSIS (70)

2.1 Scope and Management of Quality Data and Information (20)

2.2 Competitive Comparisons and Benchmarks (30)
2.3 Analysis of Quality Data and Information (20)

3.0 STRATEGIC QUALITY PLANNING (60)

3.1 Strategic Quality Planning Process (35)
3.2 Quality Goals and Plans (25)

4.0 HUMAN RESOURCE UTILIZATION (150)

4.1 Human Resource Management (20)
4.2 Employee Involvement (40)
4.3 Quality Education and Training (40)
4.4 Employee Recognition and Performance Measurement (25)
4.5 Employee Well-Being and Morale (25)

5.0 QUALITY ASSURANCE OF PRODUCTS AND SERVICES (140)

5.1 Design and Introduction of Quality Products and Services (35)
5.2 Process Quality Control (20)
5.3 Continuous Improvement of Processes (20)
5.4 Quality Assessment (15)
5.5 Documentation (10)
5.6 Business Process and Support Service Quality (20)
5.7 Supplier Quality (20)

6.0 QUALITY RESULTS (180)

6.1 Product and Service Quality Results (90)
6.2 Business Process, Operational, and Support Service Quality Results (50)
6.3 Supplier Quality Results (40)

7.0 CUSTOMER SATISFACTION (300)

7.1 Determining Customer Requirements and Expectations (30)
7.2 Customer Relationships Management (50)
7.3 Customer Service Standards (20)
7.4 Commitment to Customers (15)
7.5 Complaint Resolution for Quality Improvement (25)
7.6 Determining Customer Satisfaction (20)
7.7 Customer Satisfaction Results (70)
7.8 Customer Satisfaction Comparison (70)

TOTAL POINTS = 1000
(World Class = 850+; Average score = 400)

Appendix III Maslow's hierarchy of human needs

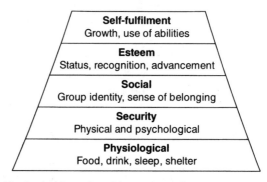

Figure 8III.1 Maslow's hierarchy of human needs

On the basis of this classification (above), Maslow made a number of propositions about the relationship between human needs and motivation.

Human needs are hierarchically ordered

As the diagram illustrates, Maslow proposed that these five basic needs are organized hierarchically. Until a lower order need is satisfied the next higher order need will not emerge to organize and direct the individual's energies. For most adults, however, the picture is not one of a single overriding need, rather one of the individual moving up and down a hierarchy of more or less satisfied needs. To understand a person's work motivation, therefore, it is important to understand this pattern of relatively satisfied or unsatisfied needs.

A satisfied need is not a source of motivation

A need once satisfied no longer provides a source of motivation. Rather it remains psychologically 'dormant'. It will emerge again to direct and organize a person's energies only if threatened by the environment. Thus a person who is satisfied by the amount of status which they receive at work will not be motivated by further incremental rewards in this area. Equally, a manager may take the security of his/her employment for granted until that security is threatened by the possibility of redundancy. In such circumstances, the manager will redefine his/her work goals and the need for security will become a source of motivation.

Higher order needs and psychological maturity

The hierarchy represents a development path from psychological immaturity to maturity, from reactive to proactive patterns of behaviour.

To deny a person the opportunity to satisfy their higher order needs is to deny them the opportunity to develop into a responsible, independent person. In work situations, therefore, we cannot deny people the opportunity to earn the respect of others and to experience a sense of achievement and yet expect them to behave in an adult and responsible manner.

Appendix IV Comparison of Maslow and Herzberg

Another theorist whose work has exerted a considerable influence on our thinking about contemporary work motivation is Herzberg. His findings are considered to be the manifestation of Maslow's hierarchy of needs in work settings.

Herzberg and his associates started their research in the late 1950s, by asking a sample of engineers and accountants to recall separate periods in their working lives when they felt particularly good and bad about work. As the chart below indicates, an analysis of the events associated respectively with these periods showed a clear pattern. The research has been replicated across different cultures and occupations and a similar pattern of work experience has been found.

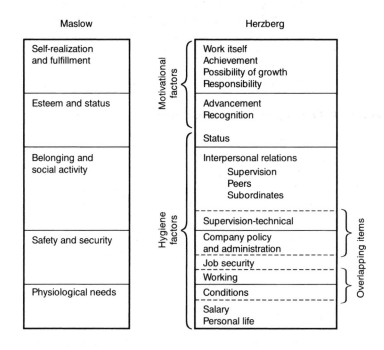

Figure 8IV.1 Maslow's need–priority model compared with Herzberg's motivation–hygiene model

Sources of job satisfaction

By contrast, the periods of satisfaction were accounted for, in most cases, by events related to the content of the job: responsibility, recognition, achievement, personal growth. It would appear that these are the factors that serve to promote feelings of job satisfaction. When they are not present in a job, however, they do not appear to give rise to feelings of dissatisfaction. Because of this, Herzberg termed them the 'motivators'.

The importance of job design

Herzberg's findings point to the importance of the way in which we design jobs. Historically, personnel practices have been concerned primarily with developing competitive and coherent policies in respect of pay, working conditions, training and supervision. These, in terms of people's experiences, serve primarily to prevent feelings of dissatisfaction.

They do not promote feelings of satisfaction. If we wish to do so then we must pay much more attention to the motivational assumptions implicit in decisions about the way we design jobs and organize work. It is these aspects of work which provide people with the opportunity to satisfy their needs for esteem and self-actualization.

9 Changing for improvement

Introduction

In this chapter, we look at the need for change in every operation. There is a need for balance in this regard of course, and we discuss how to find this balance. Too much change and people become confused; too little and the operation quickly becomes out of date or complacent. Change is driven by the marketplace and how we respond to that will dictate our business fortunes. We explore the market drivers and also the enablers of change. There are many things available to us in modern management to enable the change process to take place and we outline a number of them.

Changes always involve and need people to implement them. Those who are leaders of change need encouragement and support and we deal with the managers' responsibility to provide that encouragement to the change makers in their team.

No-one would deny the value of finding improvements within their own operation. The difficulty can be deciding which area to select for an improvement drive, so we offer some advice on how to make that selection. We outline some commonly found aspects of operations on which to base this selection process. Many markets today are dominated by the need to produce timely responses. Everyone wants instant action and if we can tune our operation to be more responsive, we stand a good chance of improved market share. We will expand on this theme in this chapter, and look in some detail at speed-related topics such as the Just-in-Time (JIT) approach to the problem.

We will briefly cover the relatively new topic of the change process known as 'business process re-engineering'. This leads to dramatic change and produces dramatic improvements, but needs careful application.

Whether we are changing the operation or not, we need a mechanism for assessing how our operation is doing compared with others. We describe 'benchmarking' as a means of doing this. It not only enables us to check how we are doing, but also provides assistance with the decisions regarding where to apply our improvement efforts. Through benchmarking we can compare ourselves with the best around, and either copy or maybe 'leapfrog' their methods and their performance.

Finally, we close the chapter by offering some tips on planning for change. By following these tips, you will increase the chances of your improvements being effective.

This Chapter relates to the following MCI Management Standards:

- M1/2.1: Contribute to the evaluation of proposed changes to services, products and systems.
- M1/2.2: Implement and evaluate changes to services, products and systems.
- M2/1.1: Identify opportunities for improvement in services, products and systems
- M2/1.2: Evaluate proposed changes for benefits and disadvantages.
- M2/1.4: Implement and evaluate changes to services, products and systems.

'If it ain't broke, don't fix it'

This old saying means that if something is running well, leave it alone. There is a lot of merit in this so long as we keep it to sensible proportions. But how do we reconcile it with the drive to make continual improvement? Chapter 4 explained that the very essence of systems such as BS5750/ISO 9000 is to ensure that we keep secure those systems in the operation that deliver successful quality. We do want people to work in a consistent way so that our operation can confidently promise its customers a level of performance that we know we can deliver. It might seem then that this subject entitled 'changing for improvement' jeopardizes this consistency aim. If we are constantly changing our systems the danger is that no-one knows exactly how to perform – constant changes can be totally disorienting. This is why we mentioned the importance of keeping sensible proportions. We cannot afford to put so much change into our operation that people are in a constant state of confusion. Similarly, in the fast-moving world of the 1990s, we cannot stand still for too long. One of the manager's jobs is to judge this balance correctly and pursue the right level of change, ensuring always that the changes will result in improvement for the business.

If an operation is left for too long in one mode, the people within it forget how to handle any change. It is something outside their day-to-day working experience. An additional effect of long periods with one operational method can be the onset of complacency. This can become something even more dangerous if the operation is successful and complacency turns into arrogance. Such feelings can blind people to seeing any reason for, and certainly no merit in, considering changes to the operation. You, as the manager, must do your utmost to avoid this both for yourself and for your staff.

When Tom Peters followed up his 'Excellence' series of books *In Search of Excellence* and *A Passion for Excellence* he eventually found an element that set the great companies apart from the ordinary ones. He described this as the eagerness with which they embraced the need for constant change. His next work was called *Thriving on Chaos*, not because there is any virtue in chaos, but because he saw successful companies then and in the future being those which know how to manage the turbulence resulting from need for continual improvement.

No organization can afford to stand still for too long because its markets and customers will not be doing so. As this is the case, managers need themselves to adopt an attitude of mind of constant change being the norm. They also need to instil this attitude into their staff. Twenty years ago change within many operations was a rare event, and they could run year in, year out along the same lines. That must not be allowed to happen now; managers and staff need to develop the skills and attitudes necessary to manage constant change. It must become the norm if your business is to survive and prosper.

We came upon a case recently where a manufacturing company adopted a policy which they called 'annual halving'. Each year, for the next few years, they would plan to halve the important, customer-perceived, performance measures. They would, for instant, halve lead times, halve costs, halve delivery times, halve error rates and halve inventory levels. This has the merit of being an easily understood plan albeit aggressive for many organizations. They believed it was necessary (and achievable) in order to hold on to their market share. Their belief was borne out in the first year when targets were met. It does illustrate, however, the continuous nature of the improvement programme they undertook – on a 'halving' programme you never get to the ultimate. There is always still something to 'halve'! However, after a few years we imagine they might need to revise the improvement factor.

Box 9.1

One of the world's best golfers, Nick Faldo, decided to 'redesign' his swing which is a fundamental 'system' for any golfer. At the time he had attained the world ranking of number 2. Most of us would have seen that as success on any measurement scale! But not Faldo. He was aiming to be number 1 and so redesigned the key system in his golfing operation. He employed a new coach and went on with his new swing to become number 1 in the world. This illustrates how radical you may need to be both to spot the opportunity and then to change a key system or operation for the improvement you need.

Factors driving change

The most obvious factor to drive change is the market, where the standards are set by the best-in-class. As individual consumers we are all responsible for driving this change by our own buying preferences.

We expect better performance today than ever before. Maybe more to the point we will no longer take our custom to sources of poor performance. These preferences more than any other are the drivers of change, and indeed change for improvement.

This does not just apply to commercial, profit-making operations. In the 1990s much is heard in Britain about the shortcomings of medical services and education and government departments. Raised standards are being demanded across the board.

Another facet of this market pressure is our shrinking world. In the past many operations only had to look locally for, and at, their competitors. In the 1990s even humble businesses are finding the competition is as likely to come from the other side of the world as from the next street. Markets have expanded through national to international and, in many cases, global arenas where the players operate on several continents. These new global players often use new approaches to gain competitive edge so we must follow or, better still, be ahead.

A further driver towards improvement exists in the financial institutions. In capitalist societies financial institutions play an ever-more important role in affecting how investors view organizations. The need to be able to show short-term results is paramount in many organizations and will drive management to seek improvements, even where results are sound. We may not always like this pressure from the City but it is part and parcel of the business environment. To survive in it, companies have to perform well against their measures of success.

The third contributor in this set of drivers for improvement comes from managers themselves. Today, management is seen as a highly competitive activity. Many managerial authorities such as the leading journals and institutions have instituted awards for 'best performance'. Governments have similarly introduced national schemes where organizations and companies can enter competitions to be judged alongside their neighbours or competitors. Winners are feted and publicized. The business press and media devote much space to them. League tables are now common (see Box 9.2 for examples).

Box 9.2
- Best factory
- Best European Business
- British Quality Awards
- The US Baldrige Quality Award
- National Training awards
- Best Construction Site award
- National Safety awards
- Best Civil Engineering project

Managers are much more aware of the need to do well, particularly when judged by others. So managers themselves are fuelling the fires of change for improvement, a very healthy attitude in our view.

Factors enabling change

Fortunately, it is probably easier to effect changes in the 1990s than at any time in history. We see a number of reasons why this is the case and we will briefly address them under the headings of staff, communication, equipment and technology, systems, suppliers and computers.

Staff

People are better educated and trained than they have ever been before. In general terms, we are more literate, numerate and better informed. Many possess technical skills and capabilities previously unheard of, and are also more accustomed to change than ever before. Our day-to-day lives embroil us in a constant round of learning new things, from the complexities of the modern motor car, to the advent of world-wide low-cost holiday packages. We are assailed on all sides with change and learn to cope with it in our daily lives.

Communication

The availability of sophisticated communication systems needs no description. Everyone knows this and sees it around them. Management have no excuse for bad communication although the new systems still need to be applied correctly to get the best from them. In our experience this is still the most badly handled aspect of change, and we will return to the topic to offer advice later in this chapter.

Equipment and technology

Great strides have been made and are being made into what can be done and the speed of development and innovation is increasing (Box 9.3). New equipment and technology often provide a ready answer to improvement moves, and need not always involve great sums of

---

Box 9.3
Agricultural revolution – 2000 years ago.
Industrial revolution   – 200 years ago.
Computer revolution   – 20 years ago.

What's next?!

money. Enhancements and add-ons can provide very worthwhile advances in performance.

Systems

Most of the new systems available to support organizations make use of the processing power and speed of computers, but not all. The whole Just-In-Time philosophy is one that can be applied to many operations and requires us to think about running our own operation in a quite different way. Booking systems for holiday and airlines, scheduling systems in factories, home-working techniques, are all examples of new working systems in action which are available to managers. You will be able to list several that have or are impacting on your operation now or in the near future.

Suppliers

All markets have been blessed by an improving, more competitive, supplier base. Suppliers are tremendous sources of ideas, capability, solutions and partnering opportunities. It needs a change of attitude by the customer to see suppliers in this light. We need to remember, for instance, that some of those global suppliers have global capabilities. We should use them. We covered this extensively in Chapter 5, but re-emphasize its importance here.

Computers

In the second half of the twentieth century computers have been the biggest single influence on business. Today unbelievable power is built into the tiny laptops we see in use everywhere. Yet we still visit operations as yet untouched by them. This may point to wasted opportunities. However, we are not advocating screens for their own sake. If an operation has carefully studied the use of computers and decided against them, we would not challenge the wisdom of that. If your system or operation does not need or cannot benefit from the use of computers, don't use them. Conversely if it does, do not shirk their inclusion out of fear, ignorance or plain meanness. They can bring major time-based advantages.

Encouraging change-makers

We have emphasized the importance of involving the operational staff in any moves to find improvements. They are closest to the work and are usually knowledgeable about problem areas, root causes and possible solutions. Their involvement breeds ownership both of the operation and of any improvement initiatives. In an enlightened atmosphere of change, promoted as much by the staff as by the management, an additional role emerges for the manager. It is to provide actual encouragement to the change makers.

This word encouragement embraces a feeling of being one step beyond mere support. Support gives the impression of management being there if needed as staff take initiatives. It has a passive ring to it. The word 'encouragement' on the other hand has an entirely different meaning. The Oxford dictionary definition includes the words 'embolden, incite, promote, assist'. The first three of these sound proactive to us, management sharing the initiative with staff in the change process. So managers need a proactive approach to offer this encouragement to their staff.

In an organization that values change for improvement, we might find that the performance measures applied during appraisals would include staff's willingness to change things. People who are prepared either to introduce or to accept change would be seen to be more highly valued, and rewarded, than those who are not. Reward in this instance does not necessarily mean with money. It could eventually mean with promotion, as management see in a person more aptitude and willingness to create improvement initiatives.

Encouragement can take the form of providing guidance or advice on a change, to help the person succeed in their venture. Maybe a short course is needed; maybe some coaching; maybe a period seconded to another department; there are many possibilities to provide positive help when needed.

Suggestion schemes

Another way in which organizations can encourage people to become change makers is through formal suggestion schemes. Such schemes provide a mechanism for people to make suggestions for improvements, usually within the sphere of their own work but not necessarily exclusively so. The most widely used suggestion schemes involve filling in forms with the essentials of the idea. Usually small committees are used to sift and assess the ideas. They usually do this in conjunction with local management and thereby lies the weakness in such schemes. As the local managers are nearly always too busy to give the ideas due consideration and assessment, most ideas lie dormant. This often has little to do with the merit of the ideas but is solely a reflection on how busy the managers are. If only they delegated some of their authority they would have more time.

Such schemes can fail to produce very much benefit, if any at all. They fall into disrepute with the workforce who no longer take any interest in them. What they most want to see are their ideas coming to fruition. When that does not happen, they lose both interest in the scheme and the confidence that the management actually want their contribution.

Whatever scheme is used, management always retain the final authority on any change being implemented. If this can be minimized, with as much authority as possible being passed down to those initiating the change, better results are possible. Many changes will not involve extensive expenditure and can be easily implemented. As a manager, you can try to ensure that you afford such ideas adequate time and that they are not held up unnecessarily. It is exactly the type of behaviour you can adapt to encourage the change-makers. Your active consideration of their proposals and the inclusion of as many ideas as is practicable, is the very best encouragement you can give.

Box 9.4

Following a redesign of the manufacturing unit of a production line of a car-seat manufacturer, a large display board was placed close to the operation. The display board depicted the new layout, showing all stages of the operation. Operators were then encouraged to make any improvements they thought of to any aspect of the new operation by writing on the wipe-clean board or by sticking comments to it on 'post-it' notes. Regular meetings of the whole team were held around the process board and they decided together whether any of the suggested changes warranted further work. Anything not wanted was cleared. Anything wanted was drawn up into a more detailed proposal which eventually went for final management approval. At all stages prior to this the working team handled the assessment and studies. This improvement scheme was designed to provide maximum encouragement to and effectiveness of workforce-led initiatives.

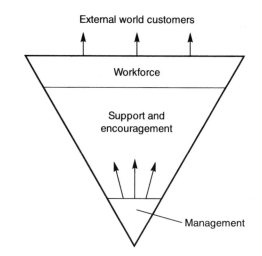

Figure 9.1 Managers as supporters

Such encouragement of change-makers does, in effect, throw into relief the changing nature of the management role. Instead of directing and policing the workforce, managers are seen as coaches and supporters. Some modern management writers see the organizational world turned upside down with the workforce at the top – doing the most important work at the interface with the customer – and the management in support. This is a useful way of looking at the management structure. It may also reflect how managers feel at times – carrying the whole world on their shoulders!

Where to start

Sometimes it may not be obvious where to start the improvement process. As we have said before, change for change sake is *not* to be recommended. If we are to endure the pain of change we need to ensure that it is worthwhile and that we will get business benefit for our efforts. We need a targeting mechanism that will help us achieve that from any improvement process, and we would recommend one that embraces four categories, or areas, of potential improvement. These are:

- Improvements in performance that customers would value greatly.
- Elimination of defects or non-conformances in the products or services.
- Improvements that will give clear cost benefits.
- Removal of hassle from the operation.

The first category requires information from the customer. This may be a combination of our direct customer and the ultimate customer if they are not one and the same. It is possible that we already have this information within the operation through good customer liaison, but if not, we must arrange to obtain it. This will give us a strong guide regarding what the customers would like to see as a result of improvements. Avoid falling into the trap of believing that you know what your customers want if you haven't been through a formal process of asking. There may be pressures or requirements that they have not discussed in informal sessions which, if you know about, you can help with. They may only emerge as you probe with questions such as 'What improvements would you like to see us make in the future?' or 'If we can adjust our operation in any ways to help you to better performance, what would those ways be?'. These are such important issues in relation to improving the operation that we would recommend that every manager has such a process as a part of their formal routines. Do remember this applies even where your own customers are an internal department.

The other three listed categories for change efforts all require information to be gathered from the operation itself. All this requires is a determination to do it, and involvement of the staff to assemble the data. It should not be difficult.

When the data has been gathered you may well then be faced with a dilemma. If you have data on a range of areas, which one should you pick for attention? Here you can make use of the Pareto effect, more commonly known as the 80/20 rule. This rule emerges where there are multiple causes for an effect. In this situation studies show that 80 per cent of the effect is as a result of 20 per cent of the causes. For instance, if customers' delivery dates are regularly missed, and the causes are logged over, say, three months, we will often find as many as ten or twenty different causes emerging (Box 9.5). However, if we count up the frequency of each of these causes, we will often find that the majority (80 per cent) of the total results from a minority (20 per cent) of the causes.

Box 9.5
Data: No. of times delivery dates missed   53

Causes and frequency ● Traffic delays for delivery vans   5
                      ● Production delays   16
                      ● Defective shipments   12
                      ● Incorrect addresses   7
                      ● Driver taken ill   1
                      ● Shortages   5
                      ● Customer relocated   1
                      ● Labelling illegible   3
                      ● Shipment not loaded on van   2
                      ● Driver could not find premises   1

In this illustration, twenty-eight failures result from only two causes: production delays and defective shipments. These two causes would be the initial target for improvement.

The 80/20 rule is extremely useful in any situation where prioritizing needs to be undertaken. It helps in the targeting process, and enables us to select the areas where our efforts are likely to produce the greatest benefit. Another consideration might be the ease with which improvements can be made. If two causes are about equal in frequency, choose to work first on the one which is easiest to handle. This is the swiftest pay-back option. This is a useful approach as it enables new change techniques to be learnt in an area of easy progress. If you tackle an intransigent problem initially, you may not succeed and you and the team will lose heart.

In areas where volume or repetitive work is undertaken in the operation, Statistical Process Control (SPC) techniques are invaluable. They are quite complex techniques which require clarity of application, but can produce dramatic results when used as part of a quality maintenance or improvement process. Statistical systems involve operators systematically recording data on the repetitive performance of the operation. Charts are plotted by operators and these provide indication and information about variability within the operation itself which, if not controlled, can lead to defects. The technique is very widely documented in detailed production and quality control tests, and institutions such as the Deming Association provide expert assistance on the subject. They are not new systems, having been in use in some companies since about 1970, but the truth is that very few operations of the many that *could* benefit are making use of them.

Global opportunities

While every operation is unique, there are areas suitable for improvement initiatives which are common to many operations. It is unlikely that all the following will apply to any single operation, but some will apply to every operation. The operational areas concerned are:

- set-up reduction;
- bottleneck elimination;
- use of 'cells';
- maintenance routines;
- white-collar lead time;
- JIT approaches;
- use of computers;
- the latest equipment; and
- the market need – speed!

Set-up reduction

In many operations, particularly of the batch type, staff have to stop what they are doing or stop what is happening in the process, and re-adjust or reset, prior to starting up to do something else. This is called reset time and the act of doing it is referred to as setting-up. The time taken to complete it is known as set-up time.

As set-up time is lost time there is great benefit in reducing it and this has become a priority area for operations improvements. It does not just apply to manufacturing areas where obvious examples involve the resetting of machines and processes to make a new batch of products. Many service industries have the same phenomena. Examples would include turning aircraft around in minimum time at an airport; reorganizing beds in a hospital between patients; a print room resetting equipment to produce A3 reports rather than A4 reports; clearing and preparing tables in a restaurant between customers. The basic framework of reducing set-up is included as Appendix I to this chapter.

One aspect of set-up reduction work is the scale of the improvements that can be made. Reductions from hours to minutes are commonplace. Set yourself really challenging targets to gain two complementary benefits. Firstly, as this is lost time, any reduction will lead to productivity improvements. Secondly, and maybe more importantly, any improvements lead to greater responsiveness of the operation to customer needs, or market changes. If set-ups between operational runs are shorter, less time is needed to prepare for product or service changes. Hence, smaller batches become economic and there is a step change in response time. The issue of response times is so important we shall return to it again later.

Bottleneck elimination

In most operations one part of the whole process will act as a bottleneck. It is the first part of the process to jam when the volume rises or the pressure increases. If it is not attended to, the whole operation is limited to that capacity level. No matter how hard anyone else works in any other part of the operation, no more output can be achieved. It might occur anywhere in the system, from receiving or placing orders, through any part of the mainstream operating core, or indeed the final delivery system. It could be in front offices, back offices, support departments or on the shopfloor. We need to understand where it is in our own operation and set a task force to removing its 'bottlenecking' effect. This might involve a variety of approaches from using extra people to the use of multiple systems or equipment. Dual lines, increased volume, more flexible systems, multi-skilling, overtime or shift working, faster equipment, might all be required to remove a bottleneck, and raise your capability or capacity.

Every operation needs a bottleneck reduction team at work from time to time. If your business is successful and grows you will need it more often than if you are static. As soon as you eliminate one bottleneck your operation will move on and be limited by another at a higher volume or throughput. While this is a never-ending battle, it is one you cannot ignore.

The use of 'cells'

Many operations were originally set up along the traditional lines of grouping together similar activities. The fitting department, the typing pool, the design department, are all examples of this approach. The trouble with this arrangement is that as the organization grows, so does each of these specialist departments. Problems now occur as a piece of work progresses from one to another through the total process. Two of the main problems are of travelling time and queuing time. If a piece of work is traced through an operation in a traditional set-up it may travel enormous distances as it moves between specialist units. All this travelling involves cost – some one or some thing to move it – and time. None of this adds value, in fact quite the reverse. There is high potential for loss and damage.

Today many operations, both manufacturing and service types, are organizing into what are described as cells. These are small units made up of all the processes required to produce the output, located close together. These cells are usually capable of providing a small range of products or services but are able to respond quickly to customer needs.

It may, on occasion, need more equipment to be provided as a number of these cells may contain the same processes, but the benefit comes in the responsiveness to the market, the reduction in lead times and a reduction in work-in-progress and inventory, as a result of elimination or reduction of queuing time.

Cells do require quite different working practices from operations staff. Multi-skilling is essential as people move around the cell with the work. Training is always an inherent part of a successful cell approach and the increased variety of work provides the operations staff with greater potential for job satisfaction.

Maintenance routines

It is common to find failures in operations caused by equipment breakdown. Too many operations fail to plan correctly the maintenance routines for the equipment they use; the result is a breakdown when the operation can least stand it.

A major cause of this situation is a belief within management that they cannot afford to lose the operational time for maintenance or upkeep routines. This is rarely the case. Correctly planned, maintenance can be organized around shut-downs or quiet periods. It need not require much time specifically set aside for that purpose alone.

Great strides can be made in this area by training operating staff to do much of the regular on-line maintenance. This can also be extended to cover the regular monitoring that should be undertaken to assess the state of equipment so that preventive maintenance can be planned accordingly. This expansion of operating staffs' responsibilities may need careful handling, but will result in them knowing their equipment very much better. This in itself can produce major benefits as they learn more about the equipment's capabilities and, as a result, are often able to achieve more with that equipment than was previously possible.

In these studies of improved maintenance approaches, maintenance is viewed as an essential aid to equipment availability. One major initiative to achieve this is called 'total productive maintenance' and addresses the issues we have outlined here.

White-collar lead time

In many operations, the core work is operative or non-office based. There is a tendency to look solely at those areas for improvements, when in fact there is often great scope in the administrative areas. Delays can be caused in office routines which go unnoticed, but offer tremendous scope for improvements. Do not just target the mainstream activity within your own operation. Do extend your improvement activities to those support areas you may have previously overlooked.

Box 9.6
An organization was asked by its customer, the UK Ministry of Defence, to produce some equipment for an emergency. Their forces were involved in some action overseas and equipment which normally took eighteen months to build was required quickly. By pulling out all the stops the manufacturing unit successfully met the requirement in eleven weeks. They had actually started to work on it as soon as the company received the request. It was amusing for them to receive the official internal order instructing them to start three weeks after they had in fact started! That is white-collar lead time at work. Eleven weeks would have been fourteen had they waited for the official go-ahead.

JIT approaches

This widely-reported topic originated from high-volume manufacturing business in Japan where they had neither the space nor the capital to cope with large volumes of work-in-progress or inventory. They developed routines that did away with work-in-progress and found ways of doing things 'just-in-time'. Products did not spend long periods in the delivery cycle, because they were made or processed just as they were needed.

This has a major impact on every aspect of the operation and requires a completely new culture, where waiting time for anything is seen as 'waste'. It flows through to suppliers where totally new supply routines are required. Warehouses are eliminated in some applications, both for raw materials and for finished goods. As the finished goods are produced just as the customer wants them, they are delivered immediately.

This 'just-in-time' thinking has expanded into service businesses where for instance it has impacted spares and stock holding routines. Better controls have enabled patients to be called to clinics a few minutes before their appointments rather than waiting hours in uninviting waiting rooms. This has required doctors to become more professional with their own planning and routines, because they take more seriously inconvenience to their 'customers' or patients.

Use of computers

Our experience shows operations sometimes do not reap the full rewards from the use of computers. Systems installed fail to provide the benefits they promised. They are often not 'user friendly', inflexible or just miss the mark where the operation is concerned.

If this is the case in your operation, perhaps you need to go and 'fight' with your IT department or your boss to get the problems resolved. Maybe the problems exist because you do not really understand the systems, in which case you must overcome that deficiency. Few managers will survive for long without the skills to get the most from computers, so start a personal campaign to raise your own capability in this area.

The latest equipment

Computers are not the only equipment you will be using. Your operation might use desks, cranes, pens, vehicles, printers, cameras, boats – the list is, of course, endless. In all cases, the latest equipment is likely to do the job better than its predecessor. So are you getting those benefits? It is claimed that investment in new technology can improve operating performance by up to 40 per cent.

Every manager needs to be alert to these opportunities. Flamboyant operations can use the latest equipment as their advertising campaign. An advertisement for Singapore Airlines referred to their complete fleet of 747s being less than three years old. They claimed this resulted in a quieter, faster, more reliable and more fuel efficient operation than their rivals. While you may not be running an airline operation, you should be continually seeking the benefits of using the latest techniques and equipment. There are always financial restrictions but the payback from new equipment can be rapid.

The market need – speed

Customers demand faster response and shorter lead times, and we need to be able to respond to marketplace changes rapidly. Product developments and product launches need to be completed in months, not years.

There is a school of thought that says that managers of operations need only address the issue of speed and everything else will follow. If you halve the time taken to do things, your costs will fall, your market share will rise, and business success will follow. While operational life may not be that simple, there is a lot to be said for this approach. If you can achieve the position where your lead time is shorter than that of your customer you are in control of your destiny. You do not need to carry stock with all its costs and potential for hidden quality problems, because you can deliver from scratch within your customers' required time-scales.

All businesses and organizations would benefit from this approach. If you only pursue one initiative, make it this one. It will give you competitive edge, assuming you hold other performance character-istics steady, such as your quality levels.

Benchmarking

It may be that you are just not sure where to seek improvements. This is an area where 'benchmarking' can be of help to you. Benchmarking is a technique for finding 'best practice'. It is suitable for looking at any and every part of an operation and can be used to identify where improvements are needed in your operation. It can be applied to any business function or sector.

One misconception often found is that benchmarking is competitor analysis. It is not. It might include it but it is not just competitor analysis. Benchmarking can be described as 'the search for better ways'. The aim is to assess ourselves against others doing similar things and then, if we find people doing something more effectively than we are, to learn how they do it. We may then copy or, better still, 'leapfrog' them, with new practices. We repeat that it can be applied to any and every function.

What to benchmark

You should benchmark key processes within the operation, as well as the overall output. All operations are made up of many parts. Benchmark some of the more important sub-operations that make a major contribution to the output. You should benchmark operations that have a major impact on your customers or have a major impact on the bottom line.

Who to benchmark

There are four categories of companies or organizations you should benchmark yourself against. Good 'benchmarkers' will use all four (Figure 9.2).

- Others within your own group: other departments doing similar things in the same company; different companies within a conglomerate; hospitals within the NHS.
- Parallel industries: organizations doing similar work but not compet-ing. Two chemical companies producing different products would be in this category.

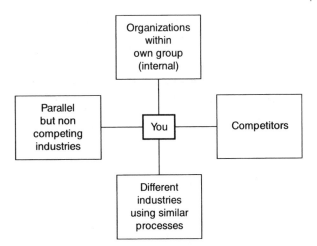

Figure 9.2 Who to benchmark

- Different industries: organizations which are using similar operational elements or processes but are in totally different industries. For instance, an airline and a sports stadium have both to check large numbers of people through ticketing in a short time. They could benchmark against one another.
- Competitors: the most difficult area in which to obtain data, but it is potentially some of the most valuable data. These are the organizations you are continually battling it out within your markets.

How to obtain the data

The most likely sources of data are:

- benchmarking research bodies;
- consultants;
- trade associations and institutions;
- suppliers and customers sharing non-confidential information;
- reverse engineering (examining competitors' products or services);
- published data – annual reports, specification sheets;
- visits;
- special task forces or benchmarking teams;
- benchmarking clubs.

How to analyse the data

The main watchword here is 'care'. Use great care when comparing any numerical data you accumulate. You need to be sure the data is comparable to your own figures. If the other 'benchmarked' organization calculates its internal costs differently from your own, then total operation costs may appear to be higher or lower than your own. In fact the prime costs might be the same, but the accountants may handle them differently. This can lead you to the wrong conclusions. Only draw conclusions when you are quite sure of your facts; ensure you are comparing 'apples with apples'. When you are doing that, the data you have will lead you to conclusions about your organization's performance compared with others.

How to use the data

When the data does show a shortfall in performance compared with others, you have a real opportunity to improve. You need to do a number of things in parallel. You need to:

- find out *how* the others are doing better than you – what are they actually doing;
- set targets for your own increased performance – will you copy or leapfrog them?
- make someone responsible for this improvement and give them the resources and support they need; and
- regularly review the progress being made.

This outline of the technique is not enough information to undertake a benchmarking exercise, but explains the principles. The technique is one which more and more organizations are adopting as they strive for world-class status. Many have been doing it for years, probably the most notable being the Rank Xerox corporation. They benchmark many operations and functions from warehousing techniques to personnel practices against organizations as diverse as 3M and Marks & Spencer. They claim it has helped them move towards greatness.

Business process re-engineering

Also called 'business redesign' this requires a radical rethink of the business and its structure. Managers are asked to regard their business as a series of processes rather than functions. In most organizations functions are the important elements and the structure is designed around them (Figure 9.3).

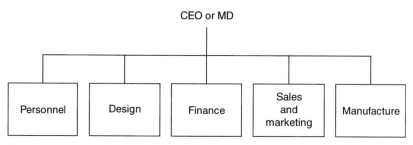

Figure 9.3 The functional structure

For customers to be served, work has to flow across all these functions and this type of structure does not make it easy or speedy. Managers are encouraged to think of their businesses or operations as a series of processes. While doing this they must remember that the main aim is to serve the customer so the key, or primary, processes will be those that enable them to do that, both in the short and the long term.

Once these key processes are identified – and there will be many in a complex operation – the second task is to review the best way of handling those processes to achieve the outcome you need. Try to ignore or forget how you are operating them today because it is very likely some of what you are doing is unnecessary. Against an objective assessment, some current practices may not be justified and should be stopped. They probably started for a good reason in the past, but the reasoning may have been faulty or is now no longer valid and that part of the process is now unnecessary. A process re-engineering approach will highlight any unnecessary operations and should also point the way to more effective ways of doing what does have to be done in the operation.

This requires you to question some fundamental assumptions and beliefs; such questioning can be used to make massive gains in performance by changing drastically the way things are done.

Your target is 30 per cent, not 5 per cent gain. Business process re-engineering is not a technique to be adopted lightly, because it will produce significant changes, and is not just tinkering with the organization. Approach it in a professional way, maybe using specialist guidance, or at least ensuring that you have the relevant education and training yourselves.

The recent proponents of this technique are headed by Mike Hammer and James Champy, two consultants from the USA whose book *Re-engineering the Corporation* is a useful guide and contains many case studies of the technique in action. These case studies target the waste that surrounds systems such as those that require numerous signatures of ever-increasing seniority to get even the smallest change authorized.

They question reconciliation procedures in areas such as accounts payable, where 95 per cent of all reconciliations pass muster, and the value of cumbersome systems to prove what we already know. There is no long-term benefit from protecting such practices, and customers are paying for the cost and delays such practices cause. Eliminating them may cost jobs in the short term, but not eliminating them may lose the company in the long term.

Planning for change

There are four aspects of planning for change:

- building improvement into the budget;
- involving staff;
- planning long, implementing short; and
- communicating change.

Building improvement into the budget

Firstly, you should be building the costs associated with any changes you plan into your budgets. They are real and must be met from somewhere. Secondly, take account in the budget of the improvements you should make, whether they be increased revenue, greater throughput, faster response, lower costs, fewer defects, lower after-sales service needs, or whatever. Your plans should reflect these costs and improvements in the appropriate place. Having them as part of the official budget will provide the impetus to make them happen.

Involving the staff

We have spoken frequently about involving the staff in many aspects of the operation. Make the improvement changes part of your regular communications agenda. That way they are not forgotten.

Planning long, implementing short

This concerns the value to be had from ensuring any change is fully planned, and everyone is involved and trained – before implementation.

Box 9.7

Sir John Egan, when head of Jaguar, described the process followed by his Japanese competitors when launching a new product and how it contrasted with that practised in the West.

He described how, as the development cycle nears completion, the number of changes increase as faults are found on prototypes and in tests (Figure 9.4). In the West, this is at its height at the product launch and all those changes and defects are inflicted on the customer.

In the world class companies in Japan, they recognize the danger of this and ensure they launch the product when the problems are resolved.

They are not launching later in time than the West; that is not the answer. Their answer is to have the hassle earlier in the launch cycle. This is an attitude of mind and means much more effort is put into the planning phase prior to implementation. They force the faults out early.

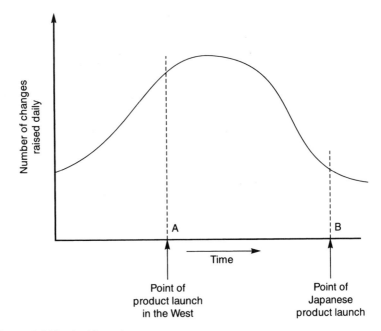

Figure 9.4 Product launch curve

Communicating change

Your plans will fail without good communication. You must learn how to do this well, particularly at the time when change is occurring. You need to make communication a key element of your plans, and allocate a substantial part of your own time to it. You can use a variety of methods including team briefings; one-to-one discussions; memos and announcements; published plans, timetables and results; and feedback sessions.

Summary

In this chapter we have highlighted the need to overcome any complacency in the operation you manage. This leads to the realization that continual change for improvement is a way of life today and how you, the manager, must encourage the change-makers.

We have outlined the factors driving and enabling change and highlighted every manager's responsibility to be exploring them all to raise capability.

There are some common areas where improvements can be identified. An example is improved speed of response to customers. These areas can be used to target your efforts. We covered the valuable part a JIT approach can play, together with the relatively new ideas behind business process re-engineering and pro-active maintenance routines for equipment. We have emphasized the need to involve, train and communicate with your staff and anyone affected by your changes. The results of your efforts can be checked through the benchmarking process and we have outlined a framework to help you. Finally we suggested a four-pronged attack on the change process you might employ to ensure that your plans for change are successful.

Management checklist

- To improve, you have to recognize the need. List any areas of your operation where you have become complacent?

  _____

  _____

  _____

- What might you do about one of them?

- What are you doing to encourage the change-makers in your operation?

- Which of the nine areas for improvement are applicable to you?
  - set-up reduction;
  - bottleneck elimination;
  - use of cells;
  - better maintenance;
  - white-collar lead time;
  - JIT approaches;
  - use of computers;
  - latest equipment; and
  - speed.

- Which one will you tackle – and how?

- Which parts of your operation would you select for benchmarking?

- Are any parts of your operation difficult to justify? Would a business process re-engineering approach help? If yes, discuss it with others, maybe your boss.

- Have you included all four aspects of our recommendations in your plans for change? They are:
  - build improvements and costs into budgets;
  - involve people fully;
  - plan long, implement short – have hassle early;
  - communicate, communicate, communicate.

Appendix to Chapter 9

Set-up reduction routine

1. Use operating staff throughout.
2. Video set-up routine as it is now. Operators do this themselves. Video several set-ups to guarantee a representative run. Operators may need training to use the video equipment.
3. Analyse video. Categorize activities into internal or external. External are those needing outside or off-line help. These external activities, such as the use of a fork-lift truck to move a heavy item, often lead to delays as the people are not instantly there.
4. Find ways to eliminate the external activities. In the fork-lift example, consider fitting an overhead block and tackle. Where external specialisms are required, provide multi-skilling training for operators.
5. Re-analyse video. Categorize activities into on-line and off-line. On-line are those that cannot be done while the operation is in action, off-line are those that can. Resetting the table for the next guests in a restaurant cannot be done while the previous people are still sitting there – it is an on-line action. However, prefolding the napkins can be done in the kitchen at any time; it is an off-line activity.
6. Find ways to eliminate as many on-line set-up activities as possible. Make them off-line as in the napkins example. This may need some extra equipment so that work can be going on on the second set while the first set is working.
7. Many set-ups require adjustments. Eliminate complex or lengthy re-adjustments. Don't ask people to measure things, or align things without special jigs, or equipment. Screw threads as part of set-up clamps should be replaced as they are very slow. Use cam clamps or magnetic clamps.
8. Eliminate the need to find hand tools, as they are frequently lost. Fasten them to the equipment, where they can't be lost.

By the use of these techniques you can make massive inroads into your set-up times, turning hours to reset into minutes. Apply the technique widely and reward excellent results. Often long set-up times can reduce availability or productivity to 60 or 70 per cent. Attack it and aim to approach 100 per cent.

10 Getting things done

Introduction

Central to any manager's job is getting things done. Here are some of the things which we see as distinguishing the effective manager:

- They know what is going on in their area.
- They know the performance factors for their operation.
- They anticipate problems.
- When a problem arises, they get to the heart of it very quickly (they deal with peripheral issues without being side-tracked by them).
- They listen.
- They are respected.
- They have time – time to deal with crises when they arise, time to take on extra responsibilities when needed.
- They take decisions.
- Above all, however, effective managers are people who get things done.

This chapter examines, in practical terms, some of the behaviour which we think is important in contributing to effective management. In doing this we shall be looking at the issues of:

- personal success;
- popularity;
- inspiration and hard work;
- improvement and change;
- making change stick;
- making decisions;
- exercising judgement, courage and determination; and
- being street-wise.

In terms of the MCI management standards, we are referring particularly to:

- MI/2.2: Implement and evaluate changes to services, products and systems.
- M2/1.4: Implement and evaluate changes to services, products and systems.
- M2/2.3: Maintain and improve operations against quality and functional specifications.

In effect, these issues will pervade the whole of the manager's job, and for a formal framework of reference it is more relevant to examine the MCI Personal Competence Model. The overview of the Personal Competence Model is reproduced in Appendix I to this chapter.

What the Personal Competence Model does is set out the behaviours which managers need to demonstrate in order to do their jobs. The management standards, to which we have referred in all the other chapters, are concerned with *what* managers should be doing. The Personal Competence Model refers to *how* managers need to behave. Effective management is a combination of doing the right things and doing them in the best possible way.

Before the publication of the MCI Standards of Management Competence, most of the work on competence – often called competency – was concerned with 'how' managers went about their job rather than 'what' they were supposed to be doing. The standards have filled that gap and provide the foundation for performance. Improved performance will result when managers are not only doing the right things but seeking to do them in a better way. We will not be referring specifically to the clusters and dimensions of the personal competences because it is better for people to familiarize themselves with the complete model and make the appropriate connections themselves.

However, some of the issues with which we shall deal will not be found in the Personal Competence Model. These are the issues which belong more to the ethical than the psychological aspects of behaviour and as such are less systematically based. It is possible that some people may not agree with everything we say, but we do believe it important to deal with issues such as popularity, integrity, courage, because they are issues which are part of managerial life. To a practising manager, textbooks often appear unreal because the bloodless scientific examination of systems and psychological analysis of behaviour never convey the reality of what happens on a day-to-day basis. If we are to discuss management effectiveness with any degree of integrity, we have to enter a number of areas which are not very well defined and for which there are fewer reference points. We do so in the knowledge that they are real and in the hope that it will help. First of all we are going to look at some of the issues concerned with personal success.

Effective managers and shooting stars

In any organization there are always managers whose progress up the management hierarchy is faster than others. We are not just talking about the effects of management development and 'fast track' promotions but of movement which is generally accepted as exceptional. Such managers are genuinely effective and, as part of their all-round management skills, they will often be seen to have strong social and political skills. Unfortunately, many people only see the political and social aspects of these careers and conclude that the key to success is to concentrate on these. Consequently, some managers' main concern is to deal with those matters which offer opportunities for self-promotion and who spend excessive time and effort on seeking personal advantage out of any situation. Such managers we have called 'shooting stars' because, although they sometimes start off by travelling spectacularly and at great speed, they eventually fizzle out.

It is quite normal for managers to look for advancement; they would not be working in management if they did not have that sort of ambition. However, undue concentration on career and self-promotion cannot make for effective management.

From time to time managers will face difficult and sometimes intractable situations which have to be resolved if work is to continue properly. Very often, whatever the solution, someone is going to be disadvantaged and the manager is going to be criticized, whatever he or she does. Shooting stars will often avoid these situations, seeing them as 'no-win' situations and potentially damaging for their career. So at the same time as avoiding the problem they lay down smoke-screens to obscure the fact that they are dodging the issue.

Effective managers will grasp the nettle but at the same time take steps to ensure that they are not unreasonably blamed if they tackle one of those intractable problems for which there are no 'right' answers and someone is bound to be dissatisfied.

Box 10.1

A valued customer has recently been very critical of your service and the quality of the goods, and virtually put you on probation. They now ask for an extra delivery at a time when stocks are low. The only way you can supply is by defaulting on an order for another valued customer. If you don't supply they will go to a competitor and the chances are that, with your recent history of poor service, you may lose them altogether. However, by defaulting on delivery for your other customer, you will seriously damage relations there. What do you decide to do?

Dilemmas such as Box 10.1 are the stuff of everyday management; solutions will be different in different organizations. There is no 'correct' answer. There are, however, some guidelines which can help.

The first rule is to recognize the dangers inherent in the problem. The example in Box 10.1 is fairly obvious; others are not always so. Sometimes there are conflicts with organizational culture – the way things are done. Sometimes there are potential conflicts with the personal views of your boss. Sometimes external contacts, such as customers or suppliers, can be stakeholders in the organization in more than one way – such as by being shareholders or as local elected representatives. You must be alive to such undertones when dealing with people.

Secondly, remember that there are two aspects to dealing with issues; what you do and the way you do it. If you know that you are in a 'no-win' situation, the only way you can come out with credit is through the way you handle it.

Thirdly, whatever you do, have a well-reasoned case for doing it. If, in the opinion of others, especially your boss, you have opted for the wrong reasoning, you have made a genuine error. This is definitely better than if you have not got a reasonably well thought-through case for your action. In these circumstances you could be seen to be guilty of rashness or irresponsibility, which are far greater sins and liable to cause long-term damage to your reputation.

Fourthly, let others know of your reasoning. In the sort of ambiguous situations which managers encounter, where there is no 'correct' solution to a problem, a well-reasoned position will always find some agreement with some people and hence you will have supporters. Effective managers who get things done must be prepared to get things wrong occasionally – 'the person who never made a mistake never made anything' – and personal damage limitation is part of the effective manager's survival kit. It is not, however, a central aspect of their behaviour.

What price popularity?

Managers get things done through other people, and the way they operate is critical. Management style has been evolving, along with changes in society, from the hierarchical and autocratic to a more democratic 'open' way of management. Within this general trend, different organizations and individuals will all practise their own particular variations of management style, but the trend is nevertheless there. 'Open' or 'democratic' management places more demands on the individual manager trying to balance the need for consultation, explanation and information against the requirement to get things done in a timely and cost-effective way. One of the dangers that does present itself is that of confusing 'open' management with 'popular' management.

Managers cannot be properly effective if they aim, consciously or unconsciously, for popularity with their staff. At a time of autocratic management when respect for rank was normal and fear was sometimes an element, it is not difficult to see how such an attitude could develop. It might also have been reasoned that if it was a sign of a weak manager to seek popularity, the reverse might be true – that an unpopular manager must be a strong manager.

If popularity is about trying to please all of the people all of the time, it is clearly impossible to achieve. The pressures to attempt this with an 'open' management style are, however, much greater than they would be with an autocratic style. With an 'open' style, staff are given information, are encouraged to offer views and opinions and generally join in decision-making. In these circumstances, managers may be tempted to actions which may not be in the best interests of the operation, simply to please or encourage their staff and avoid being considered hypocritical. For similar reasons, there is the danger of agreeing to one thing with one employee and something different with another – opinions and decisions varying, depending upon who was last spoken to. The result is inconsistency of action and, worst of all, confused staff. Where you have confusion, you cannot have effectiveness.

People, at any level, look for clarity and directness; we like to know where we stand and we look to the boss to create an unambiguous working environment. Managers therefore have to acquire the skills of commanding respect without being overbearing, and of saying 'no' without demotivating. Even the best of us find it difficult to achieve all of these things all of the time but evidence shows that employees prefer a clear and positive approach to anything else – and it is key to getting things done.

Inspiration versus perspiration

There is a great deal of management literature which documents and describes the fragmented nature of the manager's working life, constantly switching from one activity to another. Mintzberg, the distinguished American academic, concludes:

> In contrast to activities performed by most non-managers, those of the managers are characterized by brevity, variety and fragmentation. The vast majority are of brief duration, of the order of seconds for foremen and minutes for chief executives. The variety of activities to be performed is great, and the lack of pattern among subsequent activities, with the trivial interspersed with the consequential, requires that the manager shift moods quickly and frequently. In general, managerial work is fragmented and interruptions are commonplace.
>
> (Mintzberg, 1973)

This constant switching from one issue to another is frequently concerned with making decisions in order to solve problems. Much of the time these problems are minor and would be barely described as problems by the busy manager. From time to time, however, they are such as to warrant much more than an instant decision, taken 'on the hoof'. Some problems are instantly recognizable, others can be buried and deep-seated and only discernible through a series of symptoms.

When managers tackle significant problems they need a certain amount of inspiration, particularly when the problem itself is not obvious and all you see are symptoms.

Box 10.2
The management accountant becomes aware that stocks of a particular item have become surprisingly high. The item was once a best-seller but has now lost popularity. There have been no unusual orders for the item but the production department has been making very large numbers. Where is the documentation? Has the paperwork for an order gone astray and is there a frustrated customer somewhere waiting for a delivery which has not arrived? No! In its heyday the item had always been in short supply. Whenever there was a lull in production it had been generally understood that it would be made without the normal documentation and in order to utilize spare capacity. Nobody had ever withdrawn that instruction and there had been several lulls in production recently.

Finding the answer to the example in Box 10.2 is one problem. Making sure it does not happen again is another – or perhaps several problems; deciding what to do with excess stock, another. Finding answers to questions requires some ingenuity and a little inspiration. Putting the system right, making sure that it – and anything like it – does not happen again, requires the perspiration.

In a busy life there is always pressure to move on to the next problem; crisis over – where's the next one? Besides which, problems, particularly if they have an element of crisis, are always exciting. Clearing up the mess after the crisis has passed is very dull and boring. One of the most important parts of your job, however, is to improve performance and this can be done most frequently through learning from mistakes. Ensuring that mistakes are not repeated is an important function of the effective manager and this requires the perspirational qualities. We covered this in some detail in Chapter 5. In our example, it seems likely that the operative staff were not aware of the department's sales position. Perhaps they did not care; perhaps they did not want to be bothered with matters over which they had no influence; perhaps they were just anxious to be seen to be busy at all times, regardless of whether that busyness was actually going to benefit the organization. If attitudes are involved as well as just information and understanding, the manager has some serious educating to do, which may require very much more than just giving people new instructions.

The system of placing orders on the production department and also of stock-level reporting may need some amendment and this could involve what many action-orientated managers may see as the very tiresome business of negotiating with other departments. In all cases, if actions are taken and changes achieved they will have to be monitored and checked out over a period of time. These activities require the systematic application of such things as persistence, patience and diplomacy – all the dismal virtues of the administrator – allied to the motivational skills of leadership.

Continual improvement and change

Chapter 9 emphasized that no practising manager can be unaware of the need to be able to cope with and initiate change. For those working in industrial and commercial organizations, improvement and change have always been required; what is different nowadays is the frequency and speed with which they happen. The public sector, too, is being swept by a tidal wave of reform of various kinds.

Sometimes the need for change is dramatically obvious and sometimes less so. When a company changes ownership and the new Chief Executive arrives, when a public utility is privatized, when a market declines rapidly, the need for change is obvious and dramatic. When market-share is being slowly eroded by a new competitor or when the market itself is slowly shrinking, the need for change is less obvious so that the unwary and ill-informed suddenly wake up to a crisis when it has become too late to do anything about it.

When major change of the dramatic and obvious type arises, it usually means that decisions have been made at the top, and middle- and first-line managers simply have to make sure that it carries through in their particular operation. In other circumstances, when we are dealing with the need for continual improvement, middle- and first-line managers should consider themselves instigators as well as implementors of change.

Major change

Most organizations have undergone major change in the 1990s; if they have not, they may well be about to. In these circumstances, middle- and first-line managers need to:

- understand clearly what the organization is attempting to achieve;
- understand clearly what has to be achieved in their particular operation; and
- ensure that their authority and the resources available match the requirements which are being placed upon them.

These things may sound fairly obvious but remember that the reality of change is that it usually takes place at great speed. Those who make the decisions in principle cannot understand all the implications of those decisions for an operating manager and often do not have the time either to think them through or to discuss them with the managers concerned. Thus in a water company which has been privatized, it is clear to senior, middle- and first-line managers that they have to think more 'commercially'. How each manager at each of those levels interprets that idea may vary enormously. Does it mean that, if the area manager of a water authority can get pipeline maintenance carried out more cheaply by a sub-contractor, the maintenance department can be made redundant? Does it mean that as soon as a water-bill is unpaid the area manager can shut off supplies? It probably does not but the area manager needs to be clear about what he or she is permitted to do without consulting anyone and what is to be the subject of recommendation.

In many cases, senior management will have anticipated the sort of problems of interpretation and understanding which inevitably arise, and laid down procedures for dealing with them. Sometimes, either because things happen too fast or by default, they will not have done this. In these circumstances, middle- and first-line managers may find themselves having to make decisions with little guidance, and if this is the case you need a plan. Even if you have not been required to produce a plan, you need to draw one up, detailing the effects of changes on all aspects of your operation – staff, plant and equipment, output, costs.

Once made, the plan provides an agenda for discussion with appropriate senior management as to what has to be done, and an agreement on the actions you are expected to take.

Stressful situations can arise if, for whatever reason, you are not asked to produce a plan and senior management are not interested in anything which you produce on your own initiative. It may be implied that, as a manager, you should know what requires doing and you should just be getting on with it. Alternatively, it may be implied that trying to gain approval for actions at a more detailed level is a form of delaying tactic or lack of decisiveness on your part. Either way, your senior management may see this as a lack of commitment to the change which is taking place. If those are the circumstances, it is clear that you have to get on with things, but be sure that your plan is registered with your bosses. Middle- and first-line managers are often criticized as being the main impediment to change – as being unable to make the necessary adjustments to new circumstances. There may be some truth in this but we also believe that this can sometimes be caused by senior management failing to appreciate the situation in which they place middle- and first-line management in times of major change. If you feel that they are lacking in support or that the implications of what needs to be done are not fully appreciated, we can only recommend the course of careful planning, discussing the plans and clearly making the decisions. Even if it does not give answers to all your concerns, it may help to clarify the senior management position and also leave them in no doubt about what you intend to do.

Continual improvement

Change as a result of the process of continual improvement is a different matter and must be seen as a normal part of day-to-day management. Sometimes, as with issues of major change, it will be imposed from the top. However, we want to emphasize here the initiation of improvement as one of the most significant contributions which middle- and first-line managers can make to the competitiveness of their organization. There is nothing new nor particularly radical in the idea that managers should be on the alert to find ways of doing things better. What is new is the constant pressure on organizations to improve the quality of product or service or to give better value in their current position in the market. Unfortunately, organizations cannot stand still and, paradoxically, unless they are going forward and improving, they are going backwards and declining. From time to time there are breakthroughs in technology or in thinking which create a step-change in design or in process which can create a major advantage. The replacement of metal by plastic, the introduction of 'just-in-time' supply of materials or components, the application of information technology, all create major changes in organization, in business process and, hopefully, in operating efficiency. We believe, however, that the cumulative effect of small, incremental improvements carried out in every part of an organization can be just as significant. Your operation needs both types of performance improvement and you need to be seeking both types of opportunity.

Continual improvement is obviously not possible without the wholehearted support and involvement of the staff in whatever changes need to take place. Staff involvement, however, needs to be more than that of passive support. If the whole potential for improvement is to be exploited, the detailed knowledge and understanding of the operation, which is held by the people actually doing the various jobs involved, has to be harnessed. Continual improvement is not concerned with large and significant changes; it is to do with small, unspectacular changes in the everyday working arrangements of the operation:

- the saving of ten minutes a day by rearranging delivery schedules;
- the re-siting of a work-station;
- rescheduling staff meal-breaks to cope with customer overload;
- training staff in additional skills to give flexible working;
- modifying a component to speed up throughput; and
- reducing double-handling.

The saving of minutes on a routine process when multiplied throughout an organization can have dramatic effect.

It makes sense that the people actually doing the work are the people most likely to perceive how it can be improved. It is for the manager, however, to create the conditions in which those perceptions can be brought into effect. As we have said earlier, this means formal systems like quality circles and suggestion schemes; most of all, however, it requires constant contact from managers and supervisors to inform and encourage people to think positively about improvement. Are you doing enough with your own team along these lines?

Making things 'stick'

Getting things done is about making things 'stick'. If one sets about it, finding bright ideas is not that difficult (5 per cent inspiration). What is more difficult is making the ideas 'stick' (95 per cent perspiration).

In making changes, one of the first issues that needs to be considered is that of 'time'. How long will it take to put into effect? We don't know any precise rules about time, except that change, even the smallest and simplest change, takes much longer to become embedded in the organization than anyone would think reasonable. Estimate generously how long it ought to take – then treble it! The main problem is that if people have been doing things in a certain way for any length of time, they find it extraordinarily difficult to change their mind-set. This is not necessarily due to awkwardness or lack of willingness or any sort of conscious opposition. It is because, once programmed, reprogramming the human mind is a fundamental business which takes time and effort.

Box 10.3
A major international company employing ten thousand people decided to restructure the company from a centralized organization into one with five autonomous business units. Three years after the restructuring it was still being said that the biggest problem was to stop people doing their old jobs (before restructuring) and get them to behave in the spirit of the new organization.

The 'easy' way out of reprogramming people sometimes seems to be to replace them with new people who carry no baggage of previous company or industry experience. We don't believe that this is a wise option. Firstly, dismissing long-serving staff in order to replace them with more staff is both expensive and has a seriously demoralizing effect on the people remaining. Secondly, the time taken to train new staff in the organization's procedures and systems may not be much different from the time taken to train old staff into new ways. Managers expect to train new staff and probably expect to devote a considerable time to it. Managers often do not expect to train existing staff to do things differently. We believe that the benefits to the organization of devoting time and effort to retraining existing staff far outweigh similar time and effort devoted to new staff. In any case, with the need to be constantly changing things, constantly changing people cannot be a choice.

An important part of reprogramming is to get people accustomed to the idea that continual change is a normal part of working life. This may not be easy if your operation involves people doing repetitive jobs and you therefore need a type of person who can cope with humdrum, repetitive tasks. Switching people between jobs can help here, as well as helping to create a multi-skilled staff.

Once a change has been decided, serious thought must be given to the actual training or instruction required and how long it is necessary to carry it out. After that, it is a question of monitoring and coaching to ensure that new methods are absorbed and implemented. The key to retraining is in the monitoring and coaching. Once the ground has been prepared and manured and the seed sown, the key is constant watering. Managers must be constantly checking – not necessarily in an obvious manner – that people are not only doing things in the new way, but that they understand why. Performing tasks regularly means they become part of the unconscious and they are often done in an unconscious way. It is like taking a regular car-drive along a familiar route – frequently you do it and cannot remember travelling the route. You arrive at the destination uneventfully and safely, without any recollection of having passed the landmarks, driving on automatic pilot. When we have a new way of doing things we sometimes slip back to automatic pilot, and when that happens we follow the old route.

People need a great deal of encouragement to make sure that the old habits and methods have been eradicated and that reprogramming is complete. This is the reason for saying that far more time needs to be allowed than might be thought reasonable in order to make change effective. In addition, and to continue the gardening metaphor a little further, as well as constant watering there may have to be some weeding. In changed circumstances, it is likely that some people do find it impossible or refuse to adapt to new ways. Managers must face this issue – they have to grasp the nettle. It is not for this book to enter into the issues of job change and/or dismissal, but if organizations are to improve and progress there will inevitably be human casualties. Organizations cannot have their effectiveness damaged by individuals. Managers have to deal with this.

Two particular hazards need recognizing. The first concerns 'throwing out the baby with the bath water'; the second is about 'keeping your eye on the ball'.

Making changes inevitably causes hazards, if only prompted by the process of doing things differently. The worst thing that can happen is to be worse off after the change than before. There are pressures for change; it is fashionable and it sometimes gets people noticed so it can be good for the career. Our emphasis is on improvement and if, at the end of it all, you have not made an improvement, then you will have 'thrown out the baby with the bath water', making change for the sake of change.

The second hazard is the danger that making changes absorbs so much time and energy that it damages the efficiency and the effectiveness of the operation in a serious way. Making changes while still maintaining the effectiveness of the operation is one of the most testing challenges to a manager's ability. Where changes affect a whole organization, first-line and middle managers can receive a bombardment of demands from different quarters to change systems and do things differently. These can come from accountants, personnel, information technologists and the like; they are not in control of these things and often find it difficult to influence the way in which things are being done.

When managers are making changes themselves they are in control and can make the necessary judgements about what the operation can absorb without it creating a deterioration in output, quality, service and cost. As usual, in management this means careful planning to start with and careful monitoring as the changes are taking place and being embedded in the operation. It is at these times that 'tell-tales' are so useful; when attention has to be given to new activities it is absolutely invaluable to have regular and frequent signals, whether formal or informal, which can indicate how well the mainstream operation is performing. Operations which are well-organized with well-trained staff will usually run well with the lightest touch from the boss, but that touch must always be there. If it is felt that the boss's eye is off the ball completely, the operation can very quickly go to pieces. A good team can keep things going for a considerable time but eventually lack of your involvement will have a negative effect.

The other factor is not trying to do too much at one time. Objectives for improvement and change should be stretching and challenging but not so ambitious as to be unachievable. Even with careful planning and good judgement it is often not possible to achieve the right balance at once. There is a need for constant monitoring together with constant re-inforcement of messages and adjustment of actions.

Good managers don't always get things right first time but they do know when things are going wrong, and take decisive action before it is too late. We have seen many cases when managers have acted too late, hoping – in a very human way – that something will turn up to resolve a problem. It rarely does and by then the problem has become worse. These cases are often concerned with the need to dismiss staff either for lack of competence or because of redundancy. Managers who tackle these problems quickly are often seen as 'ruthless' and few people wish to be viewed in this light.

Sometimes, managers are highly committed to a particular project and because of this lose a sense of perspective. In this respect it is important to guard against becoming too subjectively involved with a particular idea or course of action. Commitment to getting things done is vital to achieving success, but if that commitment becomes obsessive it can cloud judgement and prevent managers from terminating things which are not working. Sometimes obsessiveness can be concerned with a pet theory or idea; sometimes it can be a matter of misguided stubbornness. Champions often need a sort of inner belief to keep them going, particularly if there is opposition. But causes need to make good business sense and taking a purely emotional stand must be avoided.

The MCI Personal Competence Model

In the introduction to this chapter, we referred to the MCI Personal Competence Model as a good analysis of 'how' a manager goes about doing his or her job. This complements the management standards with their 'units' and 'elements' of occupational competence which are concerned with 'what' a manager actually does.

The Personal Competence Model presents a valuable description of effective managerial behaviour, and we believe that managers will find it an extremely useful tool for analysing their own and other people's behaviour. There are other models or descriptions of personal competences but these have usually been produced for specific organizations, for their own organizational purposes. Careful comparison between the MCI Personal Competences and those developed for other organizations reveal very strong similarities – frequently the differences are mainly in the use of different words to describe the same or similar competences. The MCI model, however, is the only one which has been produced for general application and it is therefore a more appropriate reference.

In conclusion, we are going to summarize what we have been saying about effective management with reference to personal competences or behaviour. In doing this we shall be selecting and emphasizing those competences which we believe are more important than others in 'getting things done . Additionally, we shall be making some statements about competences which do not appear in the usual models.

Taking decisions

It is the job of managers to get things done and in order to do this the manager must behave positively and decisively. This means taking decisions. In taking decisions, they have to get them as right as possible for the circumstances. The competence model stresses the need to gather information, to evaluate implications and to look at options. For much of the time those processes have to be undertaken quite quickly. Important decisions usually, but not always, allow time to go through most of these steps. The day-to-day events in running operations usually demand quick decisions; quick decisions often mean that you are not in possession of all the facts and if you wait for all the facts to be assembled you will be too late. A late decision is often worse than a poor decision taken in time. So managers often have to take risks. Risks are lessened by knowledge and judgement. For success in management, you only have to be right more times than you are wrong. Striving for 100 per cent 'best' decisions every time means you will not make those decisions in time. Your own efforts will turn a mediocre decision into a good one more times than not.

Judgement

To be effective, managers really need to know about their situation, their industry, their organization, the technology, the people – and must understand the issues involved. We often talk about the importance of experience and when we do this we are simply using it as a shorthand for knowledge and understanding. If managers have encountered situations in the past, the knowledge gained from those situations can be harnessed to provide solutions for future problems. This can be of tremendous advantage, but even more so when it comes to the need to apply judgement – and managers are usually applying judgement in the most mundane of situations:

- Do you delay a decision until you have more information, or is it better to make it faster but with limited information?
- Do you carry on with an action and tell the boss afterwards – or seek his or her approval first?
- Do you send an incomplete delivery on time or wait until it is complete but thereby make it late – or do you incur extra cost by 'buying in'?
- Do you postpone a scheduled appraisal interview in order to respond to some ad hoc information request from head office?
- Do you allow a last-minute request for holiday from your secretary when you have just refused something similar from a supervisor?

Managers are not expected to hesitate with this sort of decision; they are expected to give instant answers – if they do not, the whole operational process slows down to an ineffectual bureaucratic lethargy.

But to give those decisions, managers must have knowledge, understanding and judgement quickly available. When this is born of experience – i.e. having undergone or witnessed something similar – they can be more confident of what they are doing. With greater confidence they can rely more on their judgement of the situation and act more quickly.

Determination

Once a decision is made, a course of action decided, the next problem is to make it stick. Managers need to demonstrate a quality of determination and persistence without which programmes of action will founder. Determination may be needed to get ideas across; it is certainly needed to monitor events and actions regularly to the point of monotony; it is needed to keep people constantly up to the mark until they are sufficiently trained or retrained to carry out their tasks in the required way – until they have acquired a new 'automatic pilot'.

Sometimes, however, in spite of determined efforts to make things stick, they do not. Managers can make mistakes like anyone else and if they do they must recognize and correct them as quickly as possible. Deciding to reverse a decision or abandon a project must not be done too often as it calls into question the manager's credibility, but knowing when to quit is again a matter of that judgement which is such an essential attribute of good management.

Courage

'Quitting' when it is necessary also requires a certain amount of courage and this is the third quality, along with judgement and determination, which managers need; this applies both to making decisions and to making them stick. Backing one's own judgement requires courage, especially if a manager is not following a popular course. It may be necessary to convince staff or colleagues or the boss; it is almost always necessary to withstand challenges from non-believers while programmes are put through.

Enthusiasm

To get things done, managers are working through other people and need to motivate them. Motivating people is not possible if they cannot see a very positive enthusiasm on the part of the manager. Enthusiasm is always obvious; what is more, it is highly infectious and can work wonders in raising morale and putting real 'snap' into people's attitudes to doing things.

Energy

Hand-in-hand with enthusiasm goes energy. Energetic people communicate the quality through the way they walk, the way they talk, even by the way they sit. Energetic, enthusiastic people create a crackle in the atmosphere which lasts after they have gone and gives a charge to the way the work carries on.

Integrity

Managers are people who must be trusted by their staff, by their colleagues and by their boss. To get things done, managers need the support of all of these groups of people. The first step in achieving that support is in their recognizing and trusting the managers' motives. If managers, for example:

- only do things for the sake of their CV;
- act the sycophant with their seniors;
- intrigue behind their bosses' backs;
- ask favours from colleagues but are always too busy to help out others;
- take credit for other people's work;
- make scapegoats if they have a crisis;
- do not support subordinates when they make a mistake;
- use company policy as an excuse for their own actions;

then they lose the trust and respect of those around them. In consequence, they lose the support of the people they need when they are trying to get things done.

The downside of human nature

Without saying so directly, the implications of much management literature and most behavioural study is that if the workforce does not respond it is the management which is to blame. Most people will have heard the saying that 'there are no bad workers, only bad managers'. And insofar as this places responsibility for people's performance squarely with the managers, we agree with it.

We also believe that the assumptions underlying McGregor's theory Y (that people are responsible, that they want to work and do not require coercion and policing to do so) are valid as a generalization (McGregor's theory X and theory Y are explained more fully in Appendix II to this chapter.) As a result of this sort of thinking, traditional hierarchical and autocratic views of management have become outdated. There has been a great deal of employment legislation designed to protect employees from abuse of managerial power.

One of the results of this has been to make managers feel 'under siege' by the rest of society and behave very cautiously when confronted with situations which require disciplinary action.

Managers do have to tackle very difficult problems of discipline and personality and because of both the changed attitudes to authority and the effect of legislation they sometimes feel inhibited in what they can do.

All societies include liars, fraudsters, thieves, confidence tricksters, psychopaths, drug addicts, alcoholics as well as people who are simply self-centred, awkward and anti-social. Any workforce mirrors society and within it there will always be a selection of such people. Most managers will have to deal with some, if not all, of the problems caused by these types of people during a working lifetime. Your operation needs to be managed in the belief that most people are responsible and responsive, but you need to be alert to the fact that not all are.

If you have poor performers or malingerers in the operation and you are not tackling them positively, the rest of the staff will become disillusioned and you will lose their support.

Managers cannot afford to be naive. It is right to be alert to the potential of people for improvement and development but at the same time managers cannot forget that the best of human natures has a 'downside'. Without being cynical, managers need to be realistic about human behaviour and to be prepared for the occasional 'rotten apple in the barrel', which has to be dealt with. Managers need to be street-wise, otherwise they won't survive.

Summary

Effective managers are people who get things done. Effective managers face up to difficult situations and make it clear to others what they have done and the rationale for their action. Managers cannot be effective if their aim is popularity. Managers must ensure that mistakes are not repeated and be prepared for hard work and attention to detail to ensure this. In situations of change, managers need to plan their action. Continual improvement requires constant attention to small matters and the total involvement of the workforce. Making change 'stick' sometimes takes longer than expected and requires constant attention. In making changes do not neglect the central role of your operation. Effective managers make decisions and for this they need judgement, determination, courage, enthusiasm, energy and integrity. They also need to be 'street-wise'.

Management checklist

- List all the 'no win' 'problems' you have faced recently, or that you have seen other people face. How were they resolved? Could they have been handled better?
- Do you know any managers who have a reputation for popularity? How are they viewed by superiors, by colleagues and by sub-ordinates? Are they effective managers? How important is 'popularity' to you? Does your 'popularity' have any bearing on your effectiveness?
- Does Mintzberg's description of managerial activity reflect your job? Have you ever seen examples of the same problem continually recurring? Why was this?
- Have you been involved in major change? Were you sufficiently briefed to fulfil your role? List any issues which could have been handled better; think through how you could have made improvements.
- What is on your agenda for improving your own operation? Have you experienced difficulties in
  - staff involvement and support?
  - timing?

– achieving targets?
– maintaining normal output?
Would you do things differently another time?
- Compare your own behaviour with the MCI Personal Competence Model. Do you feel that you could manage more effectively if you behaved differently? If so, list the three competences which could make the most difference and consider how you can improve over time (behaving differently takes time to achieve).
- Are you good at taking decisions? Do they take too long? Are they usually right? How can you improve your decision-making?

Appendices to Chapter 10

Appendix I Overview of the MCI Personal Competence Model

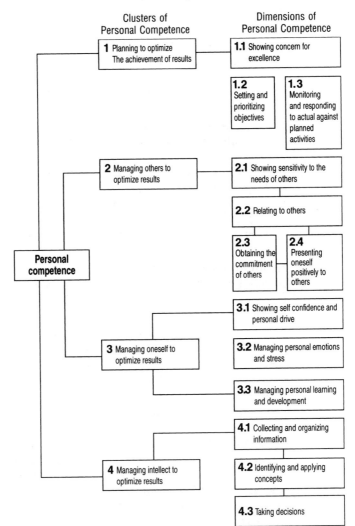

Explanation of each dimension

- **Concern for excellence** is a concern for the quality of performance. It contains the things that managers do that show they are striving for excellence in the quality of work and the way things are done. It is an approach that can be applied to most work activities and is about continually looking for improvement.

- **Setting and prioritizing objectives** is about deciding what needs to be done and making plans to achieve it. It involves setting a target and having performance indicators for the target. It can be applied to every activity from a small task to a major project. By making clear what is to be done and how it will be achieved, work can be prioritized. Each objective fits into longer term planning which involves vision in planning ahead.

- **Monitoring and responding to actual against planned activities** describes the things that managers do to check the progress and results of tasks and activities that have been scheduled. It requires following through plans to results and taking action when progress is not going to plan.

- **Showing sensitivity to the needs of others** involves developing empathy and seeing things from others' points of view, without necessarily agreeing with them. By paying attention to the needs, feelings and values of others, and encouraging them to discuss issues openly and honestly, the manager can show others that they are valued. 'Others' includes all those the manager comes into contact with, not just staff they have responsibility for.

- **Relating to others** is an approach to building up rapport and positive relationships with others through encouraging open and honest communication. It includes using interpersonal skills to resolve conflict and encourage teamwork.

- **Obtaining the commitment of others** is the presentation of facts or views to others in ways that gain their cooperation. It entails influencing others to take action willingly, yet without manipulating them. Problems and resistance are brought out into the open for discussion so that they can be resolved.

- **Presenting oneself positively to others** is about communicating to others in ways that they can relate to and positively respond to. It may involve presenting a case of getting others' support in everyday encounters or in more formal situations. It includes conveying views in terms with which the listener can identify, and adopting styles that are appropriate.

- **Showing personal confidence and personal drive** contains those behaviours concerned with initiating actions and taking responsibility for the outcome. It also covers taking control of situations and events rather than passively accepting events, demonstrating confidence and commitment and creating new oportunities for initiatives to be taken.

- **Managing personal emotions and stress** means keeping an objective view of each situation and maintaining a stable perform-ance regardless of pressure. Where stress arises, it requires taking appropriate action to minimize the effects and tackle the root causes.

Appendix II McGregor's theory X and theory Y

McGregor's theory X and theory Y is still much quoted after its publication in 1960. He states the view that underlying 'traditional' management behaviour is a set of assumptions about how people behave.

- The average human being has an inherent dislike of work and will avoid it if possible.

- Because of this human characteristic of dislike of work, most people must be coerced, controlled, directed, threatened with punishment, to get them to put forth adequate effort towards the achievement of organizational objectives.

- The average human being prefers to be directed, wishes to avoid responsibility, has relatively little ambition, and wants security above all.

This McGregor calls theory X. In summary, management's job in a theory X situation is to 'police', direct and control people.

In theory Y he challenges these assumptions with the following:

- The expenditure of physical and mental effort in work is as natural as play or rest.

- External control and the threat of punishment are not the only means of bringing about effort towards organizational objectives. We will exercise self-direction and self-control in the service of objectives to which we are committed.

- Commitment to objectives is a function of the rewards associated with their achievement (rewards are defined as satisfactions, not financial).

- The average person learns, under proper conditions, not only to accept but to seek responsibility.

- The capacity to exercise a relatively high degree of imagination, ingenuity and creativity in the solution of organizational problems is widely, not narrowly, distributed in the population.

- Under the conditions of modern industrial life, the intellectual potentialities of the average person are only partially utilized.

In summary, then, in theory Y management's role is to support people and create a climate where they can give their full contribution. Managers become mentors and supporters, not police officers.

Bibliography and further reading

Broadbent, Michael and Cullen, John (1993). *Managing Financial Resources*. Butterworth-Heinemann (in association with the Institute of Management).

Hamel, Gary and Prahalad C K (1989) 'Strategic intent'. *Harvard Business Review*. May–June.

Hammer, Mike and Champy, James (1993). *Re-engineering the Corporation*. Nicholas Brearley Publishing.

Handy, Charles (1985). *The Gods of Management*, Pan.

Health and Safety Executive (1988). *The Management of Health and Safety*. The Industrial Society.

Herzberg, Frederick, Mausner, Bernard and Boch-Snyderman, Barbara (1993). *The Motivation to Work (with a new introduction by Frederick Herzberg)*. Transaction Publishers, New Brunswick, NJ.

McGregor, Douglas (1960). *The Human Side of Enterprise*. McGraw-Hill.

Mintzberg, Henry (1973). *The Nature of Managerial Work*. Harper and Row.

Peters, Tom (1985). *A Passion for Excellence*. Random House.

Peters, Tom (1987). *Thriving on Chaos*. Alfred A Knopf.

Peters, Tom and Waterman Robert (1982). *In Search of Excellence*. Harper and Row.

Porter, Michael E (1985) *Competitive Advantage: Creating and Sustaining Superior Performance*. The Free Press.

Porter, Michael E (1989). *Competitive Advantage*. Collier MacMillan.

Porter, Lyman W, Lawler III, Edward, E and Hackman, J. Richard (1975). *Behaviour in organizations*. McGraw-Hill.

Spencer, Barbara, A (1994). 'Model of organization and total quality management: A critical evaluation'. *Academy of Management Review*, July.

Stewart, Rosemary (1991). *Managing Today and Tomorrow*. Macmillan Press.

Index